BRUNEI

POLITICAL, CONSTITUTIONAL SYSTEM AND PROCEDURES HANDBOOK

STRATEGIC INFORMATION AND REGULATIONS

International Business Publications, USA
Washington DC, USA - Bandar Seri Begawan

BRUNEI

POLITICAL, CONSTITUTIONAL SYSTEM AND PROCEDURES HANDBOOK

STRATEGIC INFORMATION AND REGULATIONS

UPDATED ANNUALLY

We express our sincere appreciation to all government agencies and international organizations which provided information and other materials for this handbook

Cover Design: **International Business Publications, USA**

2018 Updated Reprint International Business Publications, USA
ISBN 978-1-5145-3053-5

For additional analytical, business and investment opportunities information, please contact Global Investment & Business Center, USA at (703) 370-8082. Fax: (703) 370-8083. E-mail: ibpusa3@gmail.com
Global Business and Investment Info Databank - www.ibpus.com

Printed in the USA

For additional analytical, business and investment opportunities information, please contact Global Investment & Business Center, USA at (703) 370-8082. Fax: (703) 370-8083. E-mail: ibpusa3@gmail.com
Global Business and Investment Info Databank - www.ibpus.com

BRUNEI

POLITICAL, CONSTITUTIONAL SYSTEM AND PROCEDURES HANDBOOK

STRATEGIC INFORMATION AND REGULATIONS

TABLE OF CONTENTS

STRATEGIC AND BUSINESS PROFILE

BRUNEI DARUSSALAM

Capital and largest city	Bandar Seri Begawan 4°53.417′N 114°56.533′E4.890283°N 114.942217°E
Official languages	Malay
Recognised	English
Other languages	• Brunei Malay • Tutong • Kedayan • Belait • Murut • Dusun • Bisaya • Melanau • Iban • Penan
Ethnic groups (2004)	• 66.3% Malays • 11.2% Chinese • 3.4% Indigenous • 19.1% other
Demonym	Bruneian
Government	Unitary Islamic absolute monarchy
- Sultan	Hassanal Bolkiah
- Crown Prince	Al-Muhtadee Billah
Legislature	Legislative Council
	Formation
- Sultanate	14th century
- British protectorate	1888
- Independence from the United Kingdom	1 January 1984
	Area
- Total	5,765 km^2 (172nd) 2,226 sq mi
- Water (%)	8.6
	Population
- Jul 2013 estimate	415,717 (175th)
- Density	67.3/km^2 (134th) 174.4/sq mi
GDP (PPP)	2012 estimate
- Total	$21.907 billion
- Per capita	$50,440
GDP (nominal)	2012 estimate
- Total	$17.092 billion
- Per capita	$39,355
HDI (2013)	▲0.855 very high · 30th
Currency	Brunei dollar (BND)
Time zone	BDT (UTC+8)

Drives on the	left
Calling code	+673
ISO 3166 code	BN
Internet TLD	.bn

Brunei officially the **Nation of Brunei, the Abode of Peace** is a sovereign state located on the north coast of the island of Borneo in Southeast Asia. Apart from its coastline with the South China Sea, it is completely surrounded by the state of Sarawak, Malaysia; and it is separated into two parts by the Sarawak district of Limbang. It is the only sovereign state completely on the island of Borneo; the remainder of the island's territory is divided between the nations of Malaysia and Indonesia. Brunei's population was 408,786 in July 2012.

At the peak of Bruneian Empire, Sultan Bolkiah (reigned 1485–1528) is alleged to have had control over the northern regions of Borneo, including modern-day Sarawak and Sabah, as well as the Sulu archipelago off the northeast tip of Borneo, Seludong (modern-day Manila), and the islands off the northwest tip of Borneo. The maritime state was visited by Spain's Magellan Expedition in 1521 and fought against Spain in 1578's Castille War.

During the 19th century the Bruneian Empire began to decline. The Sultanate ceded Sarawak to James Brooke as a reward for his aid in putting down a rebellion and named him as rajah, and it ceded Sabah to the British North Borneo Chartered Company. In 1888 Brunei became a British protectorate and was assigned a British Resident as colonial manager in 1906. After the Japanese occupation during World War II, in 1959 a new constitution was written. In 1962 a small armed rebellion against the monarchy was ended with the help of the British.

Brunei regained its independence from the United Kingdom on 1 January 1984. Economic growth during the 1990s and 2000s, averaging 56% from 1999 to 2008, has transformed Brunei into a newly industrialised country. It has developed wealth from extensive petroleum and natural gas fields. Brunei has the second-highest Human Development Index among the South East Asia nations after Singapore, and is classified as a developed country. According to the International Monetary Fund (IMF), Brunei is ranked fifth in the world by gross domestic product per capita at purchasing power parity. The IMF estimated in 2011 that Brunei was one of two countries (the other being Libya) with a public debt at 0% of the national GDP. *Forbes* also ranks Brunei as the fifth-richest nation out of 182, based on its petroleum and natural gas fields

Brunei can trace its beginnings to the 7th century, when it was a subject state of the Srivijayan empire under the name Po-ni. It later became a vassal state of Majapahit before embracing Islam in the 15th century. At the peak of its empire, the sultanate had control that extended over the coastal regions of modern-day Sarawak and Sabah, the Sulu archipelago, and the islands off the northwest tip of Borneo. The thalassocracy was visited by Ferdinand Magellan in 1521 and fought the Castille War in 1578 against Spain. Its empire began to decline with the forced ceding of Sarawak to James Brooke and the ceding of Sabah to the British North Borneo Chartered Company. After the loss of Limbang, Brunei finally became a British protectorate in 1888, receiving a resident in

1906. In the post-occupation years, it formalised a constitution and fought an armed rebellion. Brunei regained its independence from the United Kingdom on 1 January 1984. Economic growth during the 1970s and 1990s, averaging 56% from 1999 to 2008, has transformed Brunei Darussalam into a newly industrialised country.

Brunei has the second highest Human Development Index among the South East Asia nations, after Singapore and is classified as a Developed Country. According to the International Monetary Fund (IMF), Brunei is ranked 4th in the world by gross domestic product per capita at purchasing power parity.

According to legend, Brunei was founded by Awang Alak Betatar. His move from Garang [location required] to the Brunei river estuary led to the discovery of Brunei. His first exclamation upon landing on the shore, as the legend goes, was "Baru nah!" (Which in English loosely-translates as "that's it!" or "there") and thus, the name "Brunei" was derived from his words.

It was renamed "Barunai" in the 14th Century, possibly influenced by the Sanskrit word varunai (वरुण), meaning "seafarers", later to become "Brunei". The word "Borneo" is of the same origin. In the country's full name "Negara Brunei Darussalam" "Darussalam" means "Abode of Peace" in Arabic, while "Negara" means "Country" in Malay. "Negara" derives from the Sanskrit Nagara , meaning "city".

Brunei Darussalam, the host of the 1995 BIMP-EAGA EXPO is a stable and prosperous country which offers not only a well-developed infrastructure but also a strategic location within the Asean region. The country is chugging full steam ahead to diversify its economy away from an over-dependence on oil and gas, and has put in place flexible and realistic policies to facilitate foreign and local investment. The cost of utilities are the lowest in the region, while political stability, extensive economic and natural resources and a business environment attuned to the requirements of foreign investors go towards making Brunei an excellent investment choice

At present the country's economy is dominated by the oil and liquefied natural gas industries and government expenditure patterns. Brunei exports crude oil, petroleum products and LNG mainly to Japan, the United States and the Asean countries. The second most important industry is construction, a direct result of the government's investment in development and infrastructure projects. Gearing up towards putting on the mantle of a developed country in January 1996, Brunei allocated in its 1991-95 Five Year Plan a hefty B$5 billion for national development, over a billion dollars more than in the previous budget. About B$510 million was allotted for 619 projects while B$550 million or 10 percent of the development budget went to industry and commerce. Some B$100 million alone was reserved for industrial promotion and development.

STABLE, CONDUCIVE ENVIRONMENT

The oil-rich country, lying on the north-western edge of the Borneo island, has never experienced typhoons, earthquakes or severe floods. Profitable investment can be had as the country levies no personal income tax, no sales tax, payroll, manufacturing or export tax.

Competitive investment incentives are available for investors throughout the business cycle marked by the start up, growth, maturity and expansion stages. The tax advantages at start up and the on-going incentives during growth and expansion are among the most competitive around. There is no difficulty in securing approval for foreign workers, from labourers to managers. With a small labour pool of 284,500 Brunei people and Bruneians showing a marked preference for the public sector as employer, the country has had to rely on foreign workers. These make up a third of its work force.

In line with moves to promote the private sector, it is encouraging to note the contribution from the non-oil and gas sector of the economy has risen, contributing about 25 percent to GDP compared to the oil and gas sector's 46 percent. In terms of infrastructure, Brunei is ready for vigorous economy activity. At its two main ports at Muara and Kuala Belait, goods can be shipped direct to Hong Kong, Singapore and other Asian destinations. Muara, a deep-water port 29 km away from the capital of Bandar Seri Begawan, has seen continual increase in container traffic over the past two decades.

The Brunei International Airport at Bandar offers expanded passenger and cargo facilities. Its new terminal can accommodate 1.5 million passengers and 50,000 tonnes of cargo a year, which is expected to suffice till the end of the decade. A 2,000-km road network serving the whole country undergoes continual expansion. A main highway runs the entire length of its coastline, linking Muara, the port entry point at one end, and Belait, the oil-production centre, at another end.

Telecommunications-wise, Brunei has one of the best systems in the region with plans for major upgrading. Telephone availability is about one to every three people.

Two earth satellite stations provide direct telephone, telex and facsimile links to most parts of the world. Operating systems include an analogue telephone exchange, fibreoptic cable links with Singapore and Manila, a packet switching exchange for access to high-speed computer bases overseas, cellular mobile telephone and paging systems. Direct phone links are also available in the more remote parts of the country via microwave and solar-powered telephones.

PIONEER INDUSTRY INCENTIVES

Companies granted pioneer status enjoy tax holidays of up to eight years. Brunei's regulations governing foreign participation in equity are the most flexible in the region, with 100 percent foreign ownership permitted. A pioneer company is also exempt from customs duty on items to be installed in the pioneer factory and from paying import duties on raw materials not available locally or produced in Brunei for the manufacture of pioneer products.

GEOGRAPHY

Location: Southeastern Asia, bordering the South China Sea and Malaysia
Geographic coordinates: 4 30 N, 114 40 E
Map references: Southeast Asia

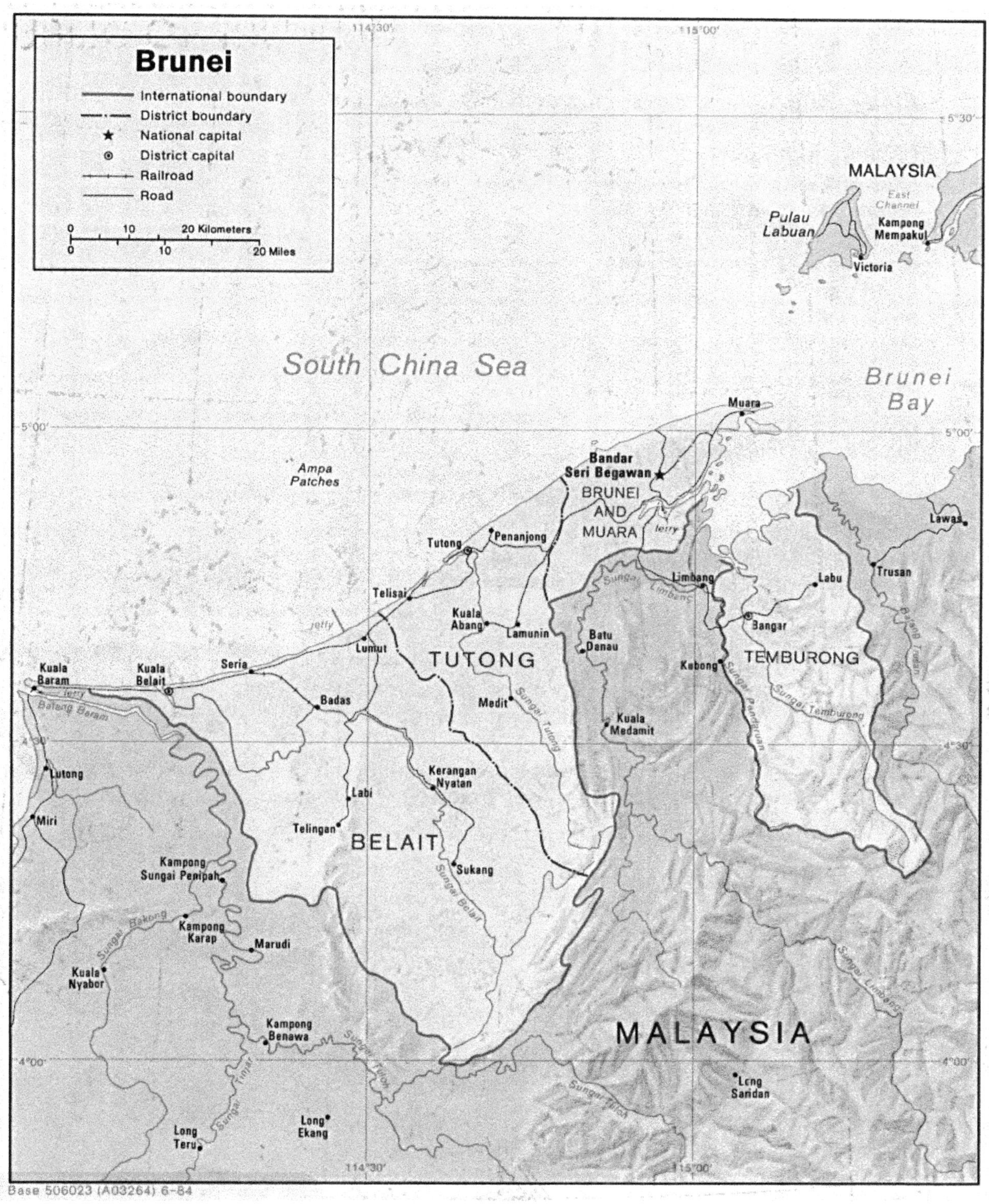

Area:
total: 5,770 sq km

land: 5,270 sq km
water: 500 sq km

Area—comparative: slightly smaller than Delaware

Land boundaries:
total: 381 km
border countries: Malaysia 381 km

Coastline: 161 km
Land use:
arable land: 1%
other: 12%

permanent crops: 1%
permanent pastures: 1%
forests and woodland: 85%

Irrigated land: 10 sq km
Natural hazards: typhoons, earthquakes, and severe flooding are very rare
Environment—current issues: seasonal smoke/haze resulting from forest fires in Indonesia

Environment—international agreements:
party to: Endangered Species, Law of the Sea, Ozone Layer Protection, Ship Pollution
signed, but not ratified: none of the selected agreements

Geography—note: close to vital sea lanes through South China Sea linking Indian and Pacific Oceans; two parts physically separated by Malaysia; almost an enclave of Malaysia

PEOPLE

Population: 322,982

Age structure:
0-14 years: 33% (male 54,154; female 51,766)
15-64 years: 63% (male 106,492; female 95,921)
65 years and over: 4% (male 7,945; female 6,704)

Population growth rate: 2.38%
Birth rate: 24.69 births/1,000 population
Death rate: 5.21 deaths/1,000 population
Net migration rate: 4.35 migrant(s)/1,000 population

Sex ratio:
at birth: 1.06 male(s)/female
under 15 years: 1.05 male(s)/female
15-64 years: 1.11 male(s)/female
65 years and over: 1.19 male(s)/female
total population: 1.09 male(s)/female

Infant mortality rate: 22.83 deaths/1,000 live births

Life expectancy at birth:
total population: 71.84 years
male: 70.35 years
female: 73.42 years

Total fertility rate: 3.33 children born/woman

Nationality:
noun: Bruneian(s)
adjective: Bruneian

Ethnic groups: Malay 64%, Chinese 20%, other 16%
Religions: Muslim (official) 63%, Buddhism 14%, Christian 8%, indigenous beliefs and other 15% (1981)
Languages: Malay (official), English, Chinese

Literacy:
definition: age 15 and over can read and write
total population: 88.2%
male: 92.6% *female:* 83.4%

GOVERNMENT

Country name:
conventional long form: Negara Brunei Darussalam
conventional short form: Brunei

Data code: BX
Government type: constitutional sultanate
Capital: Bandar Seri Begawan

Administrative divisions: 4 districts (daerah-daerah, singular—daerah); Belait, Brunei and Muara, Temburong, Tutong

Independence: 1 January 1984 (from UK)
National holiday: National Day, 23 February (1984)

Constitution: 29 September 1959 (some provisions suspended under a State of Emergency since December 1962, others since independence on 1 January 1984)

Legal system: based on English common law; for Muslims, Islamic Shari'a law supersedes civil law in a number of areas

Suffrage: none

Executive branch:
Brunei

Sultan	HASSANAL Bolkiah, Sir
Prime Minister	HASSANAL Bolkiah, Sir
Min. of Communications	Awang ABU BAKAR bin Apong
Min. of Culture, Youth, & Sports	MOHAMMAD bin Daud, Gen. (Ret.)
Min. of Defense	HASSANAL Bolkiah, Sir
Min. of Development	ABDULLAH bin Begawan
Min. of Education	Abdul RAHMAN bin Mohamed Taib
Min. of Energy	YAHYA bin Begawan
Min. of Finance	HASSANAL Bolkiah, Sir
Min. of Finance II	ABDUL RAHMAN bin Ibrahim
Min. of Foreign Affairs	MOHAMED Bolkiah, Prince
Min. of Foreign Affairs II	LIM Jock Seng
Min. of Health	SUYOI bin Osman
Min. of Home Affairs	ADANAN bin Begawan
Min. of Industry & Primary Resources	AHMAD bin Jumat, Dr.
Min. of Religious Affairs	MOHD ZAIN bin Serudin, Dr.
Senior Min. in the Prime Minister's Office	Al Muhtadee BILLAH, Crown Prince
Ambassador to the US	PUTEH ibni Mohammad Alam
Permanent Representative to the UN, New York	SHOFRY bin Abdul Ghafor

Legislative branch: unicameral Legislative Council or Majlis Masyuarat Megeri (a privy council that serves only in a consultative capacity; NA seats; members appointed by the monarch)
elections: last held in March 1962
note: in 1970 the Council was changed to an appointive body by decree of the monarch; an elected Legislative Council is being considered as part of constitutional reform, but elections are unlikely for several years

Judicial branch: Supreme Court, chief justice and judges are sworn in by the monarch for three-year terms

Political parties and leaders: Brunei Solidarity National Party or PPKB in Malay [Haji Mohd HATTA bin Haji Zainal Abidin, president]; the PPKB is the only legal political party in Brunei; it was registered in 1985, but became largely inactive after 1988; it has less than 200 registered party members; other parties include Brunei People's Party or PRB (banned in 1962) and Brunei National Democratic Party (registered in May 1985, deregistered by the Brunei Government in 1988)

International organization participation: APEC, ASEAN, C, CCC, ESCAP, G-77, IBRD, ICAO, ICRM, IDB, IFRCS, IMF, IMO, Inmarsat, Intelsat, Interpol, IOC, ISO (correspondent), ITU, NAM, OIC, OPCW, UN, UNCTAD, UPU, WHO, WIPO, WMO, WTrO

Diplomatic representation in the US:
chief of mission: Ambassador Pengiran Anak Dato Haji PUTEH Ibni Mohammad Alam
chancery: Watergate, Suite 300, 3rd floor, 2600 Virginia Avenue NW, Washington, DC 20037
telephone: (202) 342-0159
FAX: (202) 342-0158

Diplomatic representation from the US:
chief of mission: Ambassador Glen Robert RASE
embassy: Third Floor, Teck Guan Plaza, Jalan Sultan, Bandar Seri Begawan
mailing address: PSC 470 (BSB), FPO AP 96534-0001
telephone: [673] (2) 229670 *FAX:* [673] (2) 225293

Flag description: yellow with two diagonal bands of white (top, almost double width) and black starting from the upper hoist side; the national emblem in red is superimposed at the center; the emblem includes a swallow-tailed flag on top of a winged column within an upturned crescent above a scroll and flanked by two upraised hands

ECONOMY

Brunei has a small well-to-do economy that depends on revenue from natural resource extraction but encompasses a mixture of foreign and domestic entrepreneurship, government regulation, welfare measures, and village tradition. Crude oil and natural gas production account for 60% of GDP and more than 90% of exports. Per capita GDP is among the highest in Asia, and substantial income from overseas investment supplements income from domestic production. For Bruneian citizens the government provides for all medical services and free education through the university level. The government of Brunei has been emphasizing through policy and resource investments it strong desire to diversity its economy both within the oil and gas sector and to new sectors.

GDP (purchasing power parity):
$22.25 billion (2013 est.)
country comparison to the world: 128
$21.93 billion (2012 est.)
$21.73 billion (2011 est.)
note: data are in 2013 US dollars

GDP (official exchange rate):

$16.56 billion (2013 est.)

GDP - real growth rate:
1.4% (2013 est.)
country comparison to the world: 164
0.9% (2012 est.)
3.4% (2011 est.)

GDP - per capita (PPP):
$54,800 (2013 est.)
country comparison to the world: 12
$54,900 (2012 est.)
$55,200 (2011 est.)
note: data are in 2013 US dollars

GDP - composition, by end use:
household consumption: 22.1%
government consumption: 18.2%
investment in fixed capital: 14.6%
investment in inventories: 0%
exports of goods and services: 78.4%
imports of goods and services: -33.3%
(2013 est.)

GDP - composition, by sector of origin:
agriculture: 0.7%
industry: 70.9%
services: 28.4% (2013 est.)

Agriculture - products:
rice, vegetables, fruits; chickens, water buffalo, cattle, goats, eggs

Industries:
petroleum, petroleum refining, liquefied natural gas, construction, agriculture, transportation

Industrial production growth rate:
1.5% (2013 est.)
country comparison to the world: 135

Labor force:
205,800 (est.)
country comparison to the world: 169

Labor force - by occupation:

agriculture: 4.2%
industry: 62.8%
services: 33%

Unemployment rate:
2.6%
country comparison to the world: 21
2.7%

Budget:
revenues: $6.992 billion
expenditures: $5.366 billion (2013 est.)

Taxes and other revenues:
42.2% of GDP (2013 est.)
country comparison to the world: 29

Budget surplus (+) or deficit (-):
9.8% of GDP (2013 est.)
country comparison to the world: 5

Fiscal year:
1 April - 31 March

Inflation rate (consumer prices):
1% (2013 est.)
country comparison to the world: 24
0.5% (2012 est.)

Commercial bank prime lending rate:
5.5% (31 December 2013 est.)
country comparison to the world: 142
5.5% (31 December 2012 est.)

Stock of narrow money:
$3.472 billion (31 December 2013 est.)
country comparison to the world: 113
$3.509 billion (31 December 2012 est.)

Stock of broad money:
$11.92 billion (31 December 2013 est.)
country comparison to the world: 99
$11.41 billion (31 December 2012 est.)

Stock of domestic credit:

$2.846 billion (31 December 2013 est.)
country comparison to the world: 127
$2.351 billion (31 December 2012 est.)

Current account balance:
$3.977 billion
country comparison to the world: 31

Exports:
$12.75 billion
country comparison to the world: 86
$9.88 billion

Exports - commodities:
crude oil, natural gas, garments

Exports - partners:
Japan 45.7%, South Korea 15.1%, Australia 9.1%, NZ 6.6%, India 5.8%, Vietnam 4.7% (2012)

Imports:
$3.02 billion (est.)
country comparison to the world: 147

Imports - commodities:
iron and steel, motor vehicles, machinery and transport equipment, manufactured goods, food, chemicals

Imports - partners:
Singapore 26.3%, China 21.3%, UK 21.3%, Malaysia 11.8%

Debt - external:
$0 (2005)
country comparison to the world: 202

Exchange rates:
Bruneian dollars (BND) per US dollar -
1.23 (2013 est.)
1.2496 (2012 est.)
1.3635 (2010 est.)
1.45 (2009)

ENERGY

Electricity - production:
3.723 billion kWh (est.)

country comparison to the world: 126

Electricity - consumption:
3.391 billion kWh (est.)
country comparison to the world: 127

Electricity - exports:
0 kWh (est.)
country comparison to the world: 111

Electricity - imports:
0 kWh (est.)
country comparison to the world: 123

Electricity - installed generating capacity:
759,000 kW (est.)
country comparison to the world: 129

Electricity - from fossil fuels:
100% of total installed capacity (est.)
country comparison to the world: 9

Electricity - from nuclear fuels:
0% of total installed capacity (est.)
country comparison to the world: 57

Electricity - from hydroelectric plants:
0% of total installed capacity (2010 est.)
country comparison to the world: 161

Electricity - from other renewable sources:
0% of total installed capacity (est.)
country comparison to the world: 162

Crude oil - production:
141,000 bbl/day (est.)
country comparison to the world: 45

Crude oil - exports:
147,900 bbl/day (est.)
country comparison to the world: 35

Crude oil - imports:
0 bbl/day (est.)
country comparison to the world: 166

Crude oil - proved reserves:
1.1 billion bbl (1 January 2013 est.)
country comparison to the world: 41

Refined petroleum products - production:
13,500 bbl/day (est.)
country comparison to the world: 101

Refined petroleum products - consumption:
14,640 bbl/day (est.)
country comparison to the world: 144

Refined petroleum products - exports:
0 bbl/day (est.)
country comparison to the world: 159

Refined petroleum products - imports:
3,198 bbl/day (est.)
country comparison to the world: 169

Natural gas - production:
12.44 billion cu m (est.)
country comparison to the world: 38

Natural gas - consumption:
2.97 billion cu m (est.)
country comparison to the world: 73

Natural gas - exports:
9.42 billion cu m (est.)
country comparison to the world: 25

Natural gas - imports:
0 cu m (est.)
country comparison to the world: 167

Natural gas - proved reserves:
390.8 billion cu m (1 January 2013 est.)
country comparison to the world: 35

Carbon dioxide emissions from consumption of energy:
8.656 million Mt (2011 est.)

COMMUNICATION

Telephones - main lines in use:
70,933
country comparison to the world: 154

Telephones - mobile cellular:
469,700
country comparison to the world: 170

Telephone system:
general assessment: service throughout the country is good; international service is good to Southeast Asia, Middle East, Western Europe, and the US
domestic: every service available
international: country code - 673; landing point for the SEA-ME-WE-3 optical telecommunications submarine cable that provides links to Asia, the Middle East, and Europe; the Asia-America Gateway submarine cable network provides new links to Asia and the US; satellite earth stations - 2 Intelsat (1 Indian Ocean and 1 Pacific Ocean)

Broadcast media:
state-controlled Radio Television Brunei (RTB) operates 5 channels; 3 Malaysian TV stations are available; foreign TV broadcasts are available via satellite and cable systems; RTB operates 5 radio networks and broadcasts on multiple frequencies; British Forces Broadcast Service (BFBS) provides radio broadcasts on 2 FM stations; some radio broadcast stations from Malaysia are available via repeaters (2009)

Internet country code:
.bn

Internet hosts:
49,457
country comparison to the world: 96

Internet users:
314,900
country comparison to the world: 128

TRANSPORTATION

Railways:
total: 13 km (private line)
narrow gauge: 13 km 0.610-m gauge

Highways:
total: 1,150 km *paved:* 399 km *unpaved:* 751 km

Waterways: 209 km; navigable by craft drawing less than 1.2 m
Pipelines: crude oil 135 km; petroleum products 418 km; natural gas 920 km
Ports and harbors: Bandar Seri Begawan, Kuala Belait, Muara, Seria, Tutong
Merchant marine:
total: 7 liquefied gas tankers (1,000 GRT or over) totaling 348,476 GRT/340,635 DWT

Airports: 2

Airports—with paved runways:
total: 1
over 3,047 m: 1
Airports—with unpaved runways:
total: 1 *914 to 1,523 m:* 1 **Heliports:** 3

MILITARY

Military branches: Land Forces, Navy, Air Force, Royal Brunei Police
Military manpower—military age: 18 years of age
Military manpower—availability:
males age 15-49: 88,628
Military manpower—fit for military service:
males age 15-49: 51,270
Military manpower—reaching military age annually:
males: 3,078
Military expenditures—dollar figure: $343 million
Military expenditures—percent of GDP: 6%

TRANSNATIONAL ISSUES

Disputes—international: possibly involved in a complex dispute over the Spratly Islands with China, Malaysia, Philippines, Taiwan, and Vietnam; in 1984, Brunei established an exclusive fishing zone that encompasses Louisa Reef in the southern Spratly Islands, but has not publicly claimed the island.

IMPORTANT INFORMATION FOR UNDERSTANDING BRUNEI

PROFILE

OFFICIAL NAME: Negara Brunei Darussalam

Geography
Area: 5,765 sq. km. (2,226 sq. mi.), slightly larger than Delaware.
Cities: *Capital*--Bandar Seri Begawan.
Terrain: East--flat coastal plain rises to mountains; west--hilly lowland with a few mountain ridges.
Climate: Equatorial; high temperatures, humidity, and rainfall.

People
Nationality: *Noun and adjective*--Bruneian(s).
Population : 383,000.
Annual growth rate: 3.5%.
Ethnic groups: Malay, Chinese, other indigenous groups.
Religion: Islam.
Languages: Malay, English, Chinese; Iban and other indigenous dialects.
Education: *Years compulsory*--9. *Literacy* (2006)--94.7%.
Health: *Life expectancy (years)*--74.4 (men), 77.4 (women) yrs. *Infant mortality rate* --12.25/1,000.

Government
Type: Malay Islamic Monarchy.
Independence: January 1, 1984.
Constitution: 1959.
Branches: *Executive*--Sultan is both head of state and Prime Minister, presiding over a fourteen-member cabinet. *Legislative*--a Legislative Council has been reactivated after a 20-year suspension to play an advisory role for the Sultan. *Judicial* (based on Indian penal code and English common law)--magistrate's courts, High Court, Court of Appeals, Judicial Committee of the Privy Council (sits in London).
Subdivisions: *Four districts*--Brunei-Muara, Belait, Tutong, and Temburong.

Economy
Natural resources: Oil and natural gas.
Trade: *Exports*--oil, liquefied natural gas, petroleum products, garments. Major markets--Japan, Korea, ASEAN, U.S. *Imports*--machinery and transport equipment, manufactured goods. *Major suppliers*--ASEAN, Japan, U.S., EU.

PEOPLE

Many cultural and linguistic differences make Brunei Malays distinct from the larger Malay populations in nearby Malaysia and Indonesia, even though they are ethnically related and share the Muslim religion.
Brunei has hereditary nobility, carrying the title Pengiran. The Sultan can award to commoners the title Pehin, the equivalent of a life peerage awarded in the United Kingdom. The Sultan also can award his subjects the Dato, the equivalent of a knighthood in the United Kingdom, and Datin, the equivalent of damehood.

Bruneians adhere to the practice of using complete full names with all titles, including the title Haji (for men) or Hajah (for women) for those who have made the Haj pilgrimage to Mecca. Many Brunei Malay women wear the tudong, a traditional head covering. Men wear the songkok, a traditional Malay cap. Men who have completed the Haj can wear a white songkok.
The requirements to attain Brunei citizenship include passing tests in Malay culture, customs, and language. Stateless permanent residents of Brunei are given International Certificates of Identity, which allow them to travel overseas. The majority of Brunei's Chinese are permanent residents, and many are stateless. An amendment to the National Registration and Immigration Act of 2002 allowed female Bruneian citizens for the first time to transfer their nationality to their children.

Oil wealth allows the Brunei Government to provide the population with one of Asia's finest health care systems. Malaria has been eradicated, and cholera is virtually nonexistent. There are five general hospitals--in Bandar Seri Begawan, Tutong, Kuala Belait, Bangar, and Seria--and there are numerous health clinics throughout the country.

Education starts with preschool, followed by 6 years of primary education and up to 7 years of secondary education. Nine years of education are mandatory. Most of Brunei's college students attend universities and other institutions abroad, but approximately 3,674 (2005) study at the University of Brunei Darussalam. Opened in 1985, the university has a faculty of more than 300 instructors and is located on a sprawling campus overlooking the South China Sea.
The official language is Malay, but English is widely understood and used in business. Other languages spoken are several Chinese dialects, Iban, and a number of native dialects. Islam is the official religion, but religious freedom is guaranteed under the constitution.

HISTORY

Historians believe there was a forerunner to the present Brunei Sultanate, which the Chinese called Po-ni. Chinese and Arabic records indicate that this ancient trading kingdom existed at the mouth of the Brunei River as early as the seventh or eighth century A.D. This early kingdom was apparently conquered by the Sumatran Hindu Empire of Srivijaya in the early ninth century, which later controlled northern Borneo and the Philippines. It was subjugated briefly by the Java-based Majapahit Empire but soon regained its independence and once again rose to prominence.

The Brunei Empire had its golden age from the 15th to the 17th centuries, when its control extended over the entire island of Borneo and north into the Philippines. Brunei was particularly powerful under the fifth sultan, Bolkiah (1473-1521), who was famed for his sea exploits and even briefly captured Manila; and under the ninth sultan, Hassan (1605-19), who fully developed an elaborate Royal Court structure, elements of which remain today.

After Sultan Hassan, Brunei entered a period of decline due to internal battles over royal succession as well as the rising influences of European colonial powers in the region that, among other things, disrupted traditional trading patterns, destroying the economic base of Brunei and many other Southeast Asian sultanates. In 1839, the English adventurer James Brooke arrived in Borneo and helped the Sultan put down a rebellion. As a reward, he became governor and later "Rajah" of Sarawak in northwest Borneo and gradually expanded the territory under his control.

Meanwhile, the British North Borneo Company was expanding its control over territory in northeast Borneo. In 1888, Brunei became a protectorate of the British Government, retaining internal independence but with British control over external affairs. In 1906, Brunei accepted a further measure of British control when executive power was transferred to a British resident, who advised the ruler on all matters except those concerning local custom and religion.

In 1959, a new constitution was written declaring Brunei a self-governing state, while its foreign affairs, security, and defense remained the responsibility of the United Kingdom. An attempt in 1962 to introduce a partially elected legislative body with limited powers was abandoned after the opposition political party, Parti Rakyat Brunei, launched an armed uprising, which the government put down with the help of British forces. In the late 1950s and early 1960s, the government also resisted pressures to join neighboring Sabah and Sarawak in the newly formed Malaysia. The Sultan eventually decided that Brunei would remain an independent state.

In 1967, Sultan Omar abdicated in favor of his eldest son, Hassanal Bolkiah, who became the 29th ruler. The former Sultan remained as Defense Minister and assumed the royal title Seri Begawan. In 1970, the national capital, Brunei Town, was renamed Bandar Seri Begawan in his honor. The Seri Begawan died in 1986.

On January 4, 1979, Brunei and the United Kingdom signed a new treaty of friendship and cooperation. On January 1, 1984, Brunei Darussalam became a fully independent state.

GOVERNMENT AND POLITICAL CONDITIONS

Under Brunei's 1959 constitution, the Sultan is the head of state with full executive authority, including emergency powers since 1962. The Sultan is assisted and advised by five councils, which he appoints. A Council of Ministers, or cabinet, which currently consists of 14 members (including the Sultan himself), assists in the administration of the government. The Sultan presides over the cabinet as Prime Minister and also holds the positions of Minister of Defense and Minister of Finance. His son, the Crown Prince, serves as Senior Minister. One of the Sultan's brothers, Prince Mohamed, serves as Minister of Foreign Affairs.

Brunei's legal system is based on English common law, with an independent judiciary, a body of written common law judgments and statutes, and legislation enacted by the sultan. The local magistrates' courts try most cases. More serious cases go before the High Court, which sits for about 2 weeks every few months. Brunei has an arrangement with the United Kingdom whereby United Kingdom judges are appointed as the judges for Brunei's High Court and Court of Appeal. Final appeal can be made to the Judicial Committee of the Privy Council in London in civil but not criminal cases. Brunei also has a separate system of Islamic courts that apply Sharia law in family and other matters involving Muslims.
The Government of Brunei assures continuing public support for the current form of government by providing economic benefits such as subsidized food, fuel, and housing; free education and medical care; and low-interest loans for government employees.

The Sultan said in a 1989 interview that he intended to proceed, with prudence, to establish more liberal institutions in the country and that he would reintroduce elections and a legislature when he "[could] see evidence of a genuine interest in politics on the part of a responsible majority of Bruneians." In 1994, a constitutional review committee submitted its findings to the Sultan, but these have not been made public. In 2004 the Sultan re-introduced an appointed Legislative Council with minimal powers. Five of the 31 seats on the Council are indirectly elected by village leaders.

Brunei's economy is almost totally supported by exports of crude oil and natural gas. The government uses its earnings in part to build up its foreign reserves, which at one time reportedly reached more than $30 billion. The country's wealth, coupled with its membership in the United Nations, Association of Southeast Asian Nations (ASEAN), the Asia Pacific Economic Cooperation (APEC) forum, and the Organization of the Islamic Conference give it an influence in the world disproportionate to its size.

Principal Government Officials
Sultan and Yang di-Pertuan, Prime Minister, Minister of Defense, and Minister of Finance--His Majesty Sultan Hassanal Bolkiah
Senior Minister--His Royal Highness Crown Prince Billah
Minister of Foreign Affairs--His Royal Highness Prince Mohamed Bolkiah
Ambassador to the United States--Pengiran Anak Dato Haji Puteh
Ambassador to the United Nations--Dr. Haji Emran bin Bahar
Brunei Darussalam maintains an embassy in the United States at 3520 International Court, NW, Washington, DC 20008; tel. 202-237-1838.

ECONOMY

Currency	Brunei dollar BND
Fixed exchange rates	1 Brunei dollar = 1 Singapore dollar
Fiscal year	1 April – 31 March (from April 2009)
Trade organisations	APEC, ASEAN, WTO. BIMP-EAGA
	Statistics
GDP	$20.38 billion PPP Rank: 123rd
GDP growth	2.8% Q1
GDP per capita	$51,600
GDP by sector	agriculture (0.7%), industry (73.3%), services (26%)
Inflation (CPI)	1.2%
Population below poverty line	1000 person
Labour force	188,800
Labour force by occupation	agriculture 4.5%, industry 63.1%, services 32.4%
Unemployment	3.7%
Main industries	petroleum, petroleum refining, liquefied natural gas, construction
Ease-of-doing-business rank	83rd
	External
Exports	$10.67 billion
Main export partners	Japan 46.5% South Korea 15.5% Australia 9.3% India 7.0% New Zealand 6.7% (est.)
Imports	$12.055 billion c.i.f.
Main import partners	Singapore 26.3% China 21.3%

	United Kingdom 21.3%
	Malaysia 11.8%
Public finances	
Public debt	$0
Revenues	$10.49 billion
Expenses	$5.427 billion
Credit rating	Not rated

Main data source: CIA World Fact Book *All values, unless otherwise stated, are in US dollars.*

Brunei is a country with a small, wealthy economy that is a mixture of foreign and domestic entrepreneurship, government regulation and welfare measures, and village tradition. It is almost totally supported by exports of crude oil and natural gas, with revenues from the petroleum sector accounting for over half of GDP. Per capita GDP is high, and substantial income from overseas investment supplements income from domestic production. The government provides for all medical services and subsidizes food and housing. The government has shown progress in its basic policy of diversifying the economy away from oil and gas. Brunei's leaders are concerned that steadily increased integration in the world economy will undermine internal social cohesion although it has taken steps to become a more prominent player by serving as chairman for the 2000 APEC (Asian Pacific Economic Cooperation) forum. Growth in 1999 was estimated at 2.5% due to higher oil prices in the second half.

Brunei is the third-largest oil producer in Southeast Asia, averaging about 180,000 barrels per day (29,000 m^3/d). It also is the fourth-largest producer of liquefied natural gas in the world.

Brunei is the fourth-largest oil producer in Southeast Asia, averaging about 219,000 barrels a day in 2006. It also is the ninth-largest exporter of liquefied natural gas in the world. Like many oil producing countries, Brunei's economy has followed the swings of the world oil market. Economic growth has averaged around 2.8% in the 2000s, heavily dependent on oil and gas production. Oil production has averaged around 200,000 barrels a day during the 2000s, while liquefied natural gas output has been slightly under or over 1,000 trillion btu/day over the same period. Brunei is estimated to have oil reserves expected to last 25 years, and enough natural gas reserves to last 40 years.

Brunei Shell Petroleum (BSP), a joint venture owned in equal shares by the Brunei Government and the Royal Dutch/Shell group of companies, is the chief oil and gas production company in Brunei. It also operates the country's only refinery. BSP and four sister companies--including the liquefied natural gas producing firm BLNG--constitute the largest employer in Brunei after the government. BSP's small refinery has a distillation capacity of 10,000 barrels per day. This satisfies domestic demand for most petroleum products.

The French oil company Total (then known as ELF Aquitaine) became active in petroleum exploration in Brunei in the 1980s. The joint venture Total E&P Borneo BV currently produces approximately 35,000 barrels per day and 13% of Brunei's natural gas.

In 2003, Malaysia disputed Brunei-awarded oil exploration concessions for offshore blocks J and K (Total and Shell respectively), which led to the Brunei licensees ceasing exploration activities. Negotiations between the two countries are continuing in order to resolve the conflict. In 2006, Brunei awarded two on-shore blocks--one to a Canadian-led and the other to a Chinese-led consortium. Australia, Indonesia, and Korea were the largest customers for Brunei's oil exports, taking over 67% of Brunei's total crude exports. Traditional customers Japan, the U.S., and China each took around 5% of total crude exports.
Almost all of Brunei's natural gas is liquefied at Brunei Shell's Liquefied Natural Gas (LNG) plant, which opened in 1972 and is one of the largest LNG plants in the world. Some 90% of Brunei's LNG produced is sold to Japan under a long-term agreement renewed in 1993.

The agreement calls for Brunei to provide over 5 million tons of LNG per year to three Japanese utilities, namely to TEPCo, Tokyo Electric Power Co. (J.TER or 5001), Tokyo Gas Co. (J.TYG or 9531) and Osaka Gas Co. (J.OSG or 9532). The Japanese company, Mitsubishi, is a joint venture partner with Shell and the Brunei Government in Brunei LNG, Brunei Coldgas, and Brunei Shell Tankers, which together produce the LNG and supply it to Japan. Since 1995, Brunei has supplied more than 700,000 tons of LNG to the Korea Gas Corporation (KOGAS) as well. In 1999, Brunei's natural gas production reached 90 cargoes per day. A small amount of natural gas is used for domestic power generation. Since 2001, Japan remains the dominant export market for natural gas. Brunei is the fourth-largest exporter of LNG in the Asia-Pacific region behind Indonesia, Malaysia, and Australia.

The government sought in the past decade to diversify the economy with limited success. Oil and gas and government spending still account for most of Brunei's economic activity. Brunei's non-petroleum industries include agriculture, forestry, fishing, aquaculture, and banking. The garment-for-export industry has been shrinking since the U.S. eliminated its garment quota system at the end of 2004. The Brunei Economic Development Board announced plans in 2003 to use proven gas reserves to establish downstream industrial projects. The government plans to build a power plant in the Sungai Liang region to power a proposed aluminum smelting plant that will depend on foreign investors. A second major project depending on foreign investment is in the planning stage: a giant container hub at the Muara Port facilities.

The government regulates the immigration of foreign labor out of concern it might disrupt Brunei's society. Work permits for foreigners are issued only for short periods and must be continually renewed. Despite these restrictions, the estimated 100,000 foreign temporary residents of Brunei make up a significant portion of the work force. The government reported a total work force of 180,400 in 2006, with a derived unemployment rate of 4.0%.

Oil and natural gas account for almost all exports. Since only a few products other than petroleum are produced locally, a wide variety of items must be imported. Nonetheless, Brunei has had a significant trade surplus in the 2000s. Official statistics show Singapore, Malaysia, Japan, the U.S., and the U.K. as the leading importers in 2005. The United States was the third-largest supplier of imports to Brunei in 2005.

Brunei's substantial foreign reserves are managed by the Brunei Investment Agency (BIA), an arm of the Ministry of Finance. BIA's guiding principle is to increase the real value of Brunei's foreign reserves while pursuing a diverse investment strategy, with holdings in the United States, Japan, Western Europe, and the Association of Southeast Asian Nations (ASEAN) countries.

The Brunei Government encourages more foreign investment. New enterprises that meet certain criteria can receive pioneer status, exempting profits from income tax for up to 5 years, depending on the amount of capital invested. The normal corporate income tax rate is 30%. There is no personal income tax or capital gains tax.

One of the government's priorities is to encourage the development of Brunei Malays as leaders of industry and commerce. There are no specific restrictions of foreign equity ownership, but local participation, both shared capital and management, is encouraged. Such participation helps when tendering for contracts with the government or Brunei Shell Petroleum.

Companies in Brunei must either be incorporated locally or registered as a branch of a foreign company and must be registered with the Registrar of Companies. Public companies must have a minimum of seven shareholders. Private companies must have a minimum of two but not more than 50 shareholders. At least half of the directors in a company must be residents of Brunei.

The government owns a cattle farm in Australia through which the country's beef supplies are processed. At 2,262 square miles, this ranch is larger than Brunei itself. Eggs and chickens are largely produced locally, but most of Brunei's other food needs must be imported. Agriculture, aquaculture, and fisheries are among the industrial sectors that the government has selected for highest priority in its efforts to diversify the economy.

Recently the government has announced plans for Brunei to become an international offshore financial center as well as a center for Islamic banking. Brunei is keen on the development of small and medium enterprises and also is investigating the possibility of establishing a "cyber park" to develop an information technology industry. Brunei has also promoted ecotourism to take advantage of the over 70% of Brunei's territory that remains primal tropical rainforest.

DEFENSE

The Sultan is both Minister of Defense and Supreme Commander of the Armed Forces (RBAF). All infantry, navy, and air combat units are made up of volunteers. There are two infantry battalions equipped with armored reconnaissance vehicles and armored personnel carriers and supported by Rapier air defense missiles and a flotilla of coastal patrol vessels armed with surface-to-surface missiles. Brunei has ordered, but not yet taken possession of, three offshore patrol vessels from the U.K.

Brunei has a defense agreement with the United Kingdom, under which a British Armed Forces Ghurka battalion (1,500 men) is permanently stationed in Seria, near the center of Brunei's oil industry. The RBAF has joint exercises, training programs, and other military cooperation with the United Kingdom and many other countries, including the

United States. The U.S. and Brunei signed a memorandum of understanding (MOU) on defense cooperation in November 1994. The two countries conduct an annual military exercise called CARAT.

FOREIGN RELATIONS

Brunei joined ASEAN on January 7, 1984--one week after resuming full independence--and gives its ASEAN membership the highest priority in its foreign relations. Brunei joined the UN in September 1984. It also is a member of the Organization of the Islamic Conference (OIC) and of the Asia-Pacific Economic Cooperation (APEC) forum. Brunei hosted the APEC Economic Leaders' Meeting in November 2000 and the ASEAN Regional Forum (ARF) in July 2002.

U.S.-BRUNEI RELATIONS

Relations between the United States and Brunei date from the 1800s. On April 6, 1845, the U.S.S. Constitution visited Brunei. The two countries concluded a Treaty of Peace, Friendship, Commerce and Navigation in 1850, which remains in force today. The United States maintained a consulate in Brunei from 1865 to 1867.

The U.S. welcomed Brunei Darussalam's full independence from the United Kingdom on January 1, 1984, and opened an Embassy in Bandar Seri Begawan on that date. Brunei opened its embassy in Washington in March 1984. Brunei's armed forces engage in joint exercises, training programs, and other military cooperation with the U.S. A memorandum of understanding on defense cooperation was signed on November 29, 1994. The Sultan visited Washington in December 2002.

Principal U.S. Embassy Officials
Ambassador--Daniel L. Shields
Deputy Chief of Mission--John McIntyre
Management Officer--Michael Lampel

The U.S. Embassy in Bandar Seri Begawan is located on the third & fifth floors of the Teck Guan Plaza, at the corner of Jalan Sultan and Jalan MacArthur; tel: 673-2229670; fax: 673-2225293; e-mail: usembassy_bsb@state.gov

TRAVEL AND BUSINESS INFORMATION

The U.S. Department of State's Consular Information Program advises Americans traveling and residing abroad through Consular Information Sheets, Public Announcements, and Travel Warnings. **Consular Information Sheets** exist for all countries and include information on entry and exit requirements, currency regulations, health conditions, safety and security, crime, political disturbances, and the addresses of the U.S. embassies and consulates abroad. **Public Announcements** are issued to disseminate information quickly about terrorist threats and other relatively short-term conditions overseas that pose significant risks to the security of American travelers. **Travel Warnings** are issued when the State Department recommends that Americans avoid travel to a certain country because the situation is dangerous or unstable.

For the latest security information, Americans living and traveling abroad should regularly monitor the Department's Bureau of Consular Affairs Internet web site at http://www.travel.state.gov, where the current Worldwide Caution, Public Announcements, and Travel Warnings can be found. Consular Affairs Publications, which contain information on obtaining passports and planning a safe trip abroad, are also available at http://www.travel.state.gov. For additional information on international travel, see http://www.usa.gov/Citizen/Topics/Travel/International.shtml.

The Department of State encourages all U.S citizens traveling or residing abroad to register via the State Department's travel registration website or at the nearest U.S. embassy or consulate abroad. Registration will make your presence and whereabouts known in case it is necessary to contact you in an emergency and will enable you to receive up-to-date information on security conditions.

Emergency information concerning Americans traveling abroad may be obtained by calling 1-888-407-4747 toll free in the U.S. and Canada or the regular toll line 1-202-501-4444 for callers outside the U.S. and Canada.

The National Passport Information Center (NPIC) is the U.S. Department of State's single, centralized public contact center for U.S. passport information. Telephone: 1-877-4USA-PPT (1-877-487-2778). Customer service representatives and operators for TDD/TTY are available Monday-Friday, 7:00 a.m. to 12:00 midnight, Eastern Time, excluding federal holidays.

Travelers can check the latest health information with the U.S. Centers for Disease Control and Prevention in Atlanta, Georgia. A hotline at 877-FYI-TRIP (877-394-8747) and a web site at http://www.cdc.gov/travel/index.htm give the most recent health advisories, immunization recommendations or requirements, and advice on food and drinking water safety for regions and countries. A booklet entitled "Health Information for International Travel" (HHS publication number CDC-95-8280) is available from the U.S. Government Printing Office, Washington, DC 20402, tel. (202) 512-1800.

EU-BRUNEI RELATIONS

Official Name	Negara Brunei Darussalam
Population	0.38 million
Area	6000 km²
Gross Domestic Product	5 bn euros
GDP Per Capita	14.173 €
Real GDP (% growth)	3.0 %
Exports GDP %	0.85
Imports GDP %	0.27
Exports to Brunei from EU (mn €, 2001)	108 EU imports from Brunei (mn €)
Imports to EU from Brunei (mn €, 2001)	72
Human Development Index (rank of 175°)	33

Head of State	HM Paduka Seri Baginda Sultan Haji Hassanal Bolkiah Mu'izzadddin Waddaulah (Sultan, prime minister, minister of finance and defence)

FRAMEWORK

The framework for co-operation dialogue with Brunei is the EC-ASEAN Agreement of 1980. There is no bilateral cooperation agreement.

POLITICAL CONTEXT

Brunei Darussalam became independent from the United Kingdom on 1 January 1984, and a week later joined the Association of South-East Asian Nations (ASEAN). Brunei is a constitutional monarchy with the Sultan Yang Di-Pertuan – Hassanal Bolkiah as the Head of State, Prime Minister, Defence Minister, as well as Minister for Finance. The Sultan presides over a 10-member cabinet which he appoints himself. Five councils advise the Sultan on policy matters: the Religious Council, the Privy Council, the Council of Succession, the Legislative Council and the Council of Ministers (the cabinet). Since 1962 the Sultan has ruled by decree. Thus, the system of government revolves around the Sultan as the source of executive power.

On 25 September 2004, the Legislative Council met for the first time in 20 years, with 21 members appointed by the Sultan. It passed constitutional amendments, calling for a 45-seat council with 15 elected members. In a move towards political reform an appointed parliament was revived in 2004. The constitution provides for an expanded house with up to 15 elected MPs. However, no date has been set for elections.

Brunei is a Muslim country, with a Ministry of Religious Affairs established to foster and promote Islam. Brunei continues to play a peacekeeping role in the Philippines, and is taking part in efforts to monitor peace in the Indonesian region of Aceh.

EUROPEAN COMMUNITY ASSISTANCE

By virtue of its advanced level of economic development Brunei does not benefit from bilateral development or economic projects.

EC co-operation with Brunei has for the greater part been limited to joint EC- ASEAN projects.

The EC has given financial support to the ASEAN-EC Management Centre (AEMC), located in Brunei, the contract for which has come to an end.

TRADE AND ECONOMIC

Since 1929, when oil was discovered in Brunei, the country has flourished. During 1998 and as a consequence of the Asia crisis, however, both exports and imports decreased in comparison with previous years.

- **Key role of oil and gas**: Brunei suffered little directly from the Asian financial crisis of 1997. But, in 1998, the Sultanate was hit by the sharp fall in oil sales and the bankruptcy of a locally-owned oil and gas company, resulting in a contraction in GDP of 4%. Subsequently, economic activity recovered in step with the resumption of oil and gas extraction and, in recent years, the sharp rise in the oil price. The latest available data for GDP shows real annual growth around 3%. Oil reserves are officially estimated at 25 years, but, great hopes are placed in two new drilling concessions.

Economic structure: Almost everything the country needs is imported. Even the industrial labour force comes from abroad, mainly from India, the Philippines, Indonesia and Bangladesh as most of Brunei's citizens are employed as civil servants (60% of the population) and prefer the status related to that occupation. This also explains the apparent contradiction between the necessity to employ foreign manpower and the rising unemployment rate (officially at 4.7% but estimated at 9%).

- At the beginning of 2000, the government of the Sultanate announced an ambitious programme of **economic reforms** in order to reduce the dependence on oil and gas. Two initiatives have been taken up till know– to develop tourism and to support the creation of an off-shore financial centre in developing Islamic banking business.

- The tourism industry is, however, handicapped by the shortage of quality infrastructure, and the geographical insulation of the Sultanate.

Brunei's trade surplus fell by an estimated 74% in US dollar terms in 1999 as the price of oil and gas collapsed. A strengthening oil price and long-term contracts for natural gas, paid in US dollars, should, however, ensure that Brunei's trade position remains healthy.

At present Brunei produces oil and gas almost to the exclusion of other products. The government is trying hard, however, to develop manufactured exports, in particular cement and roofing (tiles) which are both protected sectors. The garment industry is struggling after the abolition of global quotas on the textile trade. The Sultan has announced financial reforms.

Brunei has signed a free-trade pact with New Zealand, Singapore and Chile. A Brunei Tourism Board has been set up

The domestic economy: Brunei's economic growth remains fairly sluggish, at 2.6% year on year but a recovery is likely to have taken place in the second quarter of 2005. The non-oil and gas sector is expanding more rapidly than the energy sector. High global oil prices have lifted transport prices, but overall inflation remains low.

Foreign trade and payments: High oil prices lay behind an increase in the merchandises-trade surplus in the first quarter of 2005.The oil and gas sector continues to account for the bulk of exports; garments exports were much lower than in the year-earlier period.

The investment policy in Brunei is largely open to foreign investors, as indicated by a favourable legal environment and a policy allowing full foreign ownership in a majority of economic sectors. Foreign investments have been more particularly in the last years as they are considered by the government as a key element to contribute to the targeted diversification of the country's economy.

As part of this strategy to attract foreign investments, an Economic Development Board (EDB) was created in 2001. The main sectors and projects promoted by the EDB and susceptible to attract foreign investments include port infrastructure, industry, communication (aviation hub), eco-tourism, and financial services. In parallel with the creation of the EDB, major policy changes have been made in the last years to promote foreign investments. August 2000 saw the introduction of an offshore legislation in Brunei. New laws were drafted covering international banking, insurance, offshore companies, trusts, limited partnerships and registered agents.

Changes in the legislation are too recent analyze its effects. The volume of FDI has doubled between 2001 and 2002, while the figures available until mid 2003 include that the trend is positive and that investments do not only target natural resources but also services.

BRUNEI GOVERNMENT AND LEGAL SYSTEM BASICS

The British Residential system was introduced in Brunei Darussalam by virtue of the Courts Enactment of 1906. Another enactment was later introduced, known as the 1908 Enactment and had repealed the 1906 Enactment. The purpose of this second Enactment was to amend the law relating to the constitution and powers of the Civil and Criminal Courts and the law and procedures to be administered in Brunei Darussalam (hereafter called the "State").

By virtue of section 3 of the 1908 Enactment, five courts were constituted in the State for the administration of Civil and Criminal justice. There were:

(1) The Court of the Resident

(2) Courts of Magistrate of the First Class

(3) Courts of Magistrate of the Second Class

(4) Courts of Native Magistrates

(5) Courts of Kathis.

The first court would be the Court of the Resident, which had and exercised original and appellate jurisdiction in civil and criminal matters. The Officer, which presided the Court of the Resident, should either be the Resident; or the District Judge of the District Court of Labuan or any District Judge of the Colony of the Straits Settlements[1].

The Court of the Resident had jurisdiction in all suits, matters and questions of a civil nature except the power to authorize any Court in the State to dissolve or annul a marriage lawfully solemnised in the United Kingdom of Great Britain and Ireland or in any British Colony, Protectorate or Possession[2].

Its appellate jurisdiction in both civil and criminal matters would be to hear and determine all appeals from the decisions of the lower Courts; and in doing so might exercise full powers or supervision and revision in respect of all proceedings in such Courts[3].

Section 8A of the 1908 Enactment stated that the Courts of Magistrates was of two kinds

i.e. Courts Magistrates of the First Class, and Courts Magistrates of the Second Class.

For the Court of Magistrate of the First Class, its criminal jurisdiction would be to try all offences for which the maximum term of imprisonment provided by law did not exceed a term of 7 years imprisonment of either description or which were punishable with fine only and for any other offence in respect of which jurisdiction was given by law; whereas

[1] Section 4 of the 1908 Enactment. [2] Section 5(i) of the 1908 Enactment. [3] Section 7 of the 1908 Enactment.

for civil jurisdiction it would hear and determine all suits when the amount in dispute or the value of the subject matter did not exceed $1,000 [4].

In addition to that, such Court had power to grant, alter, revoke and annul probates of wills and letters of administration in the estate of all persons leaving movable or immovable property in the State or the time of death having a fixed place of abode within the State where such estate does not exceed in value $2,500[5]. Such Court also had power to appoint and control guardians of infants and lunatics[6].

For its appellate jurisdiction, the Court of Magistrate of the First Class had power to hear and determine all appeals from the decisions of inferior Courts both in civil and criminal matters, and had power for revision and supervision in respect of all proceedings in such Courts[7].

For the Court of Magistrate of the Second Class, its criminal jurisdiction would be to try all offences for which the maximum term of imprisonment provided by law does not exceed 3 years imprisonment of either description or which were punishable with fine only of a sum not exceeding $100 and any offence in respect of which jurisdiction is given to the Court of a Magistrate of the Second Class.[8]

In its civil jurisdiction, the Court of Magistrate of the Second Class would hear and determine all suits when the amount in dispute or the value of the subject matter does not exceed $ 100.[9]

Unlike the Court of Magistrate of the First Class, the Court of Magistrate of the Second Class had no power to grant probate of wills or letters of administration, to appoint and control guardians of infants and lunatics, or even to hear appeals in civil or criminal matters[10].

As for the Court of a Native Magistrate, it could hear and determine all suits brought by or against Malays or other Asiatics in which the amount in dispute or the subject matter does not exceed $25 while its criminal jurisdiction would be to try and determine cases in which the maximum amount of imprisonment prescribed by law did not exceed three months[11].

And lastly, the Court of a Kathi that had such powers in all matters concerning Islamic religion, marriage and divorce as may be defined in his "Kuasa."[12].

[4] Section 8B (i) of the 1908 Enactment. [5] Section 8B (ii)(a) of the 1908 Enactment. [6] Section 8B (ii)(b) of the 1908 Enactment. [7] Section 8B (iii) of the 1908 Enactment. [8] Section 8C (i) of the 1908 Enactment. [9] Section 8C (i) of the 1908 Enactment. [10] Section 8C (ii) of the 1908 Enactment. [11] Section 9 of the 1908 Enactment. [12] Section 9 of the 1908 Enactment.

Sentences that might be imposed by the various Courts:

(1) Court of the Resident – any sentence authorized by law.

(2) Courts of Magistrate of the First Class – Imprisonment for a term not exceeding two years. Fine not exceeding $1,000. Whipping not exceeding 12 strokes.

(3) Courts of Magistrate of the Second Class – Imprisonment for a term not exceeding fourteen days. Fine not exceeding $50.

(4) Courts of Native Magistrates and Kathis – Fine not exceeding $10.[13]

Apart from the five courts mentioned earlier, there was the Supreme Court. The is court or any Judge thereof would have the original jurisdiction in the case of any offence charged to had been committed within the State for which the punishment of death is authorised by law[14].

The Supreme Court had civil appellate jurisdiction for an appeal from the final decision of the Court of the Resident in any civil action or proceeding where the amount in dispute or the subject matter exceeded$1,000 except in any of the following cases where no such appeal might be made:

(1) where the judgment or order was made by the consent of parties;

(2) where the judgment or order relates to costs only;

(3) where by any Enactment for the time being in force the judgment or order of the Court of the Resident was expressly declared to be final[15].

The criminal appellate jurisdiction of the Supreme Court would be to hear appeal from any decision of the Court of the Resident in the exercise of its original jurisdiction whereby any person had been convicted and sentenced to not less than two years imprisonment or to a fine of not less than $ 500[16].To make an appeal, the appellant would lodge a petition of appeal at the Court of the Resident addressed to the Supreme Court within seven days from the date when the judgment or order was pronounced or within such further time as may be allowed by the Court of the Resident[17]. Any judgment of order of the Court of Appeal or of the Supreme Court made under this Enactment should be executed, enforced and be given effect by the Court of the Resident[18].

However, under this Enactment there was still scope for an appeal against any judgment or order of the Court of Appeal in any civil matter. This appeal might be made to His Britannic Majesty in Council (i.e. Privy Council) subject to such rules and regulations as may be prescribed by order of His Majesty in Council[19].

[13] Section 13 of the 1908 Enactment. [14] Section 14 (i) of the 1908 Enactment. [15] Section 15 (i) of the 1908 Enactment. [16] Section 16 (1) of the 1908 Enactment. [17] Section 16(2) of the 1908 Enactment. [18] Section 17 of the 1908 Enactment. [19] Section 18 of the 1908 Enactment.

THE COMING OF ISLAM TO BRUNEI DARUSSALAM

Being a state where majority of the populations are Muslims, Islam has been made the official religion of Brunei Darussalam. To say that Islam has only been practiced in this country in recent years are quite incorrect as there are sources, which date the establishment of a Muslim sultanate rule. In fact, Islamic laws have always been the governing laws in Brunei Darussalam even before the coming of the British.

There are evidences which show that Islam had come to Brunei since the 10th century. However, its reception was slow probably because most of the populations during that time were still holding on to their beliefs in Hinduism. Muslims were comprised of just a small section of the population including those traders who came to Brunei[20]. And it was believed that the acceptance of the Sultans and nobles had started the spread of Islam among the community. Awang Alak Betatar, the first ruler of Brunei, embraced Islam when he married the princess of Johore [21]. He changed his name to Sultan Mohammad Shah and since then Islam slowly spread within Brunei.

Islam was quickly spread among most of the people in Brunei when Sultan Sharif Ali, the third Sultan of Brunei, ascended to the throne. Believed to be a descendant of the Prophet Muhammad (Peace Be Upon Him)[22], he was a pious person and was the one who had started to build mosque and had been the one who determined the direction of the Qiblat[23]. From then on Islam has become an important aspect in the life of people in Brunei where eventually it has become the official religion of Brunei Darussalam.

Other evidence that shows Brunei was indeed been governed by Islamic law can be seen in written and codified form. There exist two manuscripts, the first manuscript was called the "Hukum Kanun Brunei" which, contained 96 pages and is kept at the Language and Literature Bureau, whilst copy for reference can be found at the Brunei Museum reference no. A/BM/98/90[24]. While the second manuscript was known as "Undang-Undang dan Adat Brunei Lama" (Old Brunei Law and Custom). It consists of 68 pages and is now reserved in the Sarawak Museum[25].

The content of the first manuscript covered a wide range of laws including the Islamic laws of hudud and qisas. The overall content of the manuscript is in harmony with the Islamic law. For example: Clause One of the manuscript talks about relationship between people and its ruler, conditions of becoming a ruler, responsibilities of the people towards

[20] Prof. Dato Dr. Haji Mahmud Saedon A. Othman, *Ke Arah Pelaksanaan Undang-Undang Di Negara Brunei Darussalam*, Jurnal Undang-Undang Syariah Brunei Darussalam, Januari-Jun 2002 Jilid 2 Bil. 2 p.

[21] Pehin Jawatan Dalam Seri Maharaja Dato Seri Utama Dr. Haji Awang Mohd. Jamil Al-Sufri, *Tarsilah Brunei: Sejarah Awal dan Perkembangan Islam*, Jilid 1, Pusat Sejarah Brunei 2001, p. 33. [22] Ibid p. 80. [23] Ibid p. 90. [24] Prof. Dato' Dr. Hj Mahmud Saedon bin Awang Othman, *Undang-Undang Islam Dalam Kesultanan Melayu Brunei hingga Tahun 1959,* International Seminar on Brunei Malay Sultanate in Nusantara 1999, p.

its rulers; Clause Four talks about various kind of offences such as murder, stabbing, slaying, hitting, robbery, stealing and many other though no punishment for those

extended from the United Kingdom, some dating back as early as 1958. However, some have been notably repealed, either in whole or in part to reflect updates in the development of the law. There are however some old enactments that have been merely omitted from the Laws of Brunei as authorized by His Majesty for the Attorney General to omit. Nevertheless, its omission does not mean that they do not have the force of law and hence would still be considered valid unless it is otherwise provided.[1]

There are also a number of *Government Gazettes* which consists of: i) new laws that has not been revised to become an Act;

Since Brunei Darussalam at present pass their laws in accordance with article 83(3) of the Constitution, any new laws that has been approved by His Majesty will be published in *Government Gazette* form and will come into force on the date His Majesty approves of. Hence that new law will for the time being be referred to as an Order and not an Act.

The Law Revision Act is in place to govern the revision of such *Gazettes* to turn into Acts. After the 1st of January of every year, the Attorney General revises the law and publishes a revised edition of the new law to be included in the Laws of Brunei volumes. He also does this with existing law that has been amended so he will publish a new revised edition of that law incorporating all the recent amendments. [2]

The following constitutional and legislative documents are also considered part of the Laws of Brunei.[3] They are:

i) Treaty of Friendship and Co-operation between Brunei Darussalam and the

United Kingdom dated 7th January 1979;

ii) The Continental Shelf Proclamation 1954

iii) The North Borneo (Definition of Boundaries) Order in Council 1958; and

iv) The Sarawak (Definition of Boundaries) Order in Council 1958.

ISLAMIC LAWS

'am, the main source of law is the Holy Qur'an then followed by the tradition of the
ets or Hadith as the second source of the Islamic Laws[4]. Other sources of law in
ncludes *Ijma'* or consensus of opinion[5], *Qiyas* (Analogical Deduction)[6], *Istihsan* or
Islamic Law[7], *Maslahah Mursalah* (Consideration of Public Interest)[8], *'Urf*
[9], *Istishab* (presumption of Continuity)[10], *Saad al-Dhara'i* (Blocking the

mic laws in Brunei Darussalam are guided mainly by the principles in the
d the Prophet's tradition or Hadith as well as other sources mentioned
the official religion in Brunei Darussalam is clearly stated in the
unei Darussalam:

[2] Section 7 of the Law Revision Act [3] Schedule to the Law Revision Act [4] Mohammad Hashim Kamali, *Principles of Islamic Jurisprudence*, Second Revised Edition, Ilmiah Publishers Sdn. Bhd., Kuala Lumpur 1998, p. 58. [5] ibid p.168. [6] ibid p.197. [7] ibid p.245. [8] ibid p.267. [9] ibid p.283. [10] ibid p.297. [11] ibid p.310.

"The official religion of Brunei Darussalam shall be the Islamic Religion: Provided that all other religions may be practiced in peace and harmony by the persons professing them.[12]"

Islamic law in Brunei is still governed under the Religious Council and Kadis Courts Act (Chapter 77), an Act which consolidates the law relating to the Religious Council and the Kadis Courts, the constitution and organization of religious authorities and the regulation of religious affairs.

Apart from this Act, there are also other legislations enforced in Brunei Darussalam to govern the conduct of Muslims in this country, these legislations are for example:

i) the Syariah Courts Act (Chapter 184), an Act which make specific provisions in respect of the establishment of Syariah Courts, appointments, powers of Syar'ie Judge and jurisdiction of Syariah Courts and other matters connected with the proceedings of Syariah Courts, and for the determination and confirmation of the new moon;

ii) the Syariah Courts Evidence Order, 2001, an Order relating to the law of evidence for the Syariah Courts;

iii) the Emergency (Islamic Family Law) Order, 1999, an Order that make certain provisions relating to Islamic family law in respect of marriage, divorce, maintenance, guardianship and other matters connected with family life;

iv) the Islamic Adoption of Children Order, 2001, an Order to make certain provisions on the law of adoption of children according to Islam; and

v) the Halal Meat Act (Chapter 183) an Act which regulate the supply and importation of halal meat and related matters.

SUBSIDIARY LEGISLATION

We also have in place as part of the Laws of Brunei, a number of subsidiary legislations which include rules, regulations, orders, proclamations or other documents that has the force of law and annexed to their relevant parent Acts. Other government departments whose work is relevant to that particular legislation would usually prepare the drafts for subsidiary legislations.

The power to make subsidiary legislation is conferred under section 13 of the Interpretation and General Clauses Act (CAP. 4). Section 16 further states that the subsidiary legislation should be published in the *Government Gazette*.

CASE LAW/JUDICIAL PRECEDENT

The Supreme Court of Brunei Darussalam is largely guided by the written Constitution and the Laws of Brunei in executing their responsibility of upholding the law in Brunei Darussalam. However where there are no written laws on a particular matter, the courts would then turn to principles of law that are found in case law or judicial precedent.

[12] Article 3(1) of the Constitution of Brunei Darussalam.

Cases heard in Brunei Darussalam are compiled in annual volumes of what are called "Judgments of Brunei Darussalam." Similar to other members in the family practicing the English Legal System, Brunei Darussalam also practice the doctrine of *stare decisis,* where decisions of a higher court are binding on the lower courts. The advantages of following binding precedent include certainty, flexibility, comprehensiveness and practicality in its practice. However, it is recognized that sometimes it can be difficult for lower courts that are bound by the decision and therefore cannot alter it. For that reason also, it may create more appeals.

The courts of Brunei Darussalam would also occasionally refer to cases from Malaysia, Singapore, India and the United Kingdom, all practicing the English legal system though the decisions in those cases would not be binding but instead would only be regarded as "persuasive authority" in the courts of Brunei Darussalam.

COMMON LAW OF ENGLAND

Under the Application of Laws Act, the Common Law of England and the doctrine of equity, together with the statutes of general application that are administered or in force in England, also have the force of law in Brunei Darussalam. This provision is however on the condition that the said common law, doctrine of equity and statutes of general application does not contradict the circumstances of Brunei Darussalam, its inhabitants and subject to such qualifications or local circumstances and custom may render necessary.

GOVERNMENT AND THE STATE

THE EXECUTIVE

As stated under section 4 of the Constitution, the supreme executive authority of Brunei Darussalam is vested in and shall be exercised by His Majesty the Sultan and Yang Di-Pertuan of Brunei Darussalam who is also the Prime Minister of Brunei Darussalam. Nevertheless, His Majesty the Sultan may still appoint Ministers or Deputy Ministers to exercise that executive authority whilst solely being responsible to him in the course of their duties. These appointed ministers shall also assist and advise His Majesty the Sultan in the event His Majesty discharges his executive authority.

THE LEGISLATIVE COUNCIL

Under the Constitution, any member of the Legislative Council may introduce any bill and a bill will only become law when His Majesty the Sultan has assented, signed and sealed the bill with the Seal of the State.

The Legislative Council was temporarily suspended in 1983 but was recently reestablished at its first official meeting in September 2004. During the period where the Council was inactive, laws were passed in the form of emergency orders by His Majesty in accordance with article 83(3) of the Constitution. The normal procedure of the law making process during this period would be initiated by a particular Ministry or Government Department who would either propose or prepare the draft legislation and would then pass it to the Attorney General's Chambers to give legal advice on. Where a Ministry or Governmental Department merely propose the drafting of such legislation, the Attorney General's Chambers will then prepare the draft based on substantive points the former provides. Once the draft is ready to be adopted, it will be presented to His Majesty for his approval. The draft legislation that His Majesty approves of will be passed in an **Emergency Order** form and will be published in the *Government Gazette.*

Every order made under article 83(3) however are deemed to have been validly made, to be fully effectual and to have had full force from the date on which such Proclamation or Order was declared or made and they are deemed to have been passed by the Legislative Council.[1]

The law making process by the Legislative Council is prescribed under Part VII of the Constitution. Basically, any member of the Legislative Council may

(i) introduce a new bill;
(ii) propose a motion for the Council to debate on; or

(iii) present any petition to the Council. The bill, motion or petition will then be debated on and disposed of in accordance with the Standing Orders of the Legislative Council.

[1] Article 83A

Every bill that is going to be introduced needs to be published in the gazette and within 7 days of the publication of the bill in a gazette, the bill shall then be laid before the Legislative Council.[2]

There are certain matters however that are generally excluded from being discussed by the Legislative Council, unless His Majesty the Sultan approves otherwise, and these include matters relating to the issue of bank notes, the establishment of any bank association, amendment of the constitution in relation to both those matters. Matters that would also be disqualified are where the issues are inconsistent with any obligations imposed upon His Majesty under any international treaty or agreement with another power of state. Other disqualified matters include those having the effect of lowering or adversely affecting the rights, positions, discretions, powers, privileges, sovereignty or prerogatives of His Majesty, the standing or prominence of Brunei Darussalam's national philosophy that is Malay Islamic Monarchy and the finances or currency of Brunei Darussalam.[3]

All questions proposed to the Legislative Council to decide upon shall be concluded by way of majority vote taken from the members that are present and voting. Once a bill has been debated on, the Legislative Council will then make a decision whether or not to pass it. If the Council rejects it, which is called a "negative resolution", the Speaker of the Council will then have to submit a report to His Majesty the Sultan incorporating a summary of the debate and the reasons why the Council reached such a resolution. Nevertheless, His Majesty may still declare the Bill to have effect, notwithstanding the negative resolution and he may order it to have effect either as an Act in the form in which it was introduced or to include any amendments that he may think fit to include.[4]

When the Legislative Council decides to pass the Bill, such Bill will only become law if His Majesty the Sultan assents to it, signs it and thereafter seals the Bill with the official State Seal. Again, the bill might take effect as an Act either in its original form as to how it was introduced or His Majesty the Sultan may still make amendments to it as he thinks fit. Such law once assented, signed and sealed by His Majesty shall come into operation on the date on which such assent shall be given.[5]

All the laws made through the Legislative Council shall be styled as "Acts" which will always have the enacting words as follows: "Be it enacted by His Majesty the Sultan and Yang DI-Pertuan with the advice and consent of the Legislative Council as follows."[6]

His Majesty the Sultan also has reserved powers over any bills that was not or has not yet been passed by the Legislative Council if in his opinion, the passing or expedited passing of the Bill is in the interests of public order, good faith and good government. In such

[2] Article 41, the Constitution [3] Article 42 [4] Article 43 [5] Article 45 [6] Article 46

cases, he can declare that bill/motion/petition /business to have effect as if it had been passed or carried by that Council even though it has not been done so.[7]

THE JUDICIARY

THE SUPREME COURT

The Supreme Court of Brunei Darussalam is the body wholly responsible for the administration of justice in civil law (as opposed to "syariah law") and strictly speaking has within its hierarchical structure, the Court of Appeal and the High Court. Within the same building of the Supreme Court, we can also find the Intermediate Courts and the Courts of Magistrates (also known as the Subordinates Courts).

The head of administration for the Judiciary Department is the Chief Registrar whereas the entire judicial system is presided over and supervised by the Chief Justice.

Introduction

The Supreme Court is governed by the Supreme Court Act[8] along with its Rules annexed to the Act. The Rules of the Supreme Court regulates the practice and procedure of the High Court and the Court of Appeal. The Supreme Court consists of the President of the Court of Appeal, the Chief Justice, the Judges and the Judicial Commissioners of the Supreme Court. The jurisdiction of the Supreme Court is over any original and appellate criminal and civil cases by the High Court and also appellate criminal and civil jurisdiction by the Court of Appeal.[9]

The judges of the High Court at present consist of the Chief Justice along with two judges who are often referred to as Justices. The Court of Appeal judges are the President and two other appellate judges.

Jurisdiction

The civil jurisdiction of the High Court consists of the original jurisdiction and authority similar to that held and exercised by the Chancery, Family and Queen's Bench Divisions of the High Court of England and shall also include any other jurisdiction, original or appellate as may be conferred upon it by any other written law.[10]

The criminal jurisdiction of the High Court consists of such jurisdiction, original or appellate, as may be conferred upon it by any written law, which includes the Penal Code, the Criminal Procedure Code or the Criminal Conduct (Recovery of Proceeds) Order. In the Criminal Procedure Code specifically,[11] the High Court will have jurisdiction over any offence that was committed wholly or partly within Brunei Darussalam, or committed on board any ship or aircraft registered in Brunei Darussalam,

[7] Article 47, The Constitution [8] CAP 5 of the Laws of Brunei [9] Section 6, Supreme Court Act [10] Section 16, Supreme Court Act [11] Section 7 of the Criminal Procedure Code

or committed on the high seas if the offence is one of piracy by the law of nations. The Court will also have jurisdiction over an offence whether or not it was committed in Brunei Darussalam if it was committed by a subject of His Majesty the Sultan or by a person who abets, or enters a conspiracy to commit, an offence of Brunei Darussalam whether or not any overt act in furtherance of such conspiracy takes place within Brunei Darussalam. The High Court may also pass any sentence authorized by law. [12]

Any civil or criminal appeals from the High Court can be brought to the Court of Appeal.

The civil jurisdiction of the Court of Appeal consists of appeals from a judgment or order of the High Court in a civil cause or matter and again, such other jurisdiction conferred upon it by any other written law. The criminal jurisdiction of the Court of Appeal consists of appeals from the High Court.[13]

Appeals

Any civil appeals made from the Court of Appeal can only be referred by His Majesty the Sultan to the Judicial Committee of Her Britannic Majesty's Privy Council. For criminal cases however, no such appeals from the Court can be further made. There can be no civil appeals made if the appeal is[14]:

(i) against an order made allowing for an extension of time for appealing against a judgment or order;
(ii) a judgment that has been expressed to be final by any law;

(iii) any order made with the consent of all parties to the case;

(iv) any order relating only to costs;
(v) made without leave of the High Court of the Court of Appeal where the amount or value of the subject matter does not exceed $10,000 or where it is from any interlocutory order of judgment.

Extended jurisdiction of the High Court

Along with the exercise of its own jurisdiction as mentioned above, the High Court also has a general supervisory and revisionary jurisdiction over the Intermediate Courts and the Magistrates' Courts. Any time during a proceeding in an Intermediate Court or a Magistrates' Court, a High Court judge can always call for and check the record of proceedings and thereafter can either transfer the matter or proceedings to the High Court of he could also give directions as to the further conduct of the proceeding by the Intermediate or Magistrates' Court. Upon the High Court calling for any record in this instance, all such proceedings in the Intermediate or Subordinate Courts shall be stayed pending further what the High Court will order later on. The High Court may also feel the need to call on any decision recorded or passed by the Intermediate or Magistrates' Courts to assess the correctness, legality or propriety of the decision recorded. If they are not satisfied with their findings, they can direct for a new trial or whatever action that is necessary to secure that substantial justice is done.[15]

[12] Section 10 of the Criminal Procedure Code [13] Section 18, 19, Supreme Court Act [14] Section 20, Supreme Court Act [15] Section 20A to 20E, Supreme Court Act

INTERMEDIATE COURTS

Introduction

The Intermediate Court is governed by the Intermediate Courts Act.[16] It is an open court to which the public generally has access to.[17] However, the same provisions with regards to power to hear proceedings in camera that was are mentioned below for Magistrates Court likewise applies to the Intermediate Courts. The Intermediate Court is presided over by a Judge who sits alone.[18] There are also registrars and deputy registrar who shall also be ex-officio commissioners for oaths and notaries public.[19]

Jurisdiction

The Intermediate Court's criminal jurisdiction[20] runs concurrently with the High Court. Hence, it has all the jurisdiction, powers, duties and authority as are vested, conferred and imposed on the High Court in the exercise of its **original** criminal jurisdiction.

The Court however does not have jurisdiction in respect of any offence that is punishable with death or with imprisonment for life. Nor does it have jurisdiction in respect of any offence that imposes a period of imprisonment that is longer than 20 years. If it so happens that after the trial ends and a conviction is secured, and it appears to the Court that the imprisonment imposed should be longer than 20 years or should carry a more serious penalty, then the Intermediate Court may commit the case to the High Court for sentencing.

Where the High Court and the Intermediate Court has concurrent jurisdiction in respect of any prosecution or proceeding, the Public Prosecutor or any person expressly authorized by him in writing, can direct in which those courts the proceeding should be instituted in.

The Intermediate Court exercises its original civil jurisdiction[21] in every action where the amount claimed or the value of the subject matter in dispute exceeds $15, 000 but does not exceed $100,000 or any higher sum that the Chief Justice may further prescribe. Similarly to the provisions for the Magistrate Court, to obtain this jurisdiction, one has to further prove that the cause of action arose in Brunei Darussalam or the defendant at the time the proceedings were instituted has some form of connection with Brunei Darussalam, be it being a resident or carrying on a business etc, or the facts of the case the proceedings are based on must be alleged to have occurred in Brunei Darussalam.

[16] CAP 162 of the Laws of Brunei [17] Section 7, Intermediate Courts Act [18] Section 10, Intermediate Courts Act [19] Section 11, Intermediate Courts Act [20] See Part IV of the Intermediate Courts Act [21] See Part V of the Intermediate Courts Act

The Court does not have civil jurisdiction over the recovery of immovable property or where there is a dispute as to a title registered under the Land Code, over the interpretation of a trust instrument, the grant or revocation of probate, over the interpretation of a will, over a declaratory decree, over the legitimacy of any person, over the guardianship or custody of a minor and over the validity or dissolution of any marriage.

In an action concerning immovable property that commenced in the Intermediate Court, a defendant may within one month apply to the High Court for the action to be transferred to the High Court if he feels that there is a dispute as to a title registered under the Land code. If a High Court judge is satisfied, he may order the action to be transferred to the High Court.

Also, not taking into account that the amount claimed should not be more than $100,000, an Intermediate Court has jurisdiction over any action for the recovery of immovable property with or without a claim for rent or profits if there is no dispute as to title registered under the Land Code.

Any judgement of an Intermediate Court should be regarded by the Parties as final and conclusive between themselves.

The Intermediate Court also has jurisdiction to grant probate and letters of administration in respect of the estate within Brunei Darussalam of a deceased person and the estate in respect of which the grant is applied for but it must be exclusive of what the deceased possessed of and over what the applicant is entitled to as a trustee and not a beneficiary, and without deducting anything on the account of debts due or owing, the amount claimed must not exceeds $250,000.

When a plaintiff has a cause of action for more than $100,000, which the Intermediate Court does not have jurisdiction over, it is possible for him to abandon the excess amount in order to bring it within the jurisdiction of the Intermediate Court. However he will not be able to recover any of the excess amounts that he abandoned. Nevertheless, if the amount is more than $100,000, the Intermediate Court can still have jurisdiction when and if the parties concerned agree by a signed memorandum filed in the Intermediate Court that it shall have jurisdiction, even though the amount claimed exceeds $100,000.

In an Intermediate Court proceeding, if the counterclaim or defence of any defendant involves a matter beyond the Intermediate Court's jurisdiction, any party may apply to the High Court within one month of being served the counterclaim, for an order that the whole proceedings, or just proceedings on the counterclaim defence to be transferred to the High Court.

Appeals

Civil appeals goes straight to the Court of Appeal as if it was an appeal from the High Court. However there will be no right of appeal entertained if the parties to the action have agreed in writing that the judgment of the court shall be final and conclusive between them.[22]

Criminal appeals also go to the Court of Appeal. The Court of Appeal can also review any sentencing that has been passed by the Intermediate Court on any person or provide an opinion on a point of law that has been referred to it.[23] The practice and procedure as contained in the Supreme Court Rules for the High Court and the Court of Appeal shall also apply to the Intermediate Court.

MAGISTRATES' COURT

Introduction

The Magistrate Courts are governed by the Subordinate Courts Act[24], in terms of its civil jurisdiction and by the Criminal Procedure Code[25] in the exercise of its criminal jurisdiction. There is also in place a set of Subordinate Courts Rules regulating and prescribing the procedure (including methods for pleading) and the practice in the Magistrate Courts in the exercise of its civil jurisdiction. These Rules of Court extends to all matters of procedures, practice relating to or concerning the effect or operation in law of any procedure or practice, enforcement of judgments or orders, in any case within the cognizance of the Magistrate Court.

All magistrate courts are deemed to be open and allow public access, however there are some instances when a Court may still direct to have the whole proceedings or only in part to be in camera sitting only[26]. In particular, where references are made, whether orally or in writing, directly to any act, decision, grant, revocation, suspension, refusal, omission, authority or discretion by His Majesty the Sultan or if there are cases that intends to refer to any issue that may directly or indirectly concerns the inviolability, sanctity or interests of the position, dignity, standing, honour, eminence or sovereignty of His Majesty the Sultan, then the Magistrate Court shall hold such proceedings in camera, so long as His Majesty the Sultan has not himself issued a direction that such proceedings need not be heard in camera.

Jurisdiction

The Magistrate Court exercises its civil jurisdiction[27] over every civil proceeding where the amount claimed or the value of the subject matter in dispute does not exceed B$30,000. However, if the matter is heard before the Chief Magistrate, Chief Registrar, Deputy Chief Registrar, Senior Magistrate or the Senior Registrar this prescribed limit would be B$50,000.

[22] Section 26, Intermediate Courts Act [23] Section 27, Intermediate Courts Act [24] CAP 6 of the Laws of Brunei [25] CAP 7 of the Laws of Brunei [26] Section 7, Subordinate Courts Act [27] See Section 17 of the Subordinate Courts Act

For the court to have jurisdiction of the case, the cause of action need to have arose in Brunei Darussalam, the defendant at the time the proceedings were instituted has some form of connection with Brunei Darussalam, be it being a resident or carrying on a business etc, and the facts of the case the proceedings are based on must be alleged to have occurred in Brunei Darussalam.

Furthermore, a Magistrate Court also has jurisdiction in any proceedings for the recovery of immovable property where the rent payable in respect of such property does not exceed $500 per month. This excludes cases where there is a genuine dispute as to title registered under the Land Code.

A Magistrate Court does not have any civil jurisdiction over acts done by the order of His Majesty the Sultan, over the recovery of immovable property where there is a genuine dispute as to the title registered under the Land Code, over cases involving specific performance and rescission of contracts, over the cancellation or rectification of instruments, over the interpretation of trust instruments and the enforcement of administration of trusts, the grant of probate or letters of administration in respect of a deceased person, over the interpretation of wills, administration of estate of any deceased person and lastly it does not have civil jurisdiction over declaratory decrees.

The Magistrate's court criminal jurisdiction[28] is similar to the High Court's criminal jurisdiction as mentioned above. Namely, the court will have jurisdiction over any offence that was committed wholly or partly within Brunei Darussalam, or committed on board any ship or aircraft registered in Brunei Darussalam, or committed on the high seas if the offence is one of piracy by the law of nations. The Court will also have jurisdiction over an offence whether or not it was committed in Brunei Darussalam if it was committed by a subject of His Majesty the Sultan or by a person who abets, or enters a conspiracy to commit, an offence of Brunei Darussalam whether or not any overt act in furtherance of such conspiracy takes place within Brunei Darussalam. Furthermore, the types of offences the magistrate court may try are any offence that is shown in the eighth column of the First Schedule of the Criminal Procedure Code to be so triable. However, if the offence it is given the power to try carries a maximum punishment the court has no power to award, it shall then commit the defendant for trial by the High Court if it holds the opinion that the punishment it has power to award is inadequate.

The criminal jurisdiction of magistrates conferred by the Criminal Procedure Code include hearing, trying, determining and disposing of summarily prosecutions for offences cognized by such magistrate and inquiring into offences committed with a view to committal for trial by the High Court. Magistrates also have the power and authority to inquire into complaints of offences, summon and examine relevant witnesses, summon and issue warrants for the apprehension of criminals and offenders, and deal with them according to law, issue search warrants, hold inquests and do all other matters and things which a magistrate is empowered to do by this Code or any other Act.

[28] See section 7 of the Criminal Procedure Code

Appeals

Any appeal in a civil matter in the Magistrate Court goes to the High Court.[29] Such appeals that has right to do so are cases where a Magistrate Court has given a final judgment in any proceedings for the recovery of immovable property or in any proceedings where the amount in dispute exceeds $500. Leave for appeal is needed from a judge with respect of an interlocutory order, from a final judgment of a Magistrate Court where the amount claimed or the value of the subject matter in dispute does not exceed $500. Leave from the judge is also required from an order relating to costs and also for any orders that were made by consent of the parties.

It is important for the appellant to keep in mind that he must also fulfill all other conditions of appeal imposed in accordance with the Rules of Court of the Supreme Court Act.

In a criminal matter, if a defendant, the complainant or the Public Prosecutor is not satisfied with any judgment, sentence or order given by the magistrate, he may appeal to the High Court against such judgment, sentence or order for any error in law or in fact, or on the ground that the sentence is either to extensive or too inadequate.

A Magistrate Court can also, at any time before or during any civil proceeding, request a legal opinion from the High Court if it desires to do so. Either the Magistrate initiates the request or it can also be made on the application of any of the parties. They shall forward a statement of the facts of the case and specify the exact points on which legal opinion is being sought. The High Court will then make a declaration or order in response to the query as it thinks fit.[30]

APPOINTMENT OF JUDGES, REGISTRARS AND OTHER RELEVANT PERSONS WITHIN THE SUPREME COURTS, INTERMEDIATE COURTS AND SUBORDINATE COURTS

The High Court and Court of Appeal judges are appointed by His Majesty the Sultan by instrument under his sign manual and the State Seal.[31] To become a judge of the Supreme Court, one has to be or has been a judge of a Court having unlimited jurisdiction over civil and criminal matters in some part of the Commonwealth or a Court having jurisdiction in appeals from any such Court. He must also have been entitled to practice as an advocate in such a court for a period of not less than 7 years. The judges of the Supreme Court hold their positions until the age of 65 or at a later time where His Majesty may approve of.

His Majesty may also from time to time appoint someone who satisfies the same conditions as mentioned above for the Supreme Court judges to be a Judicial Commissioner of the Supreme Court.[32] The Judicial Commissioner has the power to act as a Judge of the Supreme Court and all things done by him in accordance with the terms

[29] Section 17, Subordinate Courts Act [30] Section 22, Subordinate Courts Act [31] Section 7, Supreme Court Act [32] Section 11, Supreme Court Act

of this appointment will be deemed to have the same validity and effect as if it has been done by a judge.

An Intermediate Court judge is also appointed by His Majesty. To qualify for appointment, he must have been entitled to practice in a court having unlimited jurisdiction in civil and criminal matters in Brunei Darussalam or some part of the Commonwealth for not less then 5 years.[33]

Finally, magistrates are also appointed by His Majesty, in particular a Chief Magistrate who shall have seniority over all other Magistrates and Coroners. His Majesty can also appoint any fit and proper person to be a Coroner who shall have the same power to act as a Magistrate for the purpose of discharging the functions of a Magistrate. Hence, their actions shall have the same validity and effect as if they had been done by a Magistrate.[34]

SYARIAH COURT

The Syariah Courts in Brunei Darussalam consist of the Syariah Subordinate Courts, the Syariah High Court and the Syariah Appeal Court. These courts will have such jurisdiction, powers, duties and authority as are conferred and imposed by the Syariah Courts Act (Chapter 184) as well as by any other written law.[35]

For appointment of Judges in the Syariah Courts, Part II of this Act, among others, talks about the appointment of Chief Syar'ie Judge, the Syariah Appeal Court Judges, Syariah High court Judges and Syariah Subordinate Courts Judges.

Section 8(1) of this Act, stated that His Majesty the Sultan and Yang Di-Pertuan may, on the advice of the President of the Majlis Ugama Islam and after consultation with the Majlis, appoint a Chief Syar'ie Judge.[36] To be qualified as a Chief Syar'ie Judge, a person must be a citizen of Brunei Darussalam; and he has served as either a Judge of a Syariah Court, or Kadi, or in both capacities, for a cumulative period of not less than 7 years prior to his appointment or that he is a person learned in *Hukum Syara'*[37] .

For Syariah Appeal Court Judges, section 9(1) of this Act, stated that His Majesty the Sultan and Yang Di-Pertuan may, on the advice of the President of the Majlis and after consultation with the Majlis, appoint and re-appoint not more than 5 Muslims to form a standing panel of Judges, for a period of not exceeding 3 years. For each proceeding in the Syariah Appeal Court, the Chief Syar'ie Judge shall elect 2 of them to constitute a quorum of Judges. Again, a person qualified to be appointed as one of the Judges in the Syariah Appeal Court must be a citizen of Brunei Darussalam and he has served as either a Judge of a Syariah Court, or Kadi, or in both capacities, for a cumulative period of not

[33] Section 10, Intermediate Courts Act [34] Section 9-11, Subordinate Courts Act [35] Section 6(1) of the Syariah Courts Act (Chapter 184). [36] Section 8(1) of the Syariah Courts Act (Chapter 184). [37] Section 8(2) of the Syariah Courts Act (Chapter 184).

less than 7 years prior to his appointment, or that he is a person learned in *Hukum Syara'*[38] .

Section 10(1) of this Act provides for appointment of Syariah High court Judges whereby His Majesty the Sultan and Yang Di-Pertuan may, on the advice of the President of the Majlis and after consultation with the Majlis, appoint Judges of the Syariah High Court. To be qualified as one, a person must be a citizen of Brunei Darussalam; and has, for a cumulative of not less than 7 years prior to his appointment, served as either a Judge of a Syariah Subordinate Court, or Kadi, or registrar, or Syar'ie Prosecutor, or in more than one of such capacities; or that he is a person learned in Hukum Syara'[39].

And for appointment of Syariah Subordinate Courts Judges, section 11 of this Act provides that His Majesty the Sultan and Yang Di-Pertuan may, on the advice of the President of the Majlis and after consultation with the Majlis, appoint Judges of the Syariah Subordinate Courts.

Under this Act, the Chief Syar'ie Judge and Syariah High Court Judges shall hold office until the age of 65 years or until such later time as may be approved by His Majesty the Sultan and Yang Di-Pertuan[40]. However, any Syar'ie Judges including the Chief Syar'ie Judge, may at any time resign from his office by sending to His Majesty the Sultan and Yang Di-Pertuan a letter of resignation under his hand, through the Majlis or the Chief Syar'ie Judge, but he may not be removed from his office or his service terminated except in accordance with the provisions of subsections (3), (4) and (5) of section 12(1) of this Act.

As mentioned earlier, Syariah Courts in Brunei Darussalam consists of Syariah Subordinate Courts, the Syariah High Court and the Syariah Appeal Court each with its own jurisdictions.

The Syariah High Court has both criminal and civil jurisdiction. In its criminal jurisdiction it shall try any offence punishable under any written law which provides for syariah criminal offences, under any written law relating to Islamic family law or under any other written law which confers on it jurisdiction to try any offence, and may impose any punishment provided therein[41].

In its civil jurisdiction, the Syariah High Court shall hear and determine all actions and proceedings relating to –

(i) betrothal, marriage (including *ta'at balik*), divorce, *khulu'*, *fasakh*, *cerai ta'liq*, determination of turns, *li'an*, *illa* or any matrimonial matter;
(ii) any disposition of or claim to any property arising out of any matter set out in the above paragraph.

[38] Section 9(2) of the Syariah Courts Act (Chapter 184). [39] Section 10(2) of the Syariah Courts Act (Chapter 184). [40] Section 12(1) of the Syariah Courts Act (Chapter 184). [41] Section 15*(a)* of the Syariah Courts Act (Chapter 184).

(iii) maintenance of dependants, legitimacy (*ithbatun nasab*) or guardianship or custody (*hadanah*) of infants;

(iv) division of or claims to *harta sepencarian*;
(v) wills or gifts during *maradal-maut* of a deceased Muslim;
(vi) gift *inter vivos* (*hibah*), or settlement (*sulh*) made without adequate monetary consideration or value by Muslim;

(vii) *waqaf* or *nazar*;

(viii) division of and inheritance of property, testate or intestate;

(ix) determination or persons entitled to part of the estate of a deceased Muslim or part of the property which such persons are respectively entitled to; or
(x) other matters in respect of which jurisdiction is conferred by any written law.[42]

For Syariah Subordinate Courts, their criminal jurisdiction are to try offence punishable under any written law which provides for syariah criminal offences, prescribing offences where the maximum punishment provided for does not exceed $10,000 or imprisonment for a period not exceeding 7 years or both and may impose any punishment provided therefor[43].

In their civil jurisdiction, the Syariah Subordinate Courts shall hear and determine all actions and proceedings which the Syariah High Court is empowered to hear and determine, where the amount or value of the subject-matter in dispute does not exceed $500,000 or is not capable of estimation in terms of money[44]. This jurisdiction may, form time to time, be increased by His Majesty the Sultan and Yang Di-Pertuan on the recommendation of the Chief Syar'ie Judge, by notifying it in the *Gazette*[45].

Jurisdiction of the Syariah Appeal Court shall be to hear and determine any appeal against any decision made by the Syariah High Court in the exercise of its original jurisdiction[46]. Whenever an appeal against a decision of the Syariah Subordinate Court has been determined by the Syariah High Court, the Syariah Appeal Court may, on application by any party, grant leave for any question of law in the public interest which has arisen in the course of the appeal, and where the decision of the Syariah High Court has affected the determination of the appeal, to be referred to the Syariah Appeal Court for its decision. Whenever leave is granted by the Syariah Appeal Court, it shall hear and determine the questions allowed to be referred for its decision and make any order which the Syariah High Court might have made, and as it thinks just for the disposal of the appeal.

[42] Section 15*(b)* –do-. [43] Section 16(1)*(a)* of the Syariah Courts Act (Chapter 184). [44] Section 16(1)*(b)* Ibid. [45] Section 16(2) Ibid. [46] Section 20(1) Ibid.

Apart from having its original jurisdiction, the Syariah High Court shall have supervisory and revisionary jurisdiction over all Syariah Subordinate Courts[47]. Similarly, the Syariah Appeal Court shall have that same power over the Syariah High Court[48].

OTHER RELEVANT LEGAL DEPARTMENTS

The Attorney General's Chambers

The Attorney General is the principal legal adviser to the Government of His Majesty the Sultan and shall advise on all legal matters connected with the affairs of Brunei Darussalam or by the Government of Brunei Darussalam.[49] He is assisted by the Solicitor General and counsels, in advising the Government and representing the Government in civil and criminal cases. The Attorney General is also responsible for the drafting of legislation. In carrying out the task of legislative drafting, the Attorney General's Chambers work closely with other Government Ministries and Departments.

The Attorney General is vested with the power under the Constitution to institute, proceed and discontinue once instituted, any criminal proceedings. All criminal prosecutions are instituted in the name of the Public Prosecutor. In carrying out this duty, the Attorney General is not subject to the direction or control of any other person or authority. He is assisted by Deputy Public Prosecutors in the conduct of criminal trials held in the Supreme Court and the Subordinate Courts.

The Attorney General basically has the exercisable power to institute, conduct or discontinue, at his discretion, any proceedings of an offence other than proceedings before a Syariah Court or a Court Martial, subject to the provisions of any other written law.

In addition, the Public Prosecutor and his Deputies also advise, and direct prosecution undertaken by the police and other law enforcement departments including rendering advice in their investigations.

Apart from carrying out the above duties, the Attorney General's Chambers also provides services to the public by maintaining the following registries; Companies, Business names, Trade Marks, Industrial designs, Inventions, Power of Attorney, Marriages, Bills of Sales.

There are five legal divisions in the Attorney-General's Chambers: Civil Division, Criminal Justice Division, International Law Division, Legislative Drafting Division and the Registry Division.

Syariah department

In 1980, a Committee of Harmonizing Laws In Accordance With Islam[50], was formed. To increase this effort, a Legal Unit[51] chaired by the Chief Kadi was established in 1988 by the Ministry of Religious Affairs its task mainly to replace the earlier committee. In 1993, a Committee for the establishment of Syariah Supreme Court known as the Action Committee Towards the Establishment of Syariah Supreme Court[52] was formed. Another committee known as the Islamic Family Law Legislative Committee[53] was later established in 1995, its tasks are to study, legislate and prepare Islamic family laws as well as other laws governed by the Kadis Court. This Legal Unit, in 1997, was eventually alleviated to its present position as a separate department in the Ministry of Religious Affairs now known as the Islamic Legal Unit.[54]

Among the duties of this Unit are to study, examine and do research on provisions in the Laws of Brunei now enforced to see whether or not there is any conflict with *Hukum Syara'*; prepare proposed draft amendment for any legal provision that conflict with *Hukum Syara'* and prepare draft legislation in accordance with *Hukum Syara'* if there is no such legislation available yet. This Unit is also appointed secretariat for several committees that had been mentioned above. Apart from that, this Unit also gives advice concerning Islamic laws to the Syariah Courts, the Faith Control Unit (Unit Kawalan Akidah), the Prosecution Section, the Investigation Section, the Family Counseling Section, the Attorney General's Chambers as well as other government departments and private firms.[55]

LEGAL PROCEDURE

CRIMINAL PROSECUTION

As stated in the Criminal Procedure Code, the general direction and control over criminal prosecutions and proceedings in Brunei Darussalam is under the responsibility of the Attorney General who is also the Public Prosecutor. His Majesty may also from time to time appoint Deputy Public Prosecutors who will be under the general control and direction of the Public Prosecutor. Deputy Public Prosecutors are conferred the powers under the Criminal Procedure Code as are delegated to them by the Public Prosecutor.

The Public Prosecutor may also by notification in the *Government Gazette* delegate all or any of his powers vested to him under the Criminal Procedure Code to any Deputy Public Prosecutor. Thus the exercise of these powers by the Deputy Public Prosecutor would be treated as if they had been exercised by the Public Prosecutor so long as Public Prosecutor does not revoke the delegation.

The Criminal Procedure Code also specifically states that every criminal prosecution and every inquiry can also be conducted by some other person expressly authorized in writing by the Public Prosecutor or His Majesty the Sultan. In those cases, a police officer or an officer of a Government Department in relation to minor cases and cases that is relevant to that particular Government Department, such as the Customs Department, the Immigration Department, the Narcotics Control Bureau and the Anti-Corruptions Bureau who do have their own prosecuting officers also conduct criminal prosecution for their relevant cases.

CRIMINAL PROCEDURE

INVESTIGATIONS

The Police are given powers to search a property and in doing so they are required to prepare a list of the things that have been seized and this document is to be signed by the officer in charge of the search and seizure. The owner of the property being searched must be present at the time the search is conducted. [1]

The police officer during the investigation stage can also take a written statement from a witness or a suspect and the person being interviewed is required to answer all questions posed to him in relation to the case being investigated on. The police officer is required to repeat the statement back to the person being questioned and he must thereafter sign the statement. [2] All statements made can be used as evidence if the person questioned becomes a witness during proceedings thereafter.[3]

[1] Section 69 of the Criminal Procedure Code [2] Section 116 of the Criminal Procedure Code [3] Section 117 of the Criminal Procedure Code

When interviewing a potential defendant, the police officer is always required to read out the defendant's rights to him after the charge is explained to him. The Courts only accept voluntarily made statements whether or not the contents of the statement are true. There is no right of silence in Brunei Darussalam as the Courts may as a consequence treat silence as a detrimental factor for the defendant.

Once a suspect is arrested, he shall be placed in remand or released on bail. If the remand is ordered by the Magistrate, the defendant cannot be remanded for more than 15 days. On the other hand, if it was ordered by the High Court, there is no time limit.[4]

PRE-TRIAL PROCEDURE

With the exception of some offences that would need the prior sanction of the Public Prosecutor or the official complaint of a concerned public servant, a Judge or magistrate may take cognizance of an offence upon receiving a complaint launched by a complainant[5], upon his own knowledge or suspicion that an such offence has been committed or when any person who is in custody without process has been brought before him for committing an offence that the Judge or magistrate has jurisdiction to inquire into or try.[6]

Once the Judge or magistrate takes cognizance of the offence and is satisfied that there is sufficient ground for proceeding, he will either issue a summons for the accused to attend court or if it is in relation to an offence that requires a warrant to be issued first, he would then issue the warrant in the first instance and also issue a summons that specifies the accused to appear at a certain time before him or some other Judge or magistrate having jurisdiction over the case. [7]

Preliminary Inquiries

Preliminary inquiries are always held for offences against the State, murder or any offence which carries a death penalty. [8]

Preliminary Inquiries are generally held for a magistrate to determine whether there is sufficient evidence to commit the case for trial in the High Court (filteration). Other cases like trafficking of drugs and rape cases go straight to the High Court without any preliminary inquiries. All other cases are generally tried summarily in the Magistrate Court.

At a preliminary inquiry, the Prosecutor will present its case and set out all the evidence, including examining witnesses, in support of its case to the Magistrate. The defendant is allowed to cross examine the witnesses who can then also be re-examined by the Prosecutor. If the magistrate, after hearing all the evidence, feels that there are insufficient grounds for committing the accused, he could either discharge him or he can

[4] Section 223 of the Criminal Procedure Code [5] Section 133 of the Criminal Procedure Code [6] Section 131 of the Criminal Procedure Code [7] Section 136 of the Criminal Procedure Code [8] Section 138 of the Criminal Procedure Code

still order that the defendant be tried before himself or before some other magistrate. In the latter case, he will consequently frame a charge and call upon the defendant to plead to those charges. [9] However if the magistrate finds that there are sufficient grounds for committing him for trial, he shall then commit the accused for trial before the High Court.[10]

If the accused is committed to trial to High Court, the magistrate will give the accused the opportunity to give a list of witnesses he wishes to be summoned to give evidence for his trial. The final list of witnesses shall be included in the record of the magistrate.[11]

Once the accused has been committed for trial, the committing magistrate shall then send the original record and all the relevant documents, weapons (if any) or any other thing which is to be produced in evidence to the Court the accused is committed to. A list of all the exhibits is also forwarded with the record. The record will specifically contain the following information[12]:

i) the serial number of the case;

ii) the date of the commission of the offence;

iii) the date of the complaint, if any;

iv) the name, age, sex, residence, if known, and nationality (or race) of the accused;

v) the offence complained of and the offence proved, and the value of the

property, if any, in respect of which the offence has been committed;

vi) the date of the summons or warrant and of the return day of the summons, if any, or on which the accused was first arrested;

vii) the date on which the accused first appeared or was brought before a magistrate;

viii) the name and title of the officer or other person conducting the prosecution;

ix) the date of making each adjournment or postponement, if any, and the date to

which such adjournment or postponement was made and the grounds for making the same;

x) the date on which the proceedings terminated;

xi) the order made;

xii) the depositions;

xiii) the statement, if any, of the accused;

xiv) the charge; and

xv) the list of witnesses as provided by the accused.

The law also allows for committal without the consideration of evidence. This method is referred to as paper committal and is done through the submission of written statements only. [13] Hence a written statement can be substituted for oral evidence and it would have

[9] Section 141 of the Criminal Procedure Code [10] Section 144 of the Criminal Procedure Code [11] Section 145 of the Criminal Procedure Code [12] Section 147 of the Criminal Procedure Code [13] Section 151A and 151B of the Criminal Procedure Code

a similar effect to be admissible under the Evidence Act. It must however satisfy the following conditions:

a) the statement must be signed by the person who made it;

b) the statement must contain a declaration by that person that the information he has written is true to the best of this knowledge and belief;

c) a copy of the statement must be given to each of the other parties to the proceedings not less then 7 days before the statement is tendered in evidence

d) none of the other parties objects to the statement being tendered in evidence.

Bail applications[14]

The defendant or his counsel may also apply for bail (whilst investigations are still being carried out) before a magistrate, High Court Judge or Intermediate Court Judge, depending on the seriousness of the case. In deciding to grant that application, the magistrate will consider two opposing factors. [15] On one hand, the Court must remember that the accused is innocent only until proved otherwise. However, the Court shall also take into consideration that the interests of justice will be perverted if the accused absconds or tampers with the witnesses.

At present, all magistrates have the power to grant bail for all type of cases by virtue of their appointments as Registrars of the Supreme Court. However, in practice, bail applications in serious cases that are triable in the High Court or Intermediate Court will be remitted to either court for such applications to be heard. These particular points will be taken into account on deciding whether or not the defendant should be released on bail:

i) Is the offence bailable or non bailable under Schedule 1 of the Criminal

Procedure Code? However, the Court still has discretion to grant bail for non-bailable offences;

ii) The nature and gravity of the offence;

iii) The number of charges;

iv) The likelihood of the accused absconding;

v) The previous record of the accused;

vi) Strength of evidence; and

vii) Other relevant factors like the age and health of the accused.

The usual conditions attached to bail are cash bail, the duty to report to the nearest police station at a prescribed number of times a week, the assurance that the accused will not tamper with witnesses and to not approach certain places, to surrender his passport and other travel documents and to remain indoors between certain hours.

Pre-Trial Review

Sometimes, a pre-trial review is also held by the High Court Judge prior to the trial. There is no legislative requirement for this and hence is not mandatory but in practice is usually held for High Court and Intermediate Court cases where the Judge will go

[14] Sections 346-353 of the Criminal Procedure Code [15] Public Prosecutor V Haji Sadikin (2000) JCBD Vol. 1 349

through the relevant documents such as the list of witnesses, list of exhibits and agreed facts (if any) with both the prosecution and the defence.

Withdrawal of Charges

At any time before a judgment is entered, charges against the defendant and all evidence against him may be discharged. If the discharge is one not amounting to an acquittal, this would mean that prosecution can be made at another time based on the same factors. [16] The power to withdraw a charge only lies with the prosecution. The person who reported the offence and initiated the prosecution cannot withdraw his claim once a police report or a statement has been prepared.

TRIAL PROCEDURE

Chapter XIX of the Criminal Procedure Code governs the procedure for trials in Brunei Darussalam.

When the defendant first appears before the Court, the charge containing the particulars to the offence or offences he is accused of shall be read out and explained to him and he shall then be asked to enter his plea, guilty or not guilty. If the accused pleads guilty, the plea will be recorded and he may be convicted thereon. However, the Judge would first need to hear the complainant and other evidence first as it considers necessary and he would also make sure the defendant truly understands the nature and consequences of his plea and intends to admit, without qualification, the offence or offences alleged against him.

Where the defendant pleads not guilty, a trial will be held ad witnesses would be called to give evidence. At the start of the trial, the prosecution will first open the case by stating briefly the nature of the offence charged and disclosing the evidence, including the appearance of witnesses, by which he proposed to prove guilt of the defendant. The burden of proof lies with the prosecution beyond reasonable doubt. If the defendant is not represented by counsel, (there is no legal aid in Brunei Darussalam with the exception of cases carrying a death penalty where the defendant will be provided a defence counsel) the Court will assist the defendant in the cross examination of witnesses.

At the close of the prosecution's case, the Court will lay down the choices for the defendant, either to given his own evidence or maintain his silence. Usually, if they choose to keep silent, and where the evidence against him is strong, a conviction will be given. However, if he decides to give his own evidence, he will then in turn open his case by stating the facts or law on which he intends to rely and make whatever comments in response to the evidence put forward by the prosecution. Before summing up his case, he would then be called upon to enter his defence and then produce his own evidence which may include witnesses that are examined on his behalf. The prosecution will then have the right of reply on the whole case.[17]

[16] Section 186 of the Criminal Procedure Code [17] Section 184 of the Criminal Procedure Code

At the end of the trial, if the Court finds the defendant not guilty, the Court shall record an order of acquittal. If the Court finds otherwise or if the defendant entered a plea of guilty, the Court shall pass sentence in accordance with the law. [18]

Sentencing

The types of sentences in Brunei Darussalam are: i) Death Penalty: The most serious punishment in Brunei Darussalam is the death penalty. In sentencing hearings dealing with the death penalty, there must be 2 judges present and both these judges must agree with the sentencing decision. Death penalties are not imposed on pregnant women who would get life imprisonment instead.

ii) Life imprisonment: The defendant will be imprisonment for as long as he shall live.

iii) Whipping: There is also whipping in Brunei Darussalam, usually a maximum of 24 whips for an adult and a maximum of 18 whips for a defendant below the age of 18.[19] Women, men above 50 years old and those that are imposed the death penalty are exempted from whipping.[20]

iv) Fines: Fines are imposed according to the relevant written law. If that does not exist, the court will decide on the appropriate amount.

v) Pay compensation: On top of the above punishments, the Court can order the defendant to pay compensation if it is satisfied that the defendant can afford to pay such amount imposed. He will be imposed imprisonment or further imprisonment on default of payment. [21]

POST-TRIAL PROCEDURE (APPEALS)

If an appeal is made from the Magistrates Court, the appeal will be heard by the High Court. Any party can make an appeal against a judgment or sentence, be it the prosecution or the defendant. Appeals made from the High Court are heard by the Court of Appeal and these are governed by the Criminal Procedure Code (Criminal Appeal Rules) 2002. A person shall commence his appeal by sending a notice of appeal to the Registrar within 14 days of the judgment or sentence made. He can at any time abandon his appeal after serving his notice of appeal by giving notice of abandonment to the Registrar. His appeal should then be dismissed.

CIVIL PROCEDURE

Civil proceedings are usually private matters between parties that relates to breach of contracts or for compensation. The civil procedure in Brunei Darussalam is governed by the Supreme Court Rules for the High Court and the Magistrates' Court Rules (Civil

[18] Section 181 of the Criminal Procedure Code [19] Section 257 of the Criminal Procedure Code [20] Section 258 of the Criminal Procedure Code [21] Section 382 of the Criminal Procedure Code

Procedure and Civil Appeals Procedure) for the Magistrate Courts. These rules mainly prescribe regulations for types of action, procedure, process, addresses and forms.

Procedure in the Magistrate Court

INTRODUCTION

Civil proceedings in the Magistrate Court would include a civil action, an order for payment of any sum or money or an order for doing or abstaining from doing any act or thing not enforceable through a mere fine or by imprisonment. All civil proceedings heard by the Magistrate Court are dealt with summarily.[22]

PRE-HEARING PROCEDURE

A person who wishes to institute civil proceedings in the Magistrate Court would need to register a written statement to the Clerk of the Court to be included in the Civil Cause Book. This written statement is often referred to as the "plaint" and it shall state the names and last known place of residence of the parties and also include a statement on the substance of the action intended to be brought. Upon doing so, he is also required to pay a prescribed fee to the Court. The magistrate has discretion to refuse the plaint if it appears that there is no cause of action. They would naturally refuse the plaint if the

The Registrar will notify the parties the date and time of the appeal hearing. If the appellant fails to appear at the appeal hearing, the case shall then be struck out and the decision shall be affirmed. If the respondent appeared at that appeal where the appellant failed to do so, the appellant shall be ordered to pay the costs of the appeal. But if the respondent did not appear, the High Court will need to consequently decide on the costs of the appeal. [33]

However if the appellant appears and whether or not the respondent appears, the High Court shall proceed with the hearing and determination of the case and shall thereafter give judgment according to the merits of the case. During the hearing, the appellant is not allowed to argue on any other points that are separate from the reasons for appeal and those set forth in his notice of appeal. But the Judge may allow amendments to the notice of appeal if he feels that there are actually other grounds than was not mentioned that should be included and also if he feels that the statement of grounds of appeal is defective.[34]

Once the Judge decides on the appeal, the High Court shall certify the judgment made and notify it to the magistrates' court. The magistrates' court will then act upon the judgment either by making such orders that are necessary and amending its own records in accordance with the judgment. The magistrate shall then have the same jurisdiction and power to enforce the High Court's judgment as if he himself made it.

[30] Rule 4 of the Magistrates' Court (Civil Appeals Procedure) Rules 2001

[31] Rule 5 of the Magistrates' Court (Civil Appeals Procedure) Rules 2001 [32] Rule 11 of the Magistrates' Court (Civil Appeals Procedure) Rules 2001 [33] Rule 12 and 13 of the Magistrates' Court (Civil Appeals Procedure) Rules 2001 [34] Rule 15 of the Magistrates' Court (Civil Appeals Procedure) Rules 2001

PROCEDURE IN THE HIGH COURT

INTRODUCTION

High Court Proceedings are initiated by writ, originating summons, originating motion or petition.[35]

There are certain proceedings that **must** be initiated by a writ and these are those relating to claims for relief or remedy for any tort (other than trespass to land), relating to an allegation of fraud, claims for damages for breach of duty (whether duty exists by virtue of a contract or of a provision made by any written law), claims for breach of promise of marriage and also relating to infringement of a patent.

Any applications that are made to a High Court Judge under any written law must be initiated by originating summons. There are also some proceedings that may be begun either by writ or by originating summons where the plaintiff can choose which is more appropriate for him. Such proceedings include those where the sole or principal question at issue is the construction of any written law, of any instrument made under any written law or of any deed, will contract or other document and also where there is unlikely to be any substantial dispute of fact in those proceedings.

PRE-HEARING PROCEDURE

Writ of Summons

All writs prior to them being issued must be indorsed with a statement of the nature of the claim made or the relief or remedy required in the action begun or a statement of the amount claimed in respect of a debt demand. It should also state that further proceedings will be stayed if the defendant pays the amount claimed to the plaintiff or the Court within a certain time limit. The Plaintiff upon presenting a writ for sealing and to be served must leave with the Registrar the original writ along with as many copies of it to be served on the defendant or defendants. The Registrar shall then assign a serial number to the writ and shall sign, seal and date the writ which shall deem the writ to be issued. [36]

Originating Summons

An originating summons must include the questions the plaintiff seeks the determination or direction of the High Court or a concise statement of the relief or remedy claimed in the proceedings with sufficient particulars to identify the cause or causes of action in respect of that claim. Similar to the process in writ of summons, the Registrar will assign a serial number to the originating summons and it will be signed, sealed and dated and thereupon issued. [37]

Originating Motion and Petition No originating motion can be made *ex parte* and without previous notice to the affected parties. However if the Court is satisfied that there will be a delay in proceedings, it may make an order *ex parte* on terms such as costs or otherwise. (Any affected party may apply to the Court to set that order aside). The notice of a motion must include a concise statement of the nature of the claim made or the relief or remedy required. The plaintiff can serve a notice of motion on the defendant together with the writ of summons or originating summons or at any time after service of such writ or summons whether or not the defendant has entered on appearance in the action.[38]

Petitions must also include a concise statement on the nature of the claim sought and the names of the persons the petition should be served with. The petition should be served on the defendant not less than 7 days before the day the Registrar has fixed to be the day and time for the hearing of the petition.[39]

Similar to writ of summons and originating summons, originating motion and petitions shall also be assigned by the Registrar a serial number and be signed, sealed and dated before it is deemed to be issued.

Service of Process[40]

All writs, originating summons to which an appearance by the defendant is required, an originating summons, notices of originating motion and petitions must be served personally on each defendant.

A plaintiff must serve a statement of claim to the defendant either when the writ or notice of writ is served on the defendant or at any time after the service of the writ or notice of writ but it must be before the expiration of 14 days after the defendant enters an appearance. Thereafter, the defendant who has entered an appearance and intends to defend himself must serve a defence on the plaintiff not more than 14 days either after the time that has been limited for him to appear or after the statement of claim is served on him, whichever is the later. Next, the plaintiff who has been served the defence must serve a reply back to the defendant. If the plaintiff was also served a counter claim from the defendant and he intends to defend it, should also serve a defence on the defendant along with the reply. In each of the pleadings served, they must contain a statement setting out summarily the material facts on which the party pleading relies for his claim or defence.[41] In particular, he must plead specifically what his claim is in relation to, for instance, performance, release, statutes of limitation, fraud or any fact showing illegality and stat that the opposite party cannot claim or defend on it. This information must always be included to avoid taking the opposite party by surprise.

It is possible for the plaintiff or the defendant to apply to the Court by summons for an order that the action be tried without pleadings or further pleadings. If the Court is satisfied that the issues in dispute can be defined without pleadings or further pleadings, then it shall direct the parties to prepare a statement of the issues in dispute or if the parties are unable to agree on such a statement, the Court may settle the statement itself.

[38] Order 8 of the Supreme Court Rules [39] Order 9 of the Supreme Court Rules [40] Order 10 of the Supreme Court Rules [41] Rule 6, Order 8 of the Supreme Court Rules

Cases involving libel, slander, breach of promise of marriage and allegations of fraud does not apply in this type of action.

Where the plaintiff fails to serve a statement of claim on the defendant, the defendant may, after the expiration of the period for him to appear apply for the Court to dismiss the action.[42] If the claim relates to a liquidated demand and if the defendant fails to serve a defence, then the plaintiff may enter a final judgment against the defendant for a sum not exceeding what is claimed in the writ and also for costs.

Entering of appearance

A defendant to an action that was begun by writ may appear in the action and defend the claim either by a solicitor or by himself. Where the defendant is a body corporate, they may not enter an appearance at the action and can only be defended by a solicitor. Entering an appearance entails completing the requisite documents, namely a memorandum of appearance and sending it along with a copy of it to the Registry.[43] A memorandum of appearance basically requests the Registry to enter an appearance for the defendant or defendants specified in the memorandum. It must specify the address of the defendant's place of residence or the business address if his solicitor.

Where the defendant fails to enter an appearance, the plaintiff may after the time limited for appearing has expired, enter final judgment against that defendant for a sum not exceeding the amount claimed by the writ and for costs and proceed with the action against other defendants, if there are any.[44] He may enter an interlocutory judgment in the case of claims for unliquidated damages.

Preparing for trial[45]

A cause or matter may be tried before a Judge or the Registrar of the Supreme Court. Notice of trial may be given by the plaintiff or the other party at any time after a reply has been delivered or after the time for delivery of a reply has expired. At least 14 days before the date for trial has been fixed, the defendant shall identify to the plaintiff those documents that are central to his case that he wishes to be included in the trial bundle. At least 2 days before the trial, the plaintiff shall have 2 bundles consisting of one copy of the following documents: a) witness statements that have been exchanged including expert's reports; b) the defendant's documents that he wishes to be included in the bundle; and c) a note agreed by the parties giving a summary of the issues involved, a summary of the propositions of law, the list of authorities to be cited and a chronology of relevant events.

A pre-trial conference may also be held at any time after the commencement of proceedings, and the Court may direct the parties to attend such a conference to discuss matters relating to the action.[46] Points to consider at this pre-trial conference would

[42] Rule 1, Order 19 [43] Rule 1, Order 12 [44] Order 13 [45] Order 34 [46] Order 34A

include any possibility of settlement, the need for the parties to furnish the Court with further information as the Court would require and the Court can also give directions as it appears necessary or desirable for securing a just, expeditious and economic disposal of the action. The parties can agree to settle at any time during the pre-trial conference on all or some of the matters in dispute. The Court can then enter judgment and make an order to give effect to that settlement.

PROCEDURE AT HEARING

At the trial, the Judge will first give directions as to which party may begin the proceedings and prescribe the orders of speeches at the trial. If the defendant decides not to adduce any evidence, the plaintiff may at the close of his case make a second speech closing his case and thereafter the defendant shall make a speech in closing his case. If the defendant does decide to adduce evidence, ha may do so at the closing of the plaintiff's case. At the close of the defendant's case, the plaintiff may make a speech in reply. Rules on evidence are prescribed under Order 38 of the rules.

Where a judgment has been given for damages and there is no provision made by the judgment in how damages are to be assessed, then the damages shall be assessed by the Registrar.[47] The Court may also make an award of provisional damages if the plaintiff has made a claim for one.[48]

Every judgment after a hearing is delivered in open Court or in Chambers, either on the conclusion of the hearing or on a subsequent day of which such notice shall be given to the parties.[49] A Judge can also give judgment and his reasons, in writing at a later date by sending a copy of it to all parties to the proceedings. In this case, the original copy of the written judgment must be signed and filed. The proper officer of the Registrar must enter into the cause book a minute of every judgment or order given by the Court.

In the enforcement of a judgment for the payment of money (and not one for the payment of money into Court), it can be enforced through writ of seizure or sale, garnishee proceedings, charging orders, appointment of a receiver, and an order of committal.[50]

To avoid hearing

Payment into and out of court[51]

In any action for a debt or damages, any defendant may pay into Court a sum of money as the plaintiff claims. Within 14 days of the payment, the plaintiff may accept the money in satisfaction of that cause of action by giving such notice to the defendant.

Offer to settle[52]

Parties to any proceeding may also serve on any other person an offer to settle any one or more of the claim in the proceedings. These can be made at any time before the Court disposes of the matter.

Summary Judgment[53]

A plaintiff can apply to the Court for a summary judgment against the defendant on the ground that that defendant has no defence to the claim included in the writ. Claims relating to libel, slander, malicious prosecution, false imprisonment, seduction or breach of promise of marriage are excluded from this application.

Application for summary judgments must be made by summons supported by an affidavit verifying the facts on which the claim, or the part of the claim, to which the application relates to is based on and it should also state the plaintiff's belief that there is no defence to that claim or no defence except as to the amount of any damages. Thereafter, the Court may dismiss the plaintiff's application especially where the defendant had satisfied the Court that there is still an issue or question in dispute which ought for some reason to be tried. On the other hand, the Court may also give such judgment for the plaintiff against the defendant on that claim.

APPEALS

Any appeal from a decision of a Registrar shall lie to a Judge in Chambers.[54] The appeal shall be brought by serving a notice on every other party to the proceedings to attend an appeal hearing before a Judge on a day specified in the notice. Appeals from a Judge shall lie to the Court of Appeal.

An appeal to the Court of Appeal shall be by way of rehearing and must be brought by a notice of appeal. Every notice of appeal must be filed and served within one month from the date when such order was pronounced (in the case of an appeal from a Judge in Chambers), from the date of refusal (in the case of an appeal against the refusal of an application), and in all other cases, from the date on which the judgment or order appealed against was pronounced.

RECIPROCAL ENFORCEMENT OF FOREIGN JUDGMENTS AND FOREIGN MAINTENANCE ORDERS

Brunei Darussalam also has in force a Maintenance Orders Reciprocal Enforcement Act[55] and a Reciprocal Enforcement of Foreign Judgments Act.[56] The Maintenance Orders Act basically provides for the enforcement in Brunei Darussalam any maintenance orders made in reciprocating countries listed in the Schedule and also for maintenance order made in Brunei Darussalam to be enforced in the listed reciprocating countries. To date, the reciprocating countries are Malaysia, Singapore, Australia and Hong Kong Special

[52] Order 23 [53] Order 14 [54] Order 56 [55] CAP 175 of the Laws of Brunei [56] CAP 176 of the Laws of Brunei

Administrative Region of the People's Republic of China. Maintenance orders are those that provide for the periodical payment of money towards the maintenance of any persons the person paying is liable to maintain.

The Foreign Judgments Act makes provision for the enforcement in Brunei Darussalam any judgments given in foreign countries listed in the Schedule who will in turn also enforce judgments given in Brunei Darussalam. Judgment in this case means a judgment or order given or made by a court in any civil proceedings, judgment in any criminal proceedings for the payment of a sum of money in respect of compensation or damages to an injured party and an award in proceedings on arbitration.[57] The countries listed for the purposes of this Act as at now are only Malaysia and Singapore, through their respective High Courts.

LEGAL PROCEDURE IN THE SYARIAH COURTS

With regards to procedure in general, the Syariah Courts Act (Chapter 184) has stated that every Syariah Court in Brunei Darussalam shall have and use where necessary a seal of such form and format as may be approved by the Majlis[58]. The language that shall be used in the Syariah Courts shall be the Malay language though it may allow the use of any other language in the interest of justice[59]. However, the courts may choose for all documents or records of proceedings to be written in jawi or rumi script[60].

PROCEDURE IN CRIMINAL PROCEEDINGS

In pre-trial procedure, section 69(1) of the Religious Council and Kadis Courts Act (Chapter 77) has laid down some guidelines concerning charge. A charge shall be framed by the prosecutor or by the Court and which shall contain sufficient particulars of the offence alleged. However in practice, during the initial stage of the case, the prosecutor would normally frame the charge, whereas at the closing of the prosecution's case, it would be up to the Court (at the stage of a prima facie) to frame or amend a charge if it thinks it is not appropriate with the charge by the prosecution based on the evidence given in Court[61].

For procedure during trial, section 70 of the Religious Council and Kadis Court (Chapter 77) has outlined procedure for hearing. Section 70(1) of this Act says that any necessary sanction to prosecute shall be proved. This is in accordance with section 62 which mentioned that for any offence under section 182, 183, 185, 186, 187 or 190, no prosecution shall be instituted except by resolution of the Majlis Ugama Islam sanctioning such prosecution.

[57] Section 2 of the Reciprocal Enforcement of Foreign Judgments Act [58] Section 7(1) of the Syariah Courts Act (Chapter 184). [59] Section 7(2)(a) Ibid. [60] Section 7(2)(b) Ibid. [61] Haji Sawas Haji Jebat, *Prosedur Perbicaraan Di Mahkamah Kadi*, Jurnal Undang-Undang Syariah Brunei Darussalam, Januari-Jun 2002 Jilid 2 Bil.2, p.35.

Section 70(2) of the Act also stated that the accused shall be charged and if he pleads guilty he may be sentenced on such plea. Though it seems too simple, in practice however, the plea will only be accepted if it is made without any qualification and that the accused understood the charge made against him as well as consequences of the charge. In addition to that, section 175(1) of the Criminal Procedure Code (Chapter 7) is also practiced whereby a charge containing the particulars of the offence of which he is accused shall be framed and explained to him, and he shall be asked whether he is guilty of the offence charged or claims to be tried. And the court before recording the plea may hear the complainant and such other evidence as it considers necessary and shall ascertain that the accused understands the nature and consequences of his plea and intends to admit, without qualification, the offence alleged against him[62].

If an accused claims trial or refuses to plead, the prosecutor shall outline the facts to be proved and the relevant law and shall then call his witnesses[63]. As laid down in section 70(4), each witness shall be examined by the party calling him[64] and this shall be called his examination-in-chief[65]; be cross-examined thereafter by the party opposing him, which shall be called his cross-examination[66] and, such cross-examination may be directed to credibility[67]. Each witness may thereafter be re-examined on matters arising out of cross-examination by the party calling him[68], and such examination shall be called his re-examination[69]. Each witness have put to him at any time any question by the Court[70] and may have any further questions put to him or be recalled at any time, by leave of the Court[71]. For particulars on examination of witnesses and in ensuring the truth of syahadah syahid reference shall be made to the Syariah Courts Evidence Order, 2001[72].

After hearing the witnesses for the prosecution the Court shall either dismiss the case or call on the accused for his defence[73]. This section is to be read together with section 177(1) of the Criminal Procedure Code (Chapter 7):

"If upon taking all evidence referred to in section 176 and making such examination (if any) of the accused under section 220 as the Court considers necessary it finds that no case against the accused has been made out which, if unrebutted, would warrant his conviction, the Court may, subject to the provisions of section 186, record an order of acquittal.

If called on for his defence, the accused may address the Court and may then either give evidence or make a statement without being sworn or affirmed, in which case he shall not

[62] Section 175(2) of the Criminal Procedure Code (Chapter 7). [63] Section 70(3) of the Religious Council and Kadis Courts Act (Chapter 77). [64] Section 70(4)*(a)* Ibid. [65] Section 120(1) of the Syariah Courts Evidence Order, 2001(S 63/2001). [66] Section 120(2) Ibid. [67] Section 70(4)*(b)* of the Religious Council and Kadis Courts Act (Chapter 77). [68] Section 70(4)*(c)* Ibid. [69] Section 120(3) of the Syariah Courts Evidence Order, 2001(S 63/2001). [70] Section 70(4)*(d)* of the Religious Council and Kadis Courts Act (Chapter 77). [71] Section 70(4)*(e)* Ibid. [72] Chapters IX and IV respectively, (S 63/2001) [73] Section 70(5) of the Religious Council and Kadis Courts Act (Chapter 77).

be liable to be cross-examined, or may stand silent provided that if the accused gives evidence, he may be cross-examined, but not as to character or as to other offences not charged[74].

In doing so the accused may then call his witnesses[75]. He may sum up his case[76], and the prosecutor may reply generally[77]. As in any other Court, the Syariah Court, after considering the case shall then either convict or acquit the accused[78]. If the accused is convicted, the court may be informed of previous offences and shall have regard to any plea of leniency[79]. The Court shall then pass sentence according to law[80].

One important section in the Religious Council and Kadis Courts Act (Chapter 77) relating to criminal procedure is section 78 where it says that in matters of practice and procedure not expressly provided for in this Act or any rules made thereunder, the Court shall have regard to the avoidance of injustice and the convenient dispatch of business and may in criminal proceedings have regard to the practice and procedure obtaining in the civil courts.

PROCEDURE IN CIVIL PROCEEDINGS

For civil proceedings, provisions used are as mentioned in the Religious Council and Kadis Courts Act (Chapter 77) in section 80 until section 93; section 95 and section 96. In practice, the Emergency (Islamic Family Law) Order, 1999 (S 12/2000) as well as relevant provisions being used in the civil courts are also applied. This is to ensure that justice is served especially for those matters not provided for in the Act or any rules thereunder. Section 96 of the Religious Council and Kadis Courts (Chapter 77) states that:

"In matters of practice and procedure, not expressly provided for in this Act or any rules made thereunder, the Court may adopt such procedure as may seem proper for the avoidance of injustice and the disposal of the matters in issue between the parties, and may in particular, but without prejudice to the generality of the foregoing, adopt the practice and procedure for the time being in force in the Magistrates' Courts in civil proceedings."

LEGAL QUALIFICATIONS FOR SYARIAH LAWYERS

Section 25 of the Syariah Courts Act (Chapter 184) has specified who may be appointed as Syar'ie Prosecutor. His Majesty the Sultan and Yang Di-Pertuan may, on the advice of the President of the Majlis Ugama Islam and after consultation with the Majlis, appoint a person who is qualified to become Syariah High Court Judge, to be the Chief Syar'ie Prosecutor[26]. The Chief Syar'ie Prosecutor shall have powers exercisable at his discretion to commence and carry out any proceedings for an offence before a Syariah Court[27]; and he shall not be subject to the direction or control of any other person or authority[28].

His Majesty the Sultan and Yang Di-Pertuan may, on the advice of the President of the Majlis and after consultation with the Chief Syar'ie Prosecutor, appoint a fit and suitable persons from members of the public service to be Syar'ie Prosecutors who shall act under the supervision and direction of the Chief Syar'ie Prosecutor and may exercise all or any right and power vested in or exercisable by the Chief Syar'ie Prosecutor himself[29].

Whereas for Syar'ie Lawyers, section 27(1) of the Syariah Courts Act (Chapter 184) says that the Chief Syar'ie Judge may, on payment of the prescribed fee, admit a person who possesses sufficient knowledge about *Hukum Syara'* and suitable to become a Syar'ie Lawyer to represent the parties in any proceedings before any Syariah Court. Subsection

(2) of section 27 also states that no person other than a Syar'ie Lawyer shall have the right to appear as a *bil-khusumah* representative in any Syariah Court on behalf of any party to any proceeding before it.

Section 28 of the Syariah Courts Act (Chapter 184), the Chief Syar'ie Judge may, with the approval of His Majesty the Sultan and Yang Di-Pertuan, make Rules of Court to provide for the procedure, qualifications and fees for admission of Syar'ie Lawyers as well as regulate, control and supervise the conduct of Syar'ie Lawyers. By virtue of that section, the Syariah Courts (Syar'ie Lawyers) Rules, 2002 has been enacted which commences on the same date as the Syariah Courts Act (Chapter 184). Part II of this Rules talks about the Establishment of Syar'ie Lawyers Committee, Part III talks about Syar'ie Lawyers, Part IV on discipline, Part V on miscellaneous provisions; whereas fees and forms under this Rules can be found in the First and Second Schedule respectively.

Rule 9 talks about admission of Syar'ie Lawyers, which shall be made by the Chief Syar'ie Judge. Rule 10 stated that a person may be admitted to be Syar'ie Lawyers if he –

(a) (i) is a Muslim and has passed the final examination which leads to a bachelor's degree in Syariah from any university or any Islamic

[26] Section 25(1) of the Syariah Courts Act (Chapter 184). [27] Section 25(2) Ibid. [28] Section 25(3) Ibid. [29] Section 25(4) Ibid.

educational institution recognized by the Government of Brunei Darussalam;

(ii) is a Muslim advocate or solicitor enrolled under the Legal Profession Act (Chapter 132) who has passed the Syar'ie Lawyer Certificate examination;

(iii) has served as a Syar'ie Judge, Kadi or Syar'ie Prosecutor for a period of not less than 3 years; or

(iv) is a Muslim who has received professional training in Islamic judicial matters which is recognized by the Government of Brunei Darussalam or who specializes in *Hukum Syara'*;

(b) has attained the age of 21 years;
(c) is of good behavior and –
(i) has never been convicted in Brunei Darussalam or in any other place of any criminal offence which makes him unfit to become a Syar'ie Lawyer;
(ii) has never been adjudged a bankrupt; and

(iii) has never been disbarred, struck off or suspended in his capacity as a legal practitioner by whatever name called in any other country.

LEGAL EDUCATION

Presently, there is no law faculty at the University of Brunei Darussalam. Most of the lawyers practicing in Brunei are either qualified in England or Malaysia.

As stated earlier in Rule 10 of the Syariah Courts (Syar'ie Lawyers) Rules, 2002, a person may be admitted as Syar'ie Lawyers if he fulfills all the necessary requirements. Therefore, in its effort to produce qualified Islamic lawyers and legal practitioners in the Syariah Court, the University of Brunei Darussalam has offered a course in Diploma In Islamic Law and Legal Practice[30], which started its first session in 2000/2001. This course stresses upon the practical aspect especially in practicality, legal administration and their executions.

Objectives of this course are, among others, to give wider opportunity for law degree holders and legal practitioners in Brunei Darussalam, in Syariah or Civil to undertake a formal program in Islamic law; to give more exposure to law graduates in Islamic law and

Administration; to produce qualified Islamic lawyers; and to minimizing government expenditure on sending students abroad by providing the course locally.

Subjects offered in the program includes the Islamic Legal System, Islamic Family Law, Syariah Political Science, Islamic Judiciary and Practice, Brunei Legal System, Islamic Law and Evidence, Islamic Criminal law, Islamic Law of Contract and Trade, Procedures in Criminal and Civil and Commercial Law.

NATIONAL DEVELOPMENT PLAN

The current National Development Plan 1996 - 2000 is the 7th in the series and primarily aims at giving an all-round enhancement to all facets of life of the people, with emphasis to economic diversification through the development of export-oriented non- oil based industries. The Government has allocated a total of $7.2 billion for this purpose, with social services taking the lion's share at $1.98 billion; Public Utilities, $1.58 billion; Transport and Communications, $1.4 billion; Industry and Commerce, $907.66 million; Public Buildings, $623.83 million; Security, $528.1 million; and Miscellaneous, $173.3 million.

COMMUNICATIONS

Airport

The present day Brunei International Airport, located at Berakas about fifteen minutes drive from Bandar Seri Begawan operates 24 hours a day, providing facilities for both regional and international air traffic. It has a 4000-metre runway that can accommodate any type of aircraft currently in service, including the 'Jumbo' 747s. Its passenger and cargo handling facilities can handle 1.5 million passengers and 50,000 tones of cargo a year. Equipped with the latest state-of the-art technology in surveillance and tracking, the airport boasts radar, flight and auxiliary data processing, 2,000-line, high-resolution color raster displays, simulation facilities, voice switching system, voice and data recording and VHF/UHF air-ground transmitters. The national air carrier is Royal Brunei Airlines founded in November 18, 1974.

Another airport, at Anduki near Seria, is used by the Brunei Shell Petroleum Company for its helicopter services.

Ports

The main Port is Muara, which is about 28 kilometers from Bandar Seri Begawan. The port can accommodate ships over 196 meters L.O.A. and take up to 7 or 8 vessels averaging 8,000 Gross Registered Tonnage {GRT} or a single ship of up to 30,000 {GRT} with a draught of not more than 9.5 meters.

Since 1973, the port has undergone extensive improvements. These include extensions to the wharf bringing the total length to 948 meters including 250 meters dedicated container wharf and 87 meters aggregate wharf. The overall storage space in the form of covered storage is 16,950 square meters, long storage warehouses 16,630 square meters and open storage space 5 hectares. Facilities for the dedicated container wharf covers an area of 92,034 square meters including 8,034 square meters covered areas.

Besides Muara Port, there are two smaller ports located one at Bandar Seri Begawan and one at Kuala Belait. The port at Bandar Seri Begawan is utilized by vessels under 93 meters LOA drawing less than 5 meters draught carrying conventional cargoes for direct deliveries and passenger launches plying between Bandar Seri Begawan, Limbang and Temburong. The wharf also accommodates various small government crafts. The port at Kuala Belait can accommodate vessels with draught of 4 meters which carries mainly general cargo for Kuala Belait and the Brunei Petroleum Shell Company.

Road

The road network in Brunei Darussalam is the primary means of movement for people, goods and services on land. It plays a vital role in the overall growth and development of the State. The network has been designed to integrate housing, commercial and industrial development. The Sultanate has constructed a good road network with various types of road throughout the country that includes highways, link roads, flyovers and round-abouts. A major road, which was completed in 1983, is a 28-kilometre highway linking Muara through Berakas and Jerudong to a point in Tutong, where it connects with the existing Bandar Seri Begawan-Tutong-Seria trunk road thus providing an alternative routes to these places.

An 11-km road between Sungai Teraban and Sungai Tujoh, makes the journey from Brunei Darussalam to Sarawak's Fourth Division such as Miri and other parts of Sarawak much easier.

The State had 2,525 kilometers (km) of roads, of which 2,328 km were covered with asphalt, 187 with pebbles, and 10 km with concrete. Of the total 1,514 km were in Brunei/Muara, 481 km in Belait, 400 km in Tutong and 130 km in Temburong district.

BRUNEI POLITICAL SYSTEM STRATEGIC INFORMATION AND DEVELOPMENTS

BASIC INFORMATION

The **politics of Brunei** take place in a framework of an absolute monarchy, where by the Sultan of Brunei is both head of state and head of government (Prime Minister of Brunei). Executive power is exercised by the government. Brunei has a Legislative Council with 36 appointed members, that only has consultative tasks. Under Brunei's 1959 constitution, His Majesty Paduka Seri Baginda Sultan Haji Hassanal Bolkiah Mu'izzaddin Waddaulah, is the head of state with full executive authority, including emergency powers since 1962. The Sultan's role is enshrined in the national philosophy known as **Melayu Islam Beraja** (**MIB**), or Malay Islamic Monarchy. The country has been under hypothetical martial law since a rebellion occurred in the early 1960s and was put down by British troops from Singapore.

EXECUTIVE BRANCH

The Sultan is the head of state and head of government in Brunei. He exercises absolute powers and full executive authority under the framework of the 1959 Constitution. The Sultan is advised by and presides over five councils, which he appoints. The five councils are the Privy Council, Council of Succession, Religious Council, Council of Ministers and the Legislative Council.[1]

PRIVY COUNCIL

According to the Constitution, the Privy Council advises the Sultan in matters concerning the exercise of authority of mercy and the amendment or revocation of provisions in the Constitution. The council also advises the Sultan on the conferring of Malay customary ranks, titles and honours. It also performs functions such as proclaiming a succession of regency. Members of the Privy Council include members of the royal family and senior government officials.[2]

COUNCIL OF SUCCESSION

The Council of Succession determines succession to the throne should that need arise. The order of succession is determined by the Constitution.[3]

RELIGIOUS COUNCIL

The Religious Council, known in full as the Brunei Islamic Religious Council (BIRC) advises the Sultan on all matters pertaining to Islam. The body in charge of Islamic administration policy. Policies determined by the council are executed by the Ministry of Religious Affairs.

Members of the Religious Council include government ministers, a pengiran cheteria, pehin manteris, state mufti, the Attorney General, the Syarie Chief Justice and additional members appointed by the Sultan.[4]

COUNCIL OF MINISTERS

Further information: Cabinet of Brunei
A Council of Ministers, or cabinet, which currently consists of nine members (including the Sultan himself as Prime Minister), perform the day-to-day administrative functions of government.[5]

LEGISLATIVE BRANCH

The **Legislative Council of Brunei** is a national unicameral legislature of Brunei. The Council holds its sitting annually in March at Legislative Council Building in Bandar Seri Begawan.

The Council is established in 1959 by virtue of Article 23 of Brunei's Constitution of 1959. Its first sitting was held at Lapau on 21 October 1959. In 1984, the Council managed to hold 32 meetings; the last one being the 21st Meeting held on 12 February 1984. Sultan Hassanal Bolkiah dissolved the Council on the following day. Hence, legislative powers were fully vested in the Sultan.

Brunei had no legislature until 25 September 2004, when the Sultan decided to reinstate the Council using the old system. Brunei, once again, had no legislature. The Sultan disestablished the Council on 1 September 2005 and, on the following day, reestablished the Council based on the amended version of Brunei's Constitution.

ROLES

Since 1959, the Council has played significant roles towards Brunei; not only to consider and approve budgets and revenue estimates, but also to advise the Sultan on the drive of the Government, to review policies implemented by the Government and to pass bills and motions brought by the Government and other members of the Council.

MEMBERSHIP

The Council comprises the Sultan, the Crown Prince,[1] cabinet ministers and three types of members: members with titles, members representing districts, and members among outstanding Bruneians. All members, other than the Sultan, are appointed by the Sultan in accordance with Article 24 of Brunei Constitution.
Since 13 January 2017, the Council has 33 members, including 13 cabinet ministers.[2]

LEGISLATIVE PROCEDURE

The Council follows the practice of other Commonwealth parliaments. All bills presented in the Council go through three readings. All bills, however, must obtain prior approval from the Cabinet prior to their presentation in the Council. Once a bill is passed, a bill must obtain Royal Assent in order to turn such bill to an Act.

BRUNEI'S CONSTITUTION

of 1959 with Amendments through 1984

PREAMBLE

In the name of GOD, the Compassionate, the Merciful, PRAISE be to GOD, the Lord of the Universe, and may the benediction and peace of God be upon Our Leader Muhammad and upon all his Relations and Friends.

BY THE GRACE OF GOD, OMAR ALI SAIFUDDIN SA'ADUL KHAIRI WADDIN IBNI ALMARHUM MOHAMED JAMAL-UL ALAM of Negara Brunei Darussalam and all its dependencies, Sultan and Yang DiPertuan, SOVEREIGN AND CHIEF OF THE MOST ESTEEMED FAMILY ORDER, SOVEREIGN AND CHIEF OF THE MOST HONOURABLE ORDER OF THE CROWN of Brunei Darussalam, ORDER OF SRI MAHKOTA NEGARA, MOST ESTEEMED FAMILY ORDER (FIRST CLASS) KELANTAN, HONORARY KNEIGHT COMMANDER OF THE MOST DISTINGUISHED ORDER OF SAINT MICHAEL AND SAINT GEORGE.

Recitals Cons. II

WHEREAS provision is being made in a separate Proclamation (in this Constitution referred to as "The Succession and regency Proclamation") for certain matters affecting His Majesty the Sultan and Yang Di-Pertuan, the Succession to the Sultanate and His Majesty the Sultan and Yang Di-Pertuan's family;

WHEREAS WE intend to govern in accordance with the provisions of this Constitution and the laws of Brunei Darussalam and, by progressive steps hereafter, to introduce further representative institutions into the government of Brunei Darussalam;

AND WHEREAS WE have, with the advice and consent of OUR traditional advisers, decided to make such provisions for the regulation of the government of Brunei Darussalam as is hereinafter contained:

NOW, THEREFORE, WE, by the rights and powers of OUR Prerogatives as Sultan of Brunei Darussalam and all its Dependencies do HEREBY PROCLAIM in OUR name and on OUR behalf and for and on behalf of OUR Successors as hereinafter follows:

PART I PRELIMINARY

This Constitution may be cited as the Constitution of Brunei Darussalam.

1. In this Constitution, unless the context otherwise requires

"Adat Istiadat Officer" means the noble and illustrious personage known as the Duli Pengiran Pemancha or any person appointed by His Majesty the Sultan and Yang Di-Pertuan to hold such appointment;

"Attorney General" means the officer appointed under subsection (1) of section 66;

"a Bruneian or a citizen of Brunei" means except where subsection (2) of section 29 i applicable, a subject of His Majesty the Sultan and Yang Di Pertuan by virtue of th provisions of any written law relating to nationality;

"Civil List" means the provision made for the maintenance of His Majesty the Sultan and Yang
Di-Pertuan or Consort out of public funds;

"Clerk to the Council of Ministers" includes any person appointed by His Majesty the Sultan and Yang Di-Pertuan to be Deputy Clerk to that Council;

"Clerk to the Legislative Council" includes any person appointed by His Majesty the Sultan and
Yang Di-Pertuan to be Deputy Clerk to that Council;

"Clerk to the Privy Council" includes any person appointed by His Majesty the Sultan and Yang
Di-Pertuan to be Deputy Clerk to that Council;

"the Commonwealth" means the countries that are independent members of the Commonwealth and territories for whose international relations any of those countries is wholly or in part responsible;

"Council of Ministers" means the Council of Cabinet Ministers established by section 10;

"Council of Regency" means a Council of Regency appointed under subsection (1) of section 13 of the Succession and Regency Proclamation;

"debt" includes any liability in respect of any obligation to repay capital sums by way of annuities and any liability under any guarantee;

"Deputy Ministers" means persons appointed under subsection (9) of section 4;

"high judicial office" means the office of a Judge of the Supreme Court, or of a court having unlimited jurisdiction in civil or criminal matters, or of a court having jurisdiction in appeals from any such court;

"His Majesty the Sultan and Yang Di-Pertuan" means His Majesty the Sultan and Yang Di-Pertuan of Negara Brunei Darussalam and includes-where appropriate, a Council of Regency; and

to the extent to which a Deputy to His Majesty is authorised to act that Deputy;

"His Majesty the Sultan and Yang Di-Pertuan in Council" means His Majesty the Sultan and Yang Di-Pertuan acting after consultation with the Council of Ministers but not necessarily in accordance with the advice of that Council nor necessarily in that Counci assembled.

"instrument" includes any publication in the Gazette, whether or not such publication merely purports to publish the doing of an act or the occurrence of a fact or event, or otherwise conveys or purports to convey information.

"Legislature" means the authority competent to make laws for Brunei Darussalam.

"Legislative Council" means the Legislative Council established by section 23;

"meeting" in relation to the Legislative Council, means all sittings of that Council held during a period beginning when that Council first meets after being summoned at any time and ending when that Council is next thereafter either adjourned sine die or prorogued or dissolved without having been prorogued;

"Ministers" means persons appointed under subsection (4) of section 4;

"Muslim Religion" means the Muslim Religion according to the Shafeite sect of that religion;

"Muslim revenue and funds" means all revenues and funds to which Part IV of the Religious Council, State Custom and Kathis Courts Act apply;

"pension rights" includes superannuation rights and provident funds rights;

"Prime Minister" means the person appointed under subsection (6) of section 4;

"Privy Council" means the Privy Council established by subsection (1) of section 5;

"public office" means any office of emolument under the Government of Brunei Darussalam but does not include the Sultanate, the office of Regent or Wazir;

"public officer" means the holder of any public office and includes any person appointed to act in any such office;

"Regent" means a Regent duly appointed under subsection (1) of section 13 of the Succession and Regency Proclamation;

"Religious Adviser" means the person duly appointed by His Majesty the Sultan and Yang Di Pertuan to hold that office;

"Seal of the State" means the National Seal of Negara Brunei Darussalam referred to in section 79;

"Senior Wazir or Kepala Wazir" means the noble and illustrious personage known as the Duli Pengiran Perdana Wazir Shibol Himmah Wal-Waqar; and "the Wazirs" means the Duli Pengiran Perdana Wazir Sahibol Himmah Wal-Waqat, the Pengiran Bendahara Seri Maharaja Permaisurara, the Pengiran DiGadong Sahibol Maai, the Pengiran Pemancha Sahibol Rae Walmashuraran and the Pengiran Temenggong Sahibol Bahar;

"Session", in relation to the Legislative Council, means the meeting of that Council commencing when it first meets after being constituted under the Constitution, or after its prorogation or

dissolution at any time, and terminating when that Council is prorogued or is dissolved without having been prorogued;

"sitting", in relation to the Legislative Council, means the period during which the Council is sitting continuously without adjournment, and includes any period during which that Council is in Committee;

"Standing Orders" means the Standing Orders of the Legislative Council made in pursuance of section 48;

"Supreme Court" means the Supreme Court of Brunei Darussalam;

"tax" includes an impost or a duty but does not include a rate levied for local purposes or a fee for services rendered;

"Welfare Officer" means the officer appointed by His Majesty the Sultan and Yang Di-Pertuan to be responsible to him for the welfare of Muslims in Brunei Darussalam;

"written law" includes all Acts, Enactments, Proclamations and subsidiary legislation, or any part thereof, but does not include any Act or Parliament of the United Kingdom nor any Order of Her Britannic Majesty in Council Royal Charter or Royal Letters Patent nor any Law which no authority in Brunei Darussalam is empowered to amend.

Where in this Constitution reference is made to any public officer by the term designating his office, such reference shall be construed as a reference to the officer for the time being discharging the functions of that office.

For the purpose of this Constitution, a person shall not be considered to hold a public office by reason only of the fact that he is in receipt of a pension or other like allowance in respect of service under Her Britannic Majesty or the Government.

No person shall be appointed to be Prime Minister unless he is a Brunei Malay professing the Muslim religion and belonging to the sect of that religion.

The Prime Minister and other Ministers shall be appointed by His Majesty the Sultan and Yang Di-Pertuan by Instrument under His Sign Manual and the National Seal and shall hold office during the pleasure of His Majesty the Sultan and Yang Di-Pertuan.

The Attorney General shall be appointed by His Majesty the Sultan and Yang Di-Pertuan by notification in the Gazette and shall old office during the pleasure of His Majesty the Sultan and Yang Di-Pertuan.

The remuneration of the Prime Minister, Ministers and Deputy Ministers shall be such as may be provided by the Legislature.

His Majesty the Sultan and Yang Di-Pertuan may appoint Deputy Ministers who shall assist the Ministers in the discharge of their duties and functions.

PART IV PRIVY COUNCIL

5. ESTABLISHMENT OF A PRIVY COUNCIL.

There shall be in and for Brunei Darussalam a Privy Council, to be styled in Malay the Majlis Meayuar at Di-Raja, constituted in accordance with this Part.

The Privy Council, the Members of which shall be styled Privy Councillors, shall consist of-

Regents, if a Council of Regency has been appointed;

fficio Members, namely, the Prime Minister, the Wazirs, Members of the Council ters, and the person who holds such other office as may from time to time be ed by His Majesty the Sultan and Yang Di-Pertuan by Proclamation in the ent Gazette;

er person (who shall be styled "Appointed Members") as His Majesty the

uan, may, by Instrument under the Seal of Brunei Darussalam, appoint.

ointed Member of the Privy Council shall hold office during His Majesty the Yang Di-Pertuan's pleasure and subject thereto for such period and upon ons as may be specified in the Instrument appointing him.

r of the Privy Council shall, before entering on the duties of his office, scribe before His Majesty the Sultan and Yang Di-Pertuan, or, if a ency has been appointed, before the senior male Regent, or before n as His Majesty the Sultan and Yang Di-Pertuan or, as the case may be, the senior male Regent may decide, an oath or declaration in the form set out as Form 1 in the Schedule.

Notwithstanding that he is not a Member of the Privy Council, the Attorney General-

a. shall have the right to attend meetings of that Council for the purpose of assisting the Council in advising His Majesty the Sultan and Yang Di-Pertuan on the exercise of the power vested in His Majesty the Sultan Yang DiPertuan by subsection (1) of section 9; and

b. may, if requested by His Majesty the Sultan and Yang Di-Pertuan or by any other person
presiding in that Council, attend any meeting of that Council for the purpose of advising the
Council in connection with any other matter.

6. FUNCTIONS OF THE PRIVY COUNCIL.

1. The Privy Council-

a. shall advise His Majesty the Sultan and Yang Di-Pertuan in relation to the amendment or
revocation of any of the provisions of this Constitution, in accordance with sections 9 and 85
respectively;

b. shall, subject to the provisions of any written law, advise His Majesty the Sultan and Yang
Di-Pertuan on the appointment of persons to Malay customary ranks, titles, honours and dignities and the designation of the functions appertaining thereto; and

c. shall perform such other functions as may be conferred on it by any other written law or by His
Majesty the Sultan and Yang Di-Pertuan.

Minutes shall be kept of all proceedings of the Privy Council.

His Majesty the Sultan and Yang Di-Pertuan shall appoint some fit and proper person to be clerk to the Privy Council, and such person shall, before entering upon the duties of his office, make and subscribe before His Majesty the Sultan and Yang Di-Pertuan or the senior male Regent, as the case may be, an oath or declaration in the form set out as Form 11 in the Schedule.

Subject to any provision contained in any other written law, the exercise of any power conferred on, or the doing of any act or thing by, the Privy Council may be signified under the h and of the Clerk to the Privy Council.

7. SUMMONING AND QUORUM

The Privy Council shall not be summoned except by the authority of His Majesty the Sultan and Yang DI-Pertuan, or, if a Council of Regency has been appointed, by the senior male Regent or, if His Majesty the Sultan and Yang Di-Pertuan is not present in Brunei Darussalam and if no Council of Regency has been appointed, by the Kepale Wazir.

a. No business shall be transacted at any meeting of the Privy Council if there are less than one-third of the Members of the Council (besides His Majesty the Sultan and Yang Di-Pertuan or other person presiding) present at the meeting, and His Majesty the Sultan and Yang D-Pertuan or any other Member of the Council present at the meeting has objected to the transaction of business on that account.

If the number of members of the Privy Council is not a multiple of three then, for the purpose of this subsection the number of members shall be deemed to be the next highest multiple of three.

Any proceedings in the Privy Council shall be valid notwithstanding that some person who was not entitled to do so took part in the proceedings.

8. PRESIDING IN THE PRIVY COUNCIL.

His Majesty the Sultan and Yang Di-Pertuan, so far as practicable, preside at meetings of the Privy Council.

In the absence of His Majesty the Sultan and Yang Di-Pertuan, the person who shall preside shall be-

a. if a Council of Regency has been appointed, the senior male regent presents;

b. if no Council of regency has been appointed, such Member of the Privy Council as His Majesty the Sultan and Yang Di-Pertuan may appoint or, in the absence of such Member or where no such Member has been appointed, the Kepala Wazir; and

c. in any other case, the ex-officio Member of the Privy Council present who stands first in the
order in which those Officers are referred to in paragraph (b) of subsection (2) of section 5.

9. PREROGATIVE OF MERCY.

1. His Majesty the Sultan and Yang Di-Pertuan may, at any time, exercise, in respect of any offence for which the offender may be tried in Brunei Darussalam, such one or more of the following powers as he may think kit, namely power to-

a. grant to any person concerned in, or convicted of, any such offence a pardon either free or
subject to lawful conditions;

b. grant to any person a respite, either indefinite or for a specified period, of the execution of any
sentence passed on that person for such an offence;

c. substitute a less severe form of punishment for that imposed by any sentence for such an
offence;

d. remit the whole or any part of any sentence passed for such an offence or of any sum of money imposed as a penalty or forfeiture, or otherwise due to B-unei Darussalam, His Majesty the
Sultan and Yang Di-Pertuan or any other person on account of such offence; or

His Majesty the Sultan and Yang Di-Pertuan shall not pardon or reprieve any offender under subsection (1) unless it shall appear to him expedient to do so upon receiving the advice of the Privy Council thereon; but, in all such cases, he shall decide either to extend or to withhold a pardon or reprieve according to his own deliberate judgement, whether the Members of the Privy Council concur, therein or otherwise, but, if he should decide any question in opposition to the judgement of the majority of such Members, he shall record his reasons at length in the minutes of the Privy Council.

Repealed.

It shall be the duty of the Attorney General to supply to the Privy Council any information which the prosecution may have in relation to any offender who has been sentenced to death which may be material to the exercise in relation to that offender of the powers vested in His Majesty the Sultan and Yang Di-Pertuan by subsection (1).

PART V THE COUNCIL OF MINISTERS

10. ESTABLISHMENT OF COUNCIL OF MINISTERS

There shall be in and for Brunei Darussalam a Council of Ministers to be styled in Malay the Majlis Mesyuart, Menteri, Menteri, constituted in accordance with the provisions of this Part.

Brunei 1959 (rev. 1984) Page 7

11. CONSTITUTION OF COUNCIL OF MINISTERS.

The Council of Ministers shall be presided over by His Majesty the Sultan and Yang Di Pertuan and shall consist of the Ministers appointed under subsection (6) of section 4.

12. TENURE OF OFFICE AND VACATION OF SEATS.

Subject to this Constitution every member shall hold his seat in the Council of Ministers during His Majesty the Sultan and Yang Di-Pertuan's pleasure.

13. Repealed.

14. ATTENDANCE AT COUNCIL OF MINISTERS OF NON-MEMBERS.

Whenever His Majesty the Sultan and Yang Di-Pertuan or other person presiding desires to obtain the advice of any person touching the affairs of government, he may require such person to attend any meeting of the Council of Ministers for such purpose.

15. PRECEDENCE.

The Members of the Council of Ministers shall have seniority and precedence among themselves in that Council as His Majesty the Sultan and Yang Di-Pertuan may assign.

16. SUMMONING AND QUORUM.

The Council of Ministers shall not be summoned except by the authority of His Majesty the Sultan and Yang Di-Pertuan.

No business shall be transacted at any meeting of the Council of Ministers if there are less than one member of the Council (besides His Majesty the Sultan and Yang Di-Pertuan or other person presiding) present at the meeting, and His Majesty the Sultan and Yang Di-Pertuan or any members of the Council present at the meeting has objected to the transaction of business on that account.

The Council of Ministers shall not be disqualified for the transaction of business by reason of any vacancy among its Members, including any vacancy not filled when that Council is first constituted or is reconstituted at any time and any proceedings therein shall be valid notwithstanding that same person who was not entitled to do so took part in the proceedings reproduced on next page.

17. PRESIDING IN COUNCIL OF MINISTERS.

In the absence of His Majesty the Sultan and Yang Di-Pertuan, the person who shall preside shall be the Member of the Council of Ministers present who stands first in order of precedence according to section 15.

18. CONSULTATION WITH THE COUNCIL OF MINISTERS.

In the exercise of his powers and the performance of his duties, His Majesty the Sultan and Yang Di-Pertuan shall, subject to the provisions of this section, consult with the Council of Ministers.

Subsection (1) of this section shall not apply to the exercise or performance by His Majesty the Sultan and Yang Di-Pertuan of any power or duty (whether conferred or imposed on him by this Constitution or by any other written law) if the law by which that power or duty is conferred or imposed empowers or requires His Majesty the Sultan and Yang Di-Pertuan to exercise that power or perform that duty after consultation with ... authority other than the Council of Ministers... does not require him to consult with any authority.

Notwithstanding subsection (1) His Majesty the Sultan and Yang Di-Pertuan shall not be obliged to consult the Council of Ministers in cases-

a. which are of such a nature that, in his judgement, Brunei Darussalam would sustain material
prejudiced by his consulting the Council of Ministers thereon;

b. in which the matters to be decided are, in his judgement, too unimportant to require the advice of the Council of Ministers; or

c. in which the matters to be decided are in his judgement too urgent to admit on the advice of the Council of Ministers being given by the time within which it may be necessary for him to act;

Provided that, in every case falling within paragraph (c), His Majesty the Sultan and Yang DiPertuan shall, as soon as practicable, inform the Council of Ministers of the measures which he has adopted with the reasons therefor.

4. Only His Majesty the Sultan and Yang Di-Pertuan or the Prime Minister shall be entitled to submit questions to the Council of Ministers, but if the Prime Minister declines to submit any question to that Council when requested in writing by any Member of that Council so to do, it shall be competent to such Member to require that there be recorded upon the minutes his written application together with the answer returned by the Prime Minister thereon.

19. His Majesty the Sultan and Yang Di-Pertuan may act in opposition to the advice of the Council of Ministers.

His Majesty the Sultan and Yang Di-Pertuan may act in oppostion to the advice given to him by the majority of the Members of the Council of Ministers if he shall, in any case, consider it right so to do, but, in any case, he shall record fully in writing, for inclusion in the minutes, the reasons for his decision.

Whenever His Majesty the Sultan and Yang Di-Pertuan shall so act against the advice of the Council of Ministers, it shall be competent for any Member to require that there be recorded upon the minutes any advice or opinion he may have given upon the question together with the reasons therefor.

20. MINUTES

Minutes shall be kept of all the proceedings of the Council of Ministers.

As soon as practicable after the minutes of a meeting of the Council of Ministers have been confirmed, a full transcript thereof shall be transmitted by the Clerk to the Council of Ministers to His Majesty and Yang Di-Pertuan.

21. ORDER TO BE TAKEN BY MEMBERS

Every member of the Council of Ministers, other than His Majesty the Sultan and Yang Di-Pertuan, shall, before entering on the duties of his office, make and subscribe before His Majesty the Sultan and Yang Di-Pertuan, or some other person authorised by His Majesty the Sultan and Yang Di-Pertuan, an oath or declaration in the form set out as Form III in the Schedule:

Provided that any person who, having previously been a Member of that Council of Ministers, again becomes a Member of that Council within one month after the termination of his previous Membership thereof may enter on the duties of his office without making and subscribing such oath or declaration.

22. His Majesty the Sultan and Yang Di-Pertuan shall appoint some fit and proper person to be Clerk to the Council of Ministers, and such person shall, before entering upon the duties of this office, make and subscribe before His Majesty the Sultan and Yang Di-Pertuan or other Member presiding an oath or declaration in the form set out as Form Ii on the Schedule.

PART VI THE LEGISLATIVE COUNCIL

There shall be a Legislative Council, to be styled in Malay the "Majlis Mesyuart Negeri", constituted in accordance with the provisions of this Part.

The Legislative Council shall consist of six ex-officio Members, five Official Members and ten Nominated Members.

The ex-officio Members of the Legislative Council shall be the Prime Minister, the Minister, the Attorney General and the Religious Adviser.

The Official Members of the Legislative Council shall be persons who hold public office and shall be appointed by His Majesty the Sultan and Yang Di-Pertuan by Instrument under the Seal of the State.

Repealed.

The Nominated Members of the Legislative Council shall be persons who do not hold public office, and shall be appointed by His Majesty and Sultan and Yang Di-Pertuan by Instrument under the Seal of the State.

1. Subject to section 30, any person other than a Regent who is a Subject of His Majesty the Sultan and Yang Di-Pertuan and who has attained the age of 21 years, shall be qualified to be appointed as an Official Member or a Nominated Member of the Legislative Council.

2. For the purposes of this section, the term "a subject of His Majesty the Sultan and Yang Di-Pertuan" shall have the same meaning as that assigned to it by the Nationality Act for the time being in force.

30. DISQUALIFICATION FOR OFFICIAL AND NOMINATED MEMBERS

No person shall be qualified to be appointed as an Official Member or a Nominated Member of the Legislative Council or having been so appointed shall sit or vote therein, who-

a. is, by virtue of his own act, under acknowledgement of allegiance, obedience or adherence to

power or state outside Brunei Darussalam.

b. is a person declared to be of unsound mind under any law in force in Brunei Darussalam;

c. has been sentenced by a Court in Brunei Darussalam, in any part of the Commonwealth or in the

Republic of Ireland to death or to imprisonment (by whatever name called):

Provided that this paragraph shall not apply to any person-

i. until the time for lodging an appeal has lapsed or, if an appeal has been lodged, until such appeal

has been dismissed or has been allowed but the appellate court has imposed a sentence of death

or imprisonment (by whatever name called);

ii. who has received a free pardon;

iii. if 3 years or more have elapsed since the termination of the imprisonment; or

iv. in respect of whom His Majesty the Sultan and Yang Di-Pertuan has, after full consideration of the circumstances, directed that this paragraph shall not apply.

d. is an undischarged bankrupt, having been adjudged or otherwise declared bankrupt under any law in force in Brunei Darussalam or in any foreign country.

e. is a party to, or a partner in, a firm or a director or manager of a company, which is a party to any contract the consideration for which exceeds in value the sum of one thousand dollars with the Government for or on account of the public service, and has not disclosed to the Speaker the nature of such contract and his interest, or the interest of such firm or company therein.

Provided that a person shall not be considered to be a party to a contract with the Government for the purpose of this paragraph by reason of his holding, or acting in, any public office.

31. TENURE OF OFFICE AND VACATION OF SEATS.

Every Official and Nominated Member of the Legislative Council shall hold his seat therein during His Majesty the Sultan and Yang Di-Pertuan's pleasure.

Every Official and Nominated Member of the Legislative Council shall cease to be a Member at the next dissolution of the Council after he has been appointed or previously thereto if his seat shall become vacant under this Constitution.

The seat of the Official or Nominated Member shall become vacant-

a. if he shall be appointed as a Regent.

b. if he shall, by writing under his hand addressed to the Clerk of the Legislative Council; resign his seat in the Legislative Council, and, in the case of an Official Member, his resignation shall be accepted by His Majesty the Sultan and Yang Di-Pertuan;

c. if he shall be absent from two consecutive meetings of the Legislative Council without having obtained from the Speaker, before the termination of either or such meetings, permission to be or to remain absent therefrom;

d. if, being an Official Member, he shall cease to hold public office;

e. if, being a Nominated Member, he shall be appointed permanently to any public office; or

f. if any circumstances arise which, if he were not a Member of the Legislative Council, would cause him to be disqualified under section 30.

If a Nominated Member shall be appointed temporarily to any public office or to act in any such office, he shall not sit as a Member or take part in the proceedings of the Legislative Council by virtue of his appointment as a Nominated Member so long as he continues to hold or act in that office.

His Majesty the Sultan and Yang Di-Pertuan may, for such reason as may appear to him to be good and sufficient, by Instrument under the Seal of the State, declare any Member, other than an ex-officio Member, to be incapable of discharging his functions as a Member of the Legislative Council, and thereupon, such Member shall not sit in or take part in the proceedings of the Legislative Council until he is declared, in manner aforesaid, again to be capable of discharging his said functions.

His Majesty the Sultan and Yang Di-Pertuan may, for such reason as may appear to him good and sufficient, by Instrument under the Seal of the State suspend any Member, other than an ex-officio Member from the exercise of his functions as such, and, thereupon such Member shall not sit in or take part in the proceedings of the Legislative Council so long as his suspension remains in force; and every such suspension shall remain in force until it shall be removed by His Majesty the Sultan and Yang Di-Pertuan by Instrument under the Seal of the State, or the person suspended ceases to be a Member of the Legislative Council.

If any ex-officio Member of the Legislative Council is appointed Regent and continues to hold the office by virtue of which he is an ex-officio member of the Legislative Council, he shall not, so long as he is a Regent, sit or take part in the proceedings of the Legislative Council as an ex-officio Member thereof.

Any person vacating a seat as a Member of the Legislative Council may, if qualified, be again appointed as, or elected to be, as the case may be, a Member from time to time.

32. DECISIONS OF QUESTIONS AS TO MEMBERSHIP OF LEGISLATIVE COUNCILS, ETC.

1. His Majesty the Sultan and Yang Di-Pertuan shall have exclusive jurisdiction to determine any question whether-

a. any Official Member or any Nominated Member of the Legislative Council has been validly
appointed as a Member of the Council; or

b. any such Member has vacated his seat therein.

2. Repealed.

33. TEMPORARY APPOINTMENTS.

1. Where for the time being-

a. one of the Members is appointed to act as regent.

b. the functions of the offices qualifying for ex-officio membership of the Legislative Council are
being discharged by less than 8 persons;

c. an Official Member is discharging the functions of any of those offices;

d. the seat of an Official Member or a Nominated Member is vacant otherwise than by reason of a dissolution of the Council.

e. a Member is unable to sit in the Legislative Council in consequence of a declaration by His
Majesty the Sultan and Yang Di-Pertuan, as provided in subsection (5) of section 31, that he is
incapable of discharging his functions as a Member;

f. a Member, other than an ex-officio Member or an Elected Member, is unable to sit in the Legislative Council in consequence of his suspension as provided in subsection (6) of section 31;

g. a Nominated Member has been appointed temporarily to a public office or to act in any such
office; or

h. an Official Member or a Nominated Member is absent from Brunei Darussalam.

His Majesty Sultan and Yang Di-Pertuan may, by Instrument under the Seal of the State, appoint a person to be a Member for the period of such vacancy.

If the deficiency is in the number of ex-officio Members or Official Members, the person so appointed shall be a person who is a public officer.

Every person so appointed shall, so long as his appointment shall subsist, be to all intents and purposes-

a. in the case of a deficiency in the number of persons sitting in the Legislative Council as ex-officio Members or Official Members an Official Member; and

b. in the case of a deficiency in the number of persons sitting in the Legislative Council as Nominated Members, a Nominated Member, and, subject to this section, section 31 shall apply accordingly.

Any such temporary appointment shall case to have effect on notification by the Clerk of the Legislative Council to the person appointed of the revocation of the appointment, or on the supersession of the appointment by the definitive appointment of a person to fill the vacancy, or when the deficiency shall otherwise cease to exist.

A temporary appointment shall cease to have effect on notification by the Clerk of the Legislative Council to the person appointed of the revocation of the appointment, or on the supersession of the appointment by the definitive appointment of a person to fill the vacancy, or when the deficiency shall otherwise cease to exist.

34. ATTENDANCE OF LEGISLATIVE COUNCIL OF NON-MEMBERS.

Whenever the Speaker desires to obtain the advice of any person in Brunei Darussalam touching any business about to be brought before the Legislative Council, he may summon any such person to attend the Legislative Council for such purpose.

Any person so required may, with the permission of the Speaker and subject to Standing Orders, address the Legislative Council but, save as aforesaid, shall take no part in the proceedings thereof.

35. FILLING OF VACANCIES.

Whenever the seat of an Official Member or a Nominated Member of the Legislative Council becomes vacant the vacancy shall be filled by appointment by His Majesty the Sultan and Yang Di-Pertuan in accordance with this Constitution.

Repealed.

36. PRECEDENCE.

1. The Members of the Legislative Council shall have seniority and precedence in the Council as follows-

First, the ex-officio Member in the order in which their offices are referred to in section 25;

Secondly, the Official Members and the Nominated Members according to the date of the Instruments by which they were respectively appointed, or if appointed on the same day, in such order as His Majesty the Sultan and Yang Di-Pertuan shall assign; and Majesty the Sultan and Yang Di-Pertuan shall assign; and

Thirdly the temporary Members in such order as His Majesty the Sultan and Yang Di-Pertuan
shall assign.

2. When any person is re-appointed to the Legislative Council to fill the vacancy caused by the termination of his own term of office, any interval between such termination and re-appointment shall be disregarded in calculating for the purpose of this section, the length of time for which such person has been continuously a Member of the Council.

37. SPEAKER.

His Majesty the Sultan and Yang Di-Pertuan may, be Instrument under the Seal of Brunei Darussalam, appoint a Speaker of the Legislative Council either from among the Members thereof; but, unless and until a Speaker is so appointed or if any time there is no subsisting appointment of a Speaker, references in this Constitution (other than in this section) to the Speaker shall be construed as references to the Prime Minister.

Any person appointed as Speaker shall hold office at His Majesty the Sultan and Yang Di-Pertuan's pleasure and, subject thereto, for such period as may be specified in the Instrument by which he is appointed:

Provided that the Speaker may, by writing under his hand addressed to His Majesty the Sultan and Yang Di-Pertuan, resign his office and, in the case of a Speaker appointed from among the Members of the Legislative Council, shall vacate his office if he ceases to be a Member of the Council.

38. SPEAKER TO ATTEND AND PRESIDE.

The Speaker shall, so far as is practicable, attend and preside at all meetings of the Legislative Council and in his absence such Member of the Legislative Council as the Speaker may, after consultation with His Majesty the Sultan and Yang Di-Pertuan, generally or specially appoint, or, in the absence of such Member or if no Member be so appointed, the Member of the Legislative Council present who stands first in the order of precedence, shall preside.

PART VII LEGISLATION AND PROCEDURE IN THE LEGISLATIVE COUNCIL

39. POWER TO MAKE LAWS.

1. It shall be lawful for His Majesty the Sultan and Yang Di-Pertuan, with the advice and consent of the Legislative Council, and subject to the provisions of this Constitution, to make laws for the peace, order and good government of Brunei Darussalam.

40. INTRODUCTION OF BILLS, ETC.

Subject to this Constitution and to Standing Orders, any Member of the Legislative Council may introduce any Bill or propose any motion for debate in, or may present any petition to, the Legislative Council, and such Bill, motion or petition shall be debated and disposed of in accordance with Standing Orders.

Except with the prior approval of His Majesty the Sultan and Yang Di-Pertuan, the Legislative Council shall not proceed upon any Bill, motion or petition which would provide for or affect:

a. the finance or currency of Brunei Darussalam;

b. the compounding or remitting of any dept due to Brunei Darussalam;

c. the custody of the Consolidated Fund, the charging of any money on the Consolidated Fund or
the abolition of any such charge;

d. the payment of moneys into the Consolidated Fund or the payment, issue or withdrawal from the Consolidated Fund of any moneys not charged thereon, or any alteration in any such payment, issue or withdrawal otherwise than by reducing it;

e. the receipt of moneys on account of the Consolidated Fund or the custody or issue of such
moneys, or the audit of the accounts of Brunei Darussalam;

f. the borrowing of money, or the giving of any guarantee by Brunei Darussalam, or the amendment of the law relating to the financial obligations of Brunei Darussalam; or

g. the assignment of any tax or fee.

3. A Bill or an amendment to a Bill shall not be deemed to make provision for any of the matters specified in subsection (2) by reason only that it provides-

a. for the imposition or alteration of any fine or other pecuniary penalty or for the payment or
demand of a license fee or a fee or charge for any service rendered.

b. for the imposition, alteration or regulation of any tax or rate by any local authority or body for
local purposes.

41. PUBLICATION OF BILLS.

Save in case of urgency to be certified in writing by the Prime Minister, every Bill shall be published for general information in the Gazette at least 14 days prior to its introduction into the Legislative Council.

42. DESCRIPTION OF BILLS, ETC., NOT TO BE PROCEEDED WITHOUT APPROVAL.

1. Except with the prior approval of His Majesty the Sultan and Yang Di-Pertuan signified thereto, the Legislative Council shall not proceed upon any Bill or upon any amendment to any Bill which, in the opinion of the Speaker, falls within any of the following classes-

a. any Bill relating to the issue of Bank Notes or the establishment of any Bank Association or the
amendment of the constitution thereof;

b. any Bill the provision of which shall appear inconsistent with obligations imposed upon Him
Majesty the Sultan and Yang Di-Pertuan or Her Majesty by Treaty or Agreement; or

c. any Bill relating to questions of defence or public security.

The approval of His Majesty the Sultan and Yang Di-Pertuan in relation to any Bill or any amendment to any Bill under this section may be expressed at any time before His Majesty the Sultan and Yang Di-Pertuan has assented thereto, and may, if given while the Legislative Council is sitting, be given verbally throughout the Prime Minister and, if given at any other time, shall be given in writing under the hand of the Prime Minister.

The Speaker may, at any time in his discretion, adjourn the Legislative Council or suspend the sitting so as to obtain the advice of His Majesty the Sultan and Yang Di-Pertuan under subsection (1) on any Bill, or any amendment to any Bill, which may be before that Council, or may require the Legislative Council not to proceed thereon until His Majesty the Sultan and Yang Di-Pertuan has given his approval.

43. VOTING.

All questions proposed for decision in the Legislative Council shall be determined by a majority of the votes of the Members present and voting.

The Speaker, if appointed as such by Instrument under the Seal of the State from among persons who are not Members of the Legislative Council, shall not have an original vote, but he shall have and exercise a casting vote.

In the absence of the Speaker the Member presiding shall have an original vote and shall in addition, if upon any question the votes are equally divided, have and exercise a casting vote.

44. VACANCIES AND QUORUM.

The Legislative Council shall not be disqualified for the transaction of business by reason of any vacancy among the Members, including any vacancy not filed when the Council is first constituted or reconstituted at any time; and any proceedings therein shall be valid notwithstanding that some person who was not entitled to do so sat or voted in that Council, or otherwise took part in those proceedings.

If, at any sitting of the Legislative Council, any Member who is present draws the attention of the person presiding at the sitting to the fact that less than 7 members are present apart from any Member presiding and, after such interval, if any, as may be provided for by the Standing Orders the person presiding is satisfied that there are less than that number of Members so present, the Council shall be adjourned.

45. ASSENT TO BILLS, ETC.

No Bill shall become law unless His Majesty the Sultan and Yang Di-Pertuan shall have assented thereto, and shall have signed the same, and the same shall have been sealed with the Seal of the state in token of assent.

A law assented to by His Majesty the Sultan and Yang Di-Pertuan shall come into operation on the date on which such assent shall be given, or, if it shall be enacted wither in such law or in some other law (including any law in force on the commencement of this Part) that it shall come into operation on some other date, on that date.

46. STYLE OF LAWS AND ENACTING WORDS.

All laws shall be styled Acts and the enacting words shall be "Be enacted by His Majesty the Sultan and Yang Di-Pertuan with the advice and consent of the Legislative Council as follows:"

47. RESERVED POWERS.

If His Majesty the Sultan and Yang Di-Pertuan shall consider that it is expedient in the interests of public order, good faith or good government of Brunei Darussalam that any Bill introduced, or any motion proposed, in the Legislative Council shall have effect, then, if the Council fail to pass that Bill or carry that motion within such time and in such form as His Majesty the Sultan and Yang Di-Pertuan may think reasonable and expedient, His Majesty the Sultan and Yang Di-Pertuan may, at any time, notwithstanding any provision of this Constitution or of any Standing Orders, declare that Bill or motion shall have effect as if it had been passed or carried by the Council either in the form in which it was so introduced or proposed or with such amendments as His Majesty the Sultan and Yang Di-Pertuan shall think fit which have been passed or carried.

Any such declaration, other than a declaration relating to a Bill, may be revoked by His Majesty the Sultan and Yang Di-Pertuan; and the Prime Minister shall notify such revocation in the Gazette; and from the date of such notification, any motion which shall have been deemed to have been carried by virtue of the declaration revoked shall cease to have effect; and such cession shall have the same effect as the repeal of a written law.

48. STANDING ORDERS.

Subject to this Constitution, the Legislative Council may from time to time make, amend and revoke Standing Orders for the regulation and orderly conduct of its own proceedings and the despatch of business; but no such Orders, and no amendment or revocation thereof, shall have effect unless approved by His Majesty the Sultan and Yang Di-Pertuan.

The first Standing Orders of the Legislative Council shall be made by His Majesty the Sultan and Yang Di-Pertuan and may be amended or revoked by that Council under subsection (1).

No Standing Order shall be suspended without the approval of the Speaker and such approval shall only be granted by him if he is satisfied that such suspension is necessary for the proper and expeditious conduct of the business of the Legislative Council.

49. OATH TO BE TAKEN BY MEMBERS.

Every Member of the Legislative Council shall before taking his seat make and subscribe before the Speaker or other Member presiding an oath or declaration in the form set ut as Form IV in the Schedule.

Provided that any person, who, having previously been a Member of the Legislative Council, again becomes Member of that

50. CLERK TO THE LEGISLATIVE COUNCIL.

His Majesty the Sultan and Yang Di-Pertuan shall appoint some fit and proper person to be Clerk to the Legislative Council, and such person shall, before entering upon the duties of his office, make and subscribe before the Speaker or other Member presiding an oath or declaration in the form set out as Form V in the Schedule.

51. MINUTES

Minutes shall be kept of all the proceedings of the Legislative Council.

As soon as practicable a full transcript of the minutes of every sitting of the Legislative Council shall be transmitted by the Clerk to the Legislative Council to His Majesty the Sultan and Yang Di-Pertuan.

52. SESSIONS, ETC., OF THE LEGISLATIVE COUNCIL.

There shall be a session of the Legislative Council once at least in every year, so that a period of 12 months shall not intervene between the last sitting in one session and the date appointed for its first sitting in the next session.

Each session of the Legislative Council shall be held at such place and shall commence at such time as His Majesty the Sultand and Yang Di-Pertuan may from time to time, by notice published in the Gazette, appoint.

53. PRIVILEGES OF LEGISLATIVE COUNCIL.

No person shall be lible to any proceedings in any court in respect of anything said, or any vote given, by him when taking part in any proceedings of the Legislative Councilor any committee thereof.

No person shall be liable to any proceedings in any court in respect of anything published by or under the authority of the Legislative Council.

Right of Sultan to address legislative council.

Prorogation and Dissolution.

His Majesty the Sultan and Yang Di-Pertuan shall have the right to address the Legislative Council at any time upon any matter.

His Majesty the Sultan and Yang Di-Pertuan may at any time, by Proclamation published in the Gazette, prorogue or dissolve the Legislative Council.

His Majesty the Sultan and Yang Di-Pertuan shall dissolve the Legislative Council at the expiration of 5 years from the date when it first meets after it is first constituted or is reconstituted at any time unless it has been sooner dissolved.

PART VIII FINANCE

56. NO TAXATION UNLESS AUTHORISED BY LAW.

No tax or rate shall be levied by or for the purpose of Brunei Darussalam except by or under the authority of law.

57. CIVIL LIST OF THE SULTAN AND HIS CONSORT.

The Legislative shall by law provide a Civil List of His Majesty the Sultan and Yang Di-Pertuan and a Civil List of his Consort, which Civil List shall be a charge on the Consolidated Fund.

58. CONSOLIDATED FUND.

All revenues and moneys howsoever raised or received by Brunei Darussalam from whatsoever source shall, subject to this constitution and any written law, be paid into and from one fund to be known as the Consolidated Fund.

59. EXPENDITURE CHARGED ON CONSOLIDATED FUND.

1. There shall be charged on the Consolidated Fund in addition to any grant, remuneration or other moneys so charged by any other provision of this Constitution or by any written law-

a. the costs, charges and expenses, other than the emoluments of members of the public service,
incidental to the collection and management of the revenues raised or received by Brunei
Darussalam;

b. all pensions, compensation for loss of office and gratuities for which Brunei Darussalam is liable;

c. all debt charges for which Brunei Darussalam is liable.

d. all moneys required to satisfy any judgment, decision or award against Brunei Darussalam by and court or tribunal; and

2. For the purposes of this section, "debt charges" include interest, sinking fund charges, the repayment or amortization of debt, and all expenditure in connection with the raising of loans on the security of the Consolidated Fund and the service and redemption of debt created thereby.

60. ANNUAL ESTIMATES OF REVENUE AND EXPENDITURE.

The Prime Minister shall, in respect of every financial year, cause to be paid before the Legislative Council a Statement of the estimated receipts and expenditure of Brunei Darussalam for that year, and, unless the Legislature by written law in respect of any year otherwise provides, that statement shall be so laid before the commencement of that year.

The estimates of expenditure shall show separately

a. the total sums required to meet expenditure charged on the Consolidated Fund; and

b. subject to subsection (3), the sums respectively required to meet the heads of other expenditure proposed to be met from the Consolidated Fund.

3. The sums to be shown under paragraph (b) of subsection (2) shall not include-

a. sums representing the proceeds of any loan raised by Brunei darussalam for specific purposes
and appropriated for those purposes by or under the written law authorising the raising of the
loan; and

b. sums presenting any money, or interest on money, received by Brunei darussalam subject to a
trust and to be applied in accordance with the terms of the trust.

4. That Statement shall also show, so far as practicable, the assets and liabilities of Brunei Darussalam at the end of the last completed financial year, the manner in which those assets are invested or held and the general heads in respect of which those liabilities are outstanding.

61. SUPPLY BILLS.

The heads of expenditure to be met from the Consolidated Fund but not charged thereon other than expenditure to be met by such sums as are mentioned in subsection (3) of section 60, shall be included in a Bill, to be known as the Annual Supply Bill, providing the issue from the Consolidated Fund of the sums necessary to meet that expenditure and the application of those sums of the purposes specified therein.

62. SUPPLEMENTARY AND EXCESS EXPENDITURES.

If, in respect of any financial year, it is found-

a. that the amount appropriated by the Annual Supply Act for any purpose is insufficient or that a need has arisen for expenditure for a purpose for which no amount has been appropriated by the Annual Supply Act; or

b. that any moneys have been expended for any purpose in excess of the amount, if any appropriated for that purpose by the Annual Supply Act:

a Supplementary Estimate showing the sums required or spent shall be caused by His Majesty the Sultan an Yang Di-Pertuan to be laid before the Legislative Council and the heads of any such expenditure shall be included in a Supplementary Supply Bill.

63. Power to authorise expenditure on account or for unspecified purposes.

The Legislature shall have power in respect of any financial year-

a. before the passing of the Annual Supply Bill to authorise by written law expenditure for part of
the year; and

b. to authorise by written law expenditure for the whole or part of the year otherwise than in accordance with sections 59 to 62 inclusive if, owing to the magnitude or indefinite character of any services or to circumstances of unusual urgency, it appears to be desirable so to do.

64. CONTENGENCIES FUND.

The Legislature may by law provide for the creation of a Contingencies Fund and for authorising the Prime Minister if satisfied that there has arisen an urgent and unforeseen need for expenditure for which no other provision exists, to make advances from the Contingencies Fund to meet that need.

Where any advance is made in accordance with subsection (1), a Supplementary Estimate shall be presented and a Supplementary Supply Bill introduced as soon as possible for the purpose of replacing the amount so advanced.

65. WITHDRAWALS FROM CONSOLIDATED FUNDS.

1. Subject to subsection (2), no moneys shall be withdrawn from the Consolidated Fund unless they are-

a. charged on the Consolidated Fund;

b. authorised to be issued by a Supply Act; or

c. authorised to be issued under section 63.

Subsection (1) shall not apply to any such sums as are mentioned in subsection (3) of section 60.

No moneys shall be withdrawn from the Consolidated Fund except in the manner provided by law.

66. AUDITOR GENERAL.

There shall be an Auditor General who shall be appointed by His Majesty the Sultan and Yang Di-Pertuan.

A person who has held office of Auditor General shall be eligible for reappointment but shall not, while holding that office be eligible for any other appointment in the service of Brunei Darussalam.

The Auditor General may at any time resign his office, but shall not be removed from office except on the like grounds and in the like manner as a member of the Public Service Commission.

The Legislature shall provide for the remuneration of the Auditor General and the remuneration so provided shall be charged on the Consolidated Fund.

The remuneration and other terms of office, including pension rights, of the Auditor General shall not be altered to his disadvantage after his appointment.

Subject to this section, the terms and conditions of the service of the Auditor General shall be determined by His Majesty the Sultan and Yang Di-Pertuan.

67. POWER AND DUTIES OF AUDITOR GENERAL.

The accounts of Brunei Darussalam shall be audited and reported upon by the Auditor General, who, with his subordinate staff, shall at all times be entitled to have access to all books, records, returns and reports relating to such accounts.

The Auditor General shall perform such other duties and exercise such powers in relation to the accounts of Brunei Darussalam and to the accounts of other public authorities and bodies administering public funds as may be provided by any written law.

68. REPORTS OF AUDITOR GENERAL.

The Auditor General shall submit his reports to His Majesty the Sultan and Yang Di-Pertuan who shall cause them to be laid before the Legislative Council.

69. The provisions of this Part shall not be applicable to Muslim revenues and funds.

PART IX THE PUBLIC SERVICES

70. TENURE IF OFFICE IN THE PUBLIC SERVICE.

Save as otherwise provided in this Constitution, every person holding office in the service of the Government of Brunei Darussalam shall hold office during the pleasure of His Majesty the Sultan and Yang Di Pertuan.

71. THE PUBLIC SERVICE COMMISSION.

There shall be a Public Service Commission which shall consist of a Chairman and Such number of members as His Majesty the Sultan and Yang Di-Pertuan may appoint.

Subject to subsection (3), every person who is appointed to be a member of the Public Service Commission shall, unless he earlier resigns his office or is removed therefrom hold office for a period of 3 years from the date of his appointment and shall be eligible for reappointment.

a. subject to paragraph (b), a member of the Public Service Commission may be removed from his office by His Majesty the Sultan and Yang Di-Pertuan.

b. A member of the Public Service Commission shall only be removed from his office for inability to perform the functions of his office (whether arising from infirmity of body or mind or any other cause) or for misbehaviour, and shall not be so removed unless his case has been investigated by a person who holds or has held high judicial office in Brunei Darussalam or any part of the Commonwealth, nominated for that purpose by His Majesty the Sultan and Yang DI-Pertuan, and that person has recommended that he should be so removed.

c. His Majesty the Sultan and Yang Di-Pertuan in Council may from time to time make, amend or revoke rules relating to the procedure to be followed in investigating any question under this subsection, and may make arrangements as to the remuneration to be paid to any person appointed under paragraph (b), which remuneration shall be a charge on the Consolidated Fund.

His Majesty the Sultan and Yang DI-Pertuan may grant leave of absence from his duties to any member of the Public Service Commission, and may appoint a person to be a temporary member for the period of such leave.

The procedure of the Public Service Commission shall, subject to any regulations made under section 75, be as determined by the Commission.

For the purposes of the Penal Code, a member of the Public Service Commission shall be deemed to be a public servant.

72. SECRETARY TO PUBLIC SERVICE COMMISSION

There shall be a Secretary to the Public Service Commission who shall be appointed by His Majesty the Sultan and Yang Di-Pertuan.

73. SALARIES OF MEMBER OF PUBLIC SERVICE COMMISSION.

Every person appointed to be a member of the Public Service Commission shall be paid such salary or allowances, or both, as may be determined by the Legislature; and all such salaries and allowance shall be a charge on the Consolidated Fund.

74. APPOINTMENTS IN THE PUBLIC SERVICE

The power to appoint, transfer, promote, dismiss or exercise disciplinary control over public officers is hereby vested in His Majesty the Sultan and Yang Di-Pertuan.

In the exercise of the power conferred upon him by subsection (1), His Majesty the Sultan and Yang Di-Pertuan shall, except in the case of the Prime Minister, Overseas Officers and such other public officers as His Majesty the Sultan and Yang Di-Pertuan in Council may prescribe by notification in the Gazette, and unless regulations under section 75 otherwise provide, consult and act in accordance with the recommendation of the Public Service Commission.

nothing in this section shall affect the provisions of any written law relating to members of the Royal Brunei Armed Forces, the Royal Brunei Police Force or the Prison Service of Brunei Darussalam.

75. REGULATIONS.

His Majesty the Sultan and Yang Di-Pertuan in Council may make regulations to provide for-

a. the exercise by the Public Service Commission of any of its functions; or

b. the exercise by the Public Service Commission or by any person, subject to such conditions as may be prescribed, of any of the powers vested in His Majesty the Sultan and Yang Di-Pertuan by section 74 and may further provide that any such person shall be free from the restriction imposed by subsection (2) to section 74.

76. HIS MAJESTY THE SULTAN AND YANG DI-PERTUAN TO ADMINISTER OATHS.

His Majesty the Sultan and Yang Di-Pertuan may, whenever he thinks fit, require any person in the public service of Brunei Darussalam to make and subscribe before him or such person as he may appoint an oath or declaration of allegiance in the form set out as Form VI in the Schedule.

Repealed.

Repealed.

PART X THE STATE SEAL

79. THE STATE SEAL.

His Majesty the Sultan and Yang Di-Pertuan shall keep and use the National Seal of Negara Darussalam for sealing all things whatsoever that shall pass that State Seal.

PART XI MISCELLANEOUS

80. PROVISIONS TO GIVE EFFECT TO CONSTITUTION.

1. His Majesty the Sultan and Yang Di-Pertuan may by Order, at any time within 3 years after the publication in the Gazette of this Constitution, make such provision as appears to him necessary or expedient for the purpose of bringing existing instruments into accord with the provisions of this Constitution or otherwise for giving effect, or enabling effect to be given, to those provisions; and, in particular and without prejudice to the generality of the foregoing power His Majesty the Sultan and Yang Di-Pertuan may by such Orders-

a. modify, add to or adapt any provisions in existing instruments which refer, in whatever terms, to His Majesty the Sultan and Yang Di-Pertuan in Council, the State Council or the Council of State.

b. provide for the transfer of functions, powers and duties conferred or imposed by existing instruments upon any person or authority to such other person or authority as may be specified by such Orders.

c. proceed to make any appointment which he would be authorised to make under Part VI if this
Constitution were in operation and may also, at any time after such appointments, proceed to
make any appointment which he would be authorised to make under section 11 of that section
and Part Vi were in force and the appointments made under Part VI had taken effect.

Provided that, except in so far as may be necessary to give effect to the provisions of this subsection, no appointment by virtue hereof shall have effect before the commencement of that Part;

d. provide for the financial procedure of Brunei Darussalam including, until other provision has
been made under subsection (1) of section 64, the establishment of a Contingencies Fund.

e. provide for the audit of the moneys of Brunei darussalam and of other public bodies administering public funds, and, until otherwise provided by the Legislative Council pursuant to subsection (4) of section 66, provide for the remuneration of Auditor General.

f. until otherwise provided by the Legislative Council pursuant to section 73, provide for the
remuneration of the member of the Public Service Commission.

g. provide for the incorporation of the Prime Minister for the purpose of holding and disposing of property, movable and immovable, in his corporate capacity, on behalf of Brunei Darussalam, and for the purpose of transferring to him, in that capacity on behalf of Brunei Darussalam, certain property, movable and immovable and Brunei Darussalam, at present held on behalf of Brunei Darussalam by certain other persons and bodies;

Subject to this section, the existing instruments shall until repealed by the authority having power to do so under his Constitution continue in force on and after the commencement of this Constitution, or any part thereof, with such modifications as may be made therein by any Order made under this section or by any other written law.

Notwithstanding anything in this Constitution contained, the State Council existing immediately before the commencement of this Constitution shall continue to have full legislative and executive authority until the commencement of Parts V, VI and VII.

In this section, "existing instruments" means Acts, rules, regulations, by-laws, proclamations, orders, licenses, permits and other instruments having the force of law, or issued in pursuance of statutory powers, and in force in Brunei Darussalam at the date of the Order by which they are affected.

An Order made under this section may be amended or revoked by a further Order and may be given a retrospective effect to a date not earlier than the date of the publication in the Gazette of this Constitution.

81. ATTORNEY GENERAL.

The Attorney General shall advise on all legal matters connected with the affairs of Brunei Darussalam referred to him by His Majesty the Sultan and Yang Di-Pertuan or by the Government of Brunei Darussalam.

The Attorney General shall have power exercisable at his discretion to institute, conduct or discontinue any proceedings for an offence other than-

a. proceedings before a Muslim Court, subject to the provisions of any written law to the contrary; or

b. proceedings before a Court Martial.

In the exercise of this power the Attorney General shall not be subject to the direction or control of any other person or authority.

3. The Attorney General shall have the right of audience in, and shall take precedence over any other person appearing before, any court or tribunal in Brunei Darussalam.

82. OFFICIAL LANGUAGE.

The official language of Brunei Darussalam shall be the Malay language and shall be in such script as may by written law be provided.

Notwithstanding subsection (1), for a period of 5 years after the coming into operation of this section, and thereafter until otherwise by written law provided, the English language may be used for all official purposes.

The official language of the proceedings of the Privy Council, of the Council of Ministers and of the Legislative Council shall be Malay;

Provided that-

a. with the leave of the person presiding, any Member may speak in English; and

b. whenever it shall be necessary for the better convenience of any Member of any Council as aforesaid who is not conversant with the Malay Language to do so, such Member may, with the leave of the person presiding, employ an interpreter during the proceedings of such Council; and every interpreter so employed shall, before entering upon his duties for the first time, make and subscribe before the person presiding an oath or declaration in the form set out as Form VII in the Schedule.

An official version in the English language shall be provided of anything which, by this Constitution, or by any written law, or by the Standing Orders, is required to be printed or in writing, and such version shall, in addition to the cfficial Malay version, be accepted as an authentic text.

Notwithstanding subsection (1), for a period of 5 years after the coming into operation of this section, and thereafter until otherwise by written law provided, the authoritative text of-

a. all Bills to be introduced, or amendments thereto to moved, in the Legislative Council; and

b. all written laws and instruments,

shall be printed in both the Malay and English languages; but in case of any doubt or conflict between the Malay and the English texts-

i. subject to paragraph (ii), if such conflict or doubt arises in any Bill, written law or instrument,
other than this Constitution, the Succession and Regency Proclamation or the Nationality
Legislation the English text shall prevail.

ii. if such conflict or doubt arises in this Constitution, the Succession and Regency Proclamation or the Nationality Legislation but not any Order made thereunder, the Malay text shall prevail.

83. STATE EMERGENCY.

Whenever it appears to His Majesty the Sultan and Yang Di-Pertuan that an occasion of public danger exists whereby the security or economic life of Brunei Darussalam, or any part thereof, is threatened whether by war or external aggression or internal disturbance, actual or threatened, he may by Proclamation (hereinafter referred to as a Proclamation of Emergency) declare a state of emergency either in the whole of Brunei Darussalam or part of Brunei Darussalam as may be specified in the Proclamation.

No Proclamation of Emergency shall be in force for more than 2 years, without prejudice, however, to the issue of another such proclamation at or before the end of that period

when a Proclamation of Emergency has been made and so long as such Proclamation is in force, His Majesty the Sultan and Yang Di-Pertuan may make any Orders whatsoever which he considers desirable in the public interest; and may prescribe penalties which may be imposed for any offence against any such Order, and may provide for the trial by any court of persons guilty of such offences:

Provided that no such Order shall confer any right to punish, without trial, by death, imprisonment or fine and that, except in so far as such procedure may be modified by any such Order, or of any offence created by any such Order, in respect of which breach or offence it is sought to make the offender liable to death, imprisonment or fine.

Without prejudice to the generality of subsection (3), such Orders may be made with regard to any matters coming within the classes of subject hereinafter enumerated, that is to say-

a. censorship, and the control and suppression of publications, writing, maps, plans, photographs,
communications and means of communication;

b. arrest, detention, exclusion and deportation;

c. control of the harbours, ports and territorial waters of Brunei Darussalam, and of the movements of vessels.

d. transportation by land, air or water and the control of the transport and movement of persons,
animals and things;

e. trading, storage, exportation, importation, production and manufacture;

f. supply and distribution of food, water, fuel, light and other necessities;

g. appropriation, control, forfeiture and disposition of property and the use thereof;

h. conferring powers on public officers and others;

i. requiring persons to do work or render services;

j. constituting a special police force;

k. formation of tribunals and other bodies for the purpose of deciding any matters specified in any such Orders, but having no power to inflict imprisonment or fines;

l. modification, amendment, supersession or suspension of all or any of the provisions of any
written law;

m. entry into, and search of, premises or other places, and search and interrogation of persons.

n. prescribing fees or other payments.

Notwithstanding anything contained in Part VIII His Majesty the Sultan and Yang Di-Pertuan may, by any such Order, make all such financial provisions as may be necessary during the period of the emergency, including provision for the public service, and for the payment of compensation for work required compulsorily to be undertaken, and for property compulsorily taken.

Any Order made under this section shall, unless His Majesty the Sultan and Yang Di-Pertuan otherwise directs, come into force on the day on which it is made.

Every Order made under this section shall, at the next meeting of the Legislative Council, be laid on the table of that Council and the Legislative Council may resolve that any such Order shall, to the extent and as from such date as may be specified in such resolution, cease to have effect; and any such cessation shall, if assented to by His Majesty the Sultan and Yang Di-Pertuan, have the same effect as the repeal of a written law.

Such Order shall be publicly notified as soon as circumstances permit, and any rescission of such Orders shall also be so published.

Any Order made under this section shall, if the Proclamation of Emergency specified only part of Brunei Darussalam, have effect only in such part:

Provided that, if, while a Proclamation of Emergency is in force in any part of Brunei Darussalam, another Proclamation of Emergency is made in respect of any other part of Brunei Darussalam any Order already made and still in force when the last Proclamation comes into operation shall, forthwith, have effect in the part of Brunei Darussalam specified in the last Proclamation.

Every Order made in pursuance of this section and every instrument made in pursuance of any such Order shall have effect notwithstanding anything therewith contained in the Constitution or in any written law.

84. EFFECT OF CONSTITUTION ON HIS MAJESTY THE SULTAN AND YANG DI-PERTUAN'S PREROGATIVE.

The Government of Brunei darussalam shall be regulated in accordance with the provisions of this Constitution, and the form of such Government shall not be altered save in pursuance of the power conferred by section 85.

save as provided in subsection (1), and save to such extent as may be necessary to avoid inconsistency with any of the provisions of this Constitution, nothing in this Constitution shall be deemed to derogate from the prerogative powers and jurisdiction of His Majesty the Sultan and Yang Di-Pertuan and, for the avoidance of doubt, it is declared that His Majesty the Sultan and Yang Di-Pertuan retains the power to proclaim a further Part or further Parts of the law of the Constitution as to him from time to time may seem expedient.

PART XII AMENDMENT AND INTERPRETATION OF THE CONSTITUTION

85. AMENDMENT OF CONSTITUTION.

His Majesty the Sultan and Yang Di-Pertuan may by Proclamation, amend or revoke any of the provisions of the Constitution including this section; and this Constitution shall not otherwise be amended.

His Majesty the Sultan and Yang Di-Pertuan shall consult the Privy Council in relation to the exercise of the powers vested in him by this section but shall not be obliged to act in accordance with the advice of that Council.

His Majesty the Sultan and Yang Di-Pertuan shall not make any Proclamation for the amendment or revocation of any provision of this Constitution unless a draft of the Proclamation has been approved by resolution of the Legislative Council.

86. INTERPRETATION TRIBUNAL.

His Majesty the Sultan and Yang Di-Pertuan may refer any question involving the meaning, interpretation, construction or effect of any of the provisions of the Constitution to the Interpretation Tribunal established in accordance with subsection (7) for their determination.

When any such question rises in any legal proceedings before any court, either party thereto may request that court to report such question to His Majesty the Sultan and Yang DI-Pertuan, with a submission that His Majesty the Sultan and Yang Di-Pertuan should refer that question to the Interpretation Tribunal; and, thereupon, the court shall so report such question unless in the opinion of the court the request is frivolous or vexatious, or the question has already been decided by the Interpretation Tribunal.

If His Majesty the Sultan and Yang Di-Pertuan does not refer a question reported under subsection (2), he shall cause the court by whom the report thereof was made to be so informed, and the court shall thereupon proceed with the determination of the legal proceedings before it.

The decision of a majority of the Interpretation Tribunal upon any question referred to it under this section shall be deemed to be a decision of the Tribunal and any decision of the Tribunal shall be in writing and shall be published in the Gazette, and may be proved by production of the Gazette.

In the case of a reference made by His Majesty the Sultan and Yang Di-Pertuan to the interpretation Tribunal pursuant to a report under subsection (2), His Majesty the Sultan and Yang Di-Pertuan shall cause the determination of the Interpretation Tribunal to be communicated to the court by which the question has been reported and, in such case, that court may make such provision as may be just as to the costs of, and incurred by, such reference.

The determination of the Interpretation Tribunal in any case referred to it under this section shall be binding and conclusive upon all persons, and shall not be called in question in any court.

The Interpretation Tribunal shall consist of a Chairman, who shall be a person who holds or has held high judicial office in, or has for at least 10 years been engaged in legal practice in, any part of the Commonwealth, and 2 other members, which Chairman and other members shall be appointed by His Majesty the Sultan and Yang Di-Pertuan by instrument under the Seal of the State.

His Majesty the Sultan and Yang Di-Pertuan in Council may from time to time make, amend or revoke rules relating to the procedure to be followed in referring or determining questions under this section, and may make arrangements as to the remuneration to be paid to members of the [Interpretation Tribunal]

SCHEDULE

FORM I OATH AND DECLARATION TO BE TAKEN OR MADE BY A PRIVY COUNCILLOR (Section 5 (4))

WALLAHI WA-BILLAHI WA-TAALLAHI

I, being an ex-officio Member (having been appointed a Member) of His Majesty's Privy Council swear by Almighty God (solemnly and sincerely declare) that, except with the authority of His Majesty the Sultan and Yang Di-Pertuan I will not directly or indirectly reveal the business or procedures of the Privy Council, or the nature or contents of any documents communicated to me as a Member of theCouncil, or any matter coming to my knowledge in my capacity as a Member of theCouncil and that in all things I will be a true and faithful Councillor.

Dated this day of , 19

Signature

FORM II OATH AND DECLARATION TO BE TAKEN OR MADE BY THE CLERK TO THE PRIVY COUNCIL AND THE CLERK TO THE COUNCIL OF MINISTERS (Section 6 (3), 22)

WALLAHI WA-BILLAHI WA-TAALLAHI

I, having been appointed Clerk to the Privy Council (Council ofMinisters) swear by Almighty God (solemnly and sincere declare) that I wil not directly or indirectly reveal such matters as shall be debated in the Council an committed to my secrecy but that I will well and truly serve in the said office as Clerk to the Privy Council. (Council of Ministers)

Dated this day of , 19

Signature

FORM III OATH AND DECLARATION TO BE TAKEN OR MADE BY A MEMBER OF THE COUNCIL OF MINISTERS (Section 21)

WALLAHI WA-BILLAHI WA-TAALLHI

I, (having been appointed a Member) of the Council of Ministers, swear by Almighty God (solemnly and sincerely declare) that, except with the authority of His Majesty the Sultan and Yang Di-Pertuan I, will not directly or indirectly reveal the business or proceedings of the Council of Ministers, or the nature or contents of any document communicated to me as a Member of the Council, or any matter coming to my knowledge in my capacity as a Member of the Council, and that in all things I will be a true and faithful Councillor.

Dated this day of , 19

Signature

FORM IV OATH AND DECLARATION TO BE TAKEN OR MADE BY A MEMBER OF THE LEGISLATIVE COUNCIL (Section 49)

WALLAHI WA-BILLAHI WA-TAALLAHI
I, being an ex-officio Member (having been appointed a Member) of the Legislative Council swear by

Almighty God (solemnly and sincerely declare) that I will to the best of my ability and judgement,
serve as a true and faithful Member of the Legislative Council.
Dated this day of , 19
Signature

FORM V OATH DECLARATION TO BE TAKEN OR MADE BY THE CLERK TO THE LEGISLATIVE COUNCIL (Section 50)

WALLAHI WA-BILLAHI WA-TAALLAHI

I, having been appointed Clerk to the Legislative Council swear by Almighty God (solemnly and sincerely declare) that I will well and truly serve in the said office of Clerk to the Legislative Council. Dated this day of , 19 Signature

FORM VI OATH AND DECLARATION OF ALLEGIANCE (Section 76)

WALLAHI WA-BILLAHI WA-TAALLAHI

I, swear by Almighty God (solemnly and sincerely declare) that I will be faithful and bear true allegiance to His Majesty Sultan and Yang Di-Pertuan and His successors according to law. That I will without fear or favour and to the best of my ability and judgement, serve as a true and faithful member of the public service of Brunei Darussalam.

Dated this day of , 19

Signature

FORM VII OATH AND DECLARATION TO BE TAKEN OR MADE BY AN INTERPRETER EMPLOYED IN THE PRIVY COUNCIL THE COUNCIL OF MINISTERS OR THE LEGISLATIVE COUNCIL (Section 82 (3) (b))

WALLAHI WA-BILLAHI WA-TAALLAHI

I, swear by Alight God (solemnly and sincerely declare) that I understand the Malay and languages and that I will, to the best of my skill an understanding, well and truly interpret and true explanation make between the Members of Privy Council (Council of Ministers) (Legislative Council) who are conversant with the Malay language and those who are conversant with the language(s).

Dated this day of , 19

Signature

ELECTION OFFENCES ACT

AN ACT TO PREVENT ELECTORAL OFFENCES AND ILLEGAL PRACTICES AT ELECTIONS; TO PROVIDE FOR THE APPOINTMENT OF ELECTION AGENTS AND TO CONTROL ELECTION OFFENCES; TO PROVIDE FOR ELECTION PETITIONS

Commencement: 28th April 1962

PART I PRELIMINARY

SHORT TITLE.

1. This Act may be cited as the Election Offences Act.

INTERPRETATION.

2. (1) In this Act, unless the context otherwise requires —

"authorised" means authorised by or under any written law relating to an election;

"constituency" means an area prescribed under the provisions of any written law for the purpose of electing one or more representatives to a council or board and includes an electoral college;

"election" means an election held in accordance with the provisions of any written law relating to the election of persons to be members of the Legislative Council;

"election agent" means the person appointed under section 12 by a candidate for election to be his agent for such election;

"Election Judge" means the Chief Justice or any Judge nominated by the Chief Justice under section 36;

"entitled" means entitled by or under any written law relating to an election;

B.L.R.O. 1/1984

"proper officer" means the officer or person appointed by or under any written law relating to an election to be in charge, or to have the conduct, thereof.

(2) Any word or expression used in this Act, the meaning of which is defined in any written law relating to any election, shall have the same meaning in this Act, for the purposes of and with reference to such election, as it has in the said written law; and any reference in this Act to any person or official shall be construed, for the purposes of and with reference to any election, as a reference to any equivalent person or official appointed under or by virtue of any written law relating to such election.

PART II ELECTORAL OFFENCES

OFFENCES BY ANY PERSON.

3. Any person who —

(a)

knowingly makes any false statement on or in connection with any application to be placed on any register of electors; or

(b)

forges or fraudulently defaces or fraudulently destroys any nomination paper, or delivers to a returning officer any nomination paper knowing the same to be forged; or

(c)

forges or counterfeits or fraudulently defaces or fraudulently destroys any ballot paper or the official mark on any ballot paper; or

(d)

without due authority supplies any ballot paper to any person; or

(e)

sells or offers to sell any ballot paper to any person or purchases or offers to purchase any ballot paper from any person; or

(f)

not being a person entitled to be in possession of any ballot paper which has been marked with any authorised mark has any such ballot paper in his possession; or

(g)

puts into any ballot box anything other than the ballot paper which he is authorised by law to put in; or

(h)

without due authority takes out of the polling station any ballot paper or is found in possession of any ballot paper outside a polling station; or

(i)

without due authority destroys, takes, opens, or otherwise interferes with any ballot box, ballot paper, or packet of ballot papers in use or intended to be used for the purposes of an election; or

(j)

without due authority prints any ballot paper or what purports to be or is capable of being used as a ballot paper at an election; or

(k)

for the purposes of an election, manufactures, constructs, imports into Brunei Darussalam, has in his possession, supplies or uses, or causes to be manufactured, constructed, imported into Brunei Darussalam, supplied or used, any appliance, device or mechanism by which a ballot paper may be extracted, affected or manipulated after having been deposited in a ballot box during the polling at any election; or

(l)

votes at any election when he is not entitled to vote thereat; or

(m)

prints any advertisement, hand-bill, placard or poster which refers to an election and contains a reproduction of a ballot paper, or of what purports to be a ballot paper, to be used or likely to be used at such election:

Provided that nothing in this paragraph shall be deemed to prohibit the printing in any such advertisement, hand-bill, placard or poster of the name or symbol of one candidate only, together with a reproduction of a cross or other mark indicating approval of such name or symbol,

shall be guilty of an offence: Penalty, imprisonment for 3 years and a fine of $10,000 and, subject to any provision to the contrary in any written law relating to any election, shall until the expiration of 5 years from conviction or release from such imprisonment, whichever shall be the later, be incapable of being registered or listed as an elector or of voting at any election or of being elected at any election, and if at that date he has been elected at any election, his seat shall be vacated from the date of such conviction.

B.L.R.O. 1/1984

OFFENCES BY ELECTION OFFICERS.

4. Any officer, clerk, interpreter or other person having any duty to perform pursuant to any written law relating to any election who —

(a)

makes, in any record, return or other document which he is required to keep or make under such written law, any entry which he knows or has reasonable cause to believe to be false, or does not believe to be true; or

(b)

permits any person whom he knows or has reasonable cause to believe not to be a blind person or an incapacitated person to vote in the manner provided for blind persons or incapacitated persons, as the case may be; or

(c)

refuses to permit any person whom he knows or has reasonable cause to believe to be a blind person or an incapacitated person to vote in the manner provided for blind persons or incapacitated persons, as the case may be; or

(d)

wilfully prevents any person from voting at the polling station at which he knows or has reasonable cause to believe such person is entitled to vote; or

(e)

wilfully rejects or refuses to count any ballot paper which he knows or has reasonable cause to believe is validly cast for any candidate in accordance with the provisions of such written law; or

(f)

wilfully counts any ballot paper as being cast for any candidate, which he knows or has reasonable cause to believe was not validly cast for such candidate; or

(g)

is without reasonable cause guilty of any act or omission in breach of his official duty,

shall be guilty of an offence: Penalty, imprisonment for 3 years and a fine of $10,000 and, subject to any specific provision to the contrary in any written law relating to any election, shall until the expiration of 5 years from conviction or release from such imprisonment, whichever shall be the later, be incapable of being registered or listed as an elector or of voting at any election or of being elected at any election, and if at that date he has been elected at any election, his seat shall be vacated from the date of such conviction.

MAINTENANCE OF SECRECY AT ELECTIONS.

5. (1) Every officer, clerk, interpreter, candidate, agent and any other person (hereinafter in this section referred to as an "authorised person") authorised to attend at a polling station, or at the counting of the votes, shall, before so attending make an Oath of Secrecy, substantially as in Form A in the First Schedule.

(2)

Every officer, clerk, interpreter, candidate, agent and authorised person in attendance at a polling station shall maintain, and aid in maintaining, the secrecy of the voting in such station, and shall not communicate, except for some purpose authorised by law, before the poll is closed, to any person any information as to the name or number on the register of electors of any elector who has or has not applied for a ballot paper or voted at that station, or as to the official mark, but the total number of voters who have voted at any station at any time before the poll is closed may in the discretion of the presiding officer be divulged to a candidate or his agent authorised to attend at the polling station.

(3)

No such officer, clerk, interpreter, candidate, agent or authorised person and no person whomsoever shall attempt to obtain in the polling station information as to the candidate for whom any voter in such station is about to vote or has voted, or communicate at any time to any person any information obtained in a polling station as to the candidate for whom any voter in such station is about to vote or has voted, or as to the number of the ballot paper given to any voter at such station.

(4)

Every officer, clerk, interpreter, candidate, agent and authorised person, in attendance at the counting of the votes shall maintain, and aid in maintaining, the secrecy of the voting, and shall not attempt to communicate any information obtained at such counting as to the candidate for whom any vote is given by any particular ballot paper.

(5)

No person, except a presiding officer acting for a purpose authorised by any written law relating to any election or a person authorised by the presiding officer and acting for such purpose as aforesaid, shall communicate or attempt to communicate with any voter after such voter has received a ballot paper and before he has placed the same in a ballot box.

(6)

Every person who acts in contravention of the provisions of this section shall be guilty of an offence: Penalty, imprisonment for 2 years and a fine of $5,000.

B.L.R.O. 1/1984

OFFENCES AGAINST THIS PART.

6. (1) Every person who abets the commission of or attempts to commit an offence specified in this Part shall be liable to the punishment and disqualifications prescribed for that offence.

(2)

Every offence under this Part shall be a seizable offence within the meaning of the Criminal Procedure Code (Chapter 7).

(3)

In a prosecution for an offence in relation to a nomination paper, ballot box, ballot paper or marking instrument at an election, the property in such nomination paper, ballot box, ballot paper or marking instrument, as well as the property in the counterfoil of any ballot paper, may be stated to be in the returning officer at that election.

(4)

A prosecution for an offence under this Part shall not be instituted without the sanction of the Public Prosecutor.

PART III CORRUPT PRACTICES

PERSONATION.

7. Every person who at an election applies for a ballot paper in the name of some other person, whether that name be that of a person living or dead, or of a fictitious person or who, having voted once at any such election, applies at the same election for a ballot paper in his own name, shall be guilty of the offence of personation.

TREATING.

8. Every person who, corruptly, by himself or by any other person, either before, during or after an election, directly or indirectly gives or provides or causes to be given or provided, or is accessory to the giving or providing, or pays or engages to pay wholly or in part, the expense of giving or providing any food, drink, refreshment or provision, or any money or ticket or other means or device to enable the procuring of any food, drink, refreshment or provision, to or for any person for the purpose of corruptly influencing that person or any other person to give or refrain from giving his vote at such election or on account of any such person or any other person having voted or refrained from voting or being about to vote or refrain from voting at such election, and every elector or voter who corruptly accepts or takes any such food, drink, or refreshment or provision, or any such money or ticket or who adopts such other means or device to enable the procuring of such food, drink, refreshment or provision shall be guilty of the offence of treating.

UNDUE INFLUENCE.

9. Every person who, directly or indirectly, by himself or by any other person on his behalf, makes use of or threatens to make use of any force, violence, or restraint, or inflicts or threatens to inflict, by himself or by any other person, any temporal or spiritual injury, damage, harm, or loss upon or against any person in order to induce or compel such person to vote or refrain from voting, or on account of such person having voted or refrained from voting, at any election, or who by abduction, duress, or any fraudulent device or contrivance impedes or prevents the free exercise of the franchise of any elector or voter, or thereby compels, induces, or prevails upon any elector or voter either to give or refrain from giving his vote at any election, shall be guilty of the offence of undue influence.

BRIBERY.

10. The following persons shall be deemed guilty of the offence of bribery —

(a)

every person who, directly or indirectly, by himself or by any other person on his behalf, gives, lends, or agrees to give or lend, or offers, promises, or promises to procure or to endeavour to procure, any money or valuable consideration to or for any elector or voter, or to or for any person on behalf of any elector or voter or to or for any other person, in order to induce any elector or voter to vote or refrain from voting, or corruptly does any such act as aforesaid on account of such elector or voter having voted or refrained from voting at any election;

(b)

every person who, directly or indirectly, by himself or by any other person on his behalf, gives or procures, or agrees to give or procure, or offers, promises, or promises to procure or to endeavour to procure, any office, place or employment to or for any elector or voter, or to or for any person on behalf of any elector or voter, or to or for any other person, in order to induce such elector or voter to vote or refrain from voting, or corruptly does any such act as aforesaid on

B.L.R.O. 1/1984

account of any elector having voted or refrained from voting at any election;

(c)

every person who, directly or indirectly by himself or by any other person on his behalf, makes any such gift, loan, offer, promise, procurement or agreement as aforesaid to or for any person in order to induce such person to procure or endeavour to procure the election of any person, or the vote of any elector or voter at any election;

(d)

every person who upon or in consequence of any such gift, loan, offer, promise, procurement or agreement, procures or engages, promises or endeavours to procure, the election of any person, or the vote of any elector or voter at any election;

(e)

every person who advances or pays or causes to be paid any money to, or to the use of, any other person with the intent that such money or any part thereof shall be expended in bribery at any election or who knowingly pays or causes to be paid any money to any person in discharge or repayment of any money wholly or in part expended in bribery at any such election;

(f)

every elector or voter who, before or during any election, directly or indirectly, by himself or by any other person on his behalf, receives, agrees, or contracts for any money, gift, loan, or valuable consideration, office, place or employment, for himself or for any other persons, for voting or agreeing to vote or for refraining or agreeing to refrain from voting at any such election;

(g)

every person who, after any election, directly or indirectly, by himself or by any other person on his behalf, receives any money or valuable consideration on account of any person having voted or refrained from voting or having induced any other person to vote or to refrain from voting at any such election;

(h)

every person who, directly or indirectly, by himself or by any other person on his behalf, on account of and as payment for voting or for having voted or for agreeing or having agreed to vote for any candidate at any election, or on account of and as payment for his having assisted or agreed to assist any candidate at any election, applies to such candidate, or to his agent or agents, for the gift or loan of money or valuable consideration, or for the promise of the gift or loan of any money or valuable consideration or for any office, place or employment or for the promise of any office, place or employment;

(i)

every person who, directly or indirectly, by himself or by any person on his behalf, in order to induce any other person to agree to be nominated as a candidate or to refrain from becoming a candidate or to withdraw if he has become a candidate, gives or procures any office, place or employment, or agrees to give or procure or offers or promises to procure or to endeavour to procure any office, place or employment, to or for such other person, or gives or lends, or agrees to give or lend, or offers, or promises to procure or endeavour to procure any money or valuable consideration to or for any person or to or for such other person, or to or for any person on behalf of such other person.

PUNISHMENT AND INCAPACITIES FOR CORRUPT PRACTICE.

11. (1) Every person who —

(a)

commits the offence of personation, or aids, abets, counsels or procures the commission of the offence of personation; or

(b)

commits the offence of treating, undue influence or bribery; or

(c)

prints, publishes, distributes or posts up or causes to be printed, published, distributed or posted up any advertisement, handbill, placard or poster which refers to any election and which does not bear upon its face the names and addresses of its printer and publisher; or

(d)

makes or publishes, before or during any election, for the purpose of affecting the return of any candidate, any false statement of fact in relation to the personal character or conduct of such candidate; or

(e)

makes or publishes, before or during any election, for the purpose of promoting or procuring the election of any candidate, any false statement of the withdrawal of any other candidate at such election; or

(f)

being a candidate or election agent knowingly makes the declaration as to election expenses required by section 25 falsely,

B.L.R.O. 1/1984

shall be guilty of a corrupt practice, and shall, on conviction by a magistrate, be liable, in the case referred to in paragraph *(a)* of this subsection, to imprisonment for 2 years and to a fine of not less than $3,000 and not exceeding $10,000, and, in any other case, to imprisonment for 2 years and to a fine of $5,000.

(2)

Offences under paragraphs *(a)* and *(b)* of the preceding subsection shall be seizable offences within the meaning of the Criminal Procedure Code (Chapter 7).

(3)

Every person who is convicted of a corrupt practice shall, subject to any specific provision to the contrary in any written law relating to any election, by conviction, become incapable of being registered or listed as an elector or of voting at any election or of being elected at any election, and if at that date he has been elected at any election, his seat shall be vacated from the date of such conviction:

Provided that such disability shall cease on the expiry of 5 years from conviction or release from imprisonment, whichever shall be the later.

(4)

A prosecution for a corrupt practice except any corrupt practice as defined in paragraphs *(d)* and *(e)* of subsection (1) of this section shall not be instituted without the sanction of the Public Prosecutor.

PART IV ELECTION AGENT, ELECTION EXPENSES AND ILLEGAL PRACTICES

NOMINATION OF ELECTION AGENT.

12. (1) On or before the day of nomination at an election a person shall be named in writing by or on behalf of each candidate as his agent for such election.

(2)

A candidate may name himself as election agent, and thereupon shall, so far as circumstances admit, be subject to the provisions of this Act, both as a candidate and as an election agent, and any reference in this Act to an election agent shall be construed to refer to the candidate acting in his capacity of election agent.

(3)

On or before the day of nomination the name and address of the election agent of each candidate shall be declared in writing by the candidate or some other person on his behalf to the returning officer, and the returning officer shall forthwith, by affixing a notice in a conspicuous place outside his office, give public notification of the name and address of every election agent so declared.

(4)

One election agent only shall be appointed for each candidate, but the appointment, whether the election agent appointed be the candidate himself or not, may be revoked and in the event of such revocation or of his death, whether such event is before, during or after the election, then forthwith another election agent shall be appointed, and his name and address declared in writing to the returning officer, who shall forthwith give public notice of the same in the manner aforesaid.

(5)

If no person's name and address has been declared as required by subsection (3) hereof, the candidate shall be deemed at that time to have named himself as election agent and to have revoked any appointment of another person as his election agent.

(6)

Every election agent shall have, within the constituency in which he is an election agent, an office to which all claims, notices, writs, summonses and documents may be sent and the address of such office shall be declared at the same time as the appointment of the agent to the returning officer, and shall be stated in the public notification under subsection (3) hereof with the name of the election agent and his address.

DISQUALIFICATION FOR APPOINTMENT AS ELECTION AGENT ETC.

13. (1) Subject to the provisions of subsection (2) of section 12, a person is disqualified for being appointed as an election agent, polling agent or counting agent if —

(a)

he is not a subject of His Majesty the Sultan and Yang Di-Pertuan;

(b) he is less than 21 years of age;

(c)

he has within the period of 5 years immediately preceding the day of nomination at the election been convicted of any offence involving violence or dishonesty by a court of law in Brunei Darussalam and has not received a free pardon;

B.L.R.O. 1/1984

(d)

he has within the period of 5 years immediately preceding the day of nomination at the election been convicted of or been released from prison after serving a sentence of imprisonment for any offence under this Act;

(e)

he has within the period of 5 years immediately preceding the day of nomination at the election been convicted of an offence under the Societies Act (Chapter 66);

(f)

he is a person in respect of whom an order has been made under the Societies Act.

(2) No officer, clerk, interpreter or other person having any duty to perform pursuant to any written law relating to any election shall be appointed as an election agent or act as an agent of a candidate in the conduct or management of any election.

MAKING OF APPOINTMENTS AND CONTRACTS THROUGH ELECTION AGENT.

14. (1) The election agent of a candidate shall appoint every polling agent, counting agent, clerk and messenger employed, whether for payment or not, on behalf of the candidate at an election, and hire every committee-room hired on behalf of the candidate, and shall before the opening of the poll inform the presiding officer at each polling station in writing of the name and address of the polling agent or agents appointed to act at that station and the returning officer of the constituency or electoral ward concerned in writing of the name and address of the counting agent or agents appointed to attend the counting of the votes:

Provided that the returning officer may limit the number of counting agents, so however that the number shall be the same in the case of each candidate and the number allowed to a candidate shall not, except in special circumstances, be less than the number obtained by dividing the number of clerks employed on the counting by the number of candidates.

(2) A contract whereby any expenses are incurred on account of or in respect of the conduct or management of an election shall not be enforceable against a candidate at such election, unless made by the candidate himself or by his election agent:

Provided that inability under this section to enforce such contract against the candidate shall not relieve the candidate from the consequences of any corrupt or illegal practice committed by his agent.

PAYMENT OF EXPENSES THROUGH ELECTION AGENT.

15. (1) Except as permitted by or in pursuance of this Act, no payment and no advance or deposit shall be made by a candidate at an election, or by any agent on behalf of the candidate, or by any other person at any time, whether before, during, or after such election, in respect of any expenses incurred on account of or in respect of the conduct or management of such election otherwise than by or through the election agent of the candidate; and all money provided by any person other than the candidate for any expenses incurred on account of or in respect of the conduct or management of the election, whether as gift, loan, advance, or deposit, shall be paid to the candidate or his election agent and not otherwise:

Provided that the provisions of this subsection shall not be deemed to apply to any payment by the returning officer or to any sum disbursed by any person out of his own money for any small expense legally incurred by himself, if such sum is not repaid to him.

(2) A person who makes any payment, advance, or deposit in contravention of this section or pays in contravention of this section any money so provided as aforesaid, shall be guilty of an illegal practice.

PROHIBITION OF CERTAIN EXPENSES.

16. (1) No expenses shall, with a view to promoting or procuring the election of a candidate, be incurred by any person other than the candidate, his election agent and persons authorised in writing by the election agent on account —

(a)

of holding any public meeting or public entertainment, or organising any public display;

(b)

of printing or issuing advertisements, circulars or publications; or

(c)

of otherwise presenting to the electors the candidate or his views or the extent or nature of his backing, or disparaging another candidate:

Provided that this paragraph shall not —

(i)

restrict publication in a newspaper or other periodical of any matter relating to the election;

B.L.R.O. 1/1984

(ii)

apply to expenses incurred by any person in travelling or in living away from home, or to similar personal expenses.

(2)

Where a person incurs any expenses required to be authorised by an election agent under subsection (1) of this section, he shall within 14 days after the date of publication of the result of the election in the *Gazette* send to the election agent a return, accompanied by a declaration made by him (or in the case of an association or body of persons a director, general manager, secretary or other similar officer thereof) verifying the return and giving particulars of the matters for which the expenses were incurred:

Provided that this subsection shall not apply to any person engaged or employed for payment or promise of payment by the candidate or his election agent.

(3)

The expenses shown in the return referred to in subsection (2) of this section shall be included in the return made by the election agent in accordance with subsection (1) of section 25, and the authority received from the election agent shall be annexed to and deemed to form part of such return.

(4)

Any person who incurs any expenses in contravention of this section, or who makes any declaration required by subsection (2) of this section which is false and which he either knows or believes to be false or does not believe to be true, shall be guilty of an illegal practice.

PERIOD FOR SENDING IN CLAIMS AND MAKING PAYMENTS FOR ELECTION EXPENSES.

17. (1) Every payment made by an election agent in respect of any expenses incurred on account of or in respect of the conduct and management of an election shall, except where less than $10 or where, from the nature of the case, such as travel by rail or postage, a receipt is not obtainable, be vouched for by a bill stating the particulars and by a receipt.

(2)

Every claim against a candidate at an election or his election agent in respect of any expenses incurred on account of or in respect of the conduct or management of such election, which is not sent in to the election agent within the time limited by this Act, shall be barred and shall not be paid; and subject to such exception as may be allowed in pursuance of this Act, an election agent who pays a claim in contravention of this section shall be guilty of an illegal practice.

(3)

Except as by this Act permitted, the time limited by this Act for sending in claims shall be 14 days after the date of publication of the result of the election in the *Gazette*.

(4)

All expenses incurred by or on behalf of a candidate at an election, which are incurred on account of or in respect of the conduct or management of such election shall be paid within the time limited by this Act; and, subject to such exception as may be allowed in pursuance of this Act, an election agent who makes a payment in contravention of this provision shall be guilty of an illegal practice.

(5)

Except as by this Act permitted, the time limited by this Act for the payment of such expenses as aforesaid shall be 28 days after the date of publication of the result of the election in the *Gazette*.

(6)

Where it has been proved to the satisfaction of the Election Judge by a candidate that any payment made by an election agent in contravention of this section was made without the sanction or connivance of such candidate the election of such candidate shall not be void, nor shall he be subject to any incapacity under this Act by reason only of such payment having been made in contravention of this section.

(7)

If the election agent in the case of any claim sent in to him within the time limited by this Act disputes it, or refuses or fails to pay it within the said period of 28 days, such claim shall be deemed to be a disputed claim.

(8)

The claimant may, if he thinks fit, bring an action for a disputed claim in any competent court; and any sum paid by the candidate or his agent in pursuance of the judgement or order of such court shall be deemed to be paid within the time limited by this Act, and to be an exception from the provisions of this Act, requiring claims to be paid by the election agent.

(9)

On cause shown to the satisfaction of a Judge of the High Court, such Judge on application by the claimant or by the candidate or his election agent may by order give leave for the payment by a candidate or his election agent of a disputed claim, or of a claim for any such expenses as aforesaid, although sent in after the time in this section mentioned for sending in claims, or although the same was sent in to the candidate and not to the election agent.

(10)

Any sum specified in the order of leave may be paid by the candidate or his election agent; and when paid in pursuance of such leave shall be deemed to be paid within the time limited by this Act.

B.L.R.O. 1/1984

REMUNERATION OF ELECTION AGENT.

18. So far as circumstances admit, this Act shall apply to a claim for his remuneration by an election agent and to the payment thereof in like manner as if he were any other creditor, and if any difference arises respecting the amount of such claim, the claim shall be a disputed claim within the meaning of this Act, and be dealt with accordingly.

PERSONAL EXPENSES OF CANDIDATE AND PETTY EXPENSES.

19. (1) The candidate at an election may pay any personal expenses incurred by him on account of or in connection with or incidental to such election to an amount not exceeding $1,000, but any further personal expenses so incurred by him shall be paid by his election agent.

(2)

The candidate shall send to the election agent within the time limited by this Act for sending in claims a written statement of the amount of personal expenses paid as aforesaid by such candidate.

(3)

The personal expenses of a candidate include his reasonable travelling expenses, and the reasonable expenses of his living at hotels or elsewhere for the purposes of the election.

(4)

Any person may, if so authorised in writing by the election agent of the candidate, pay any necessary expenses for stationery, postage, telegrams, and other petty expenses to a total amount not exceeding that named in the authority, but any excess above the total amount so named shall be paid by the election agent.

(5)

A statement of the particulars of payment made by any person so authorised shall be sent to the election agent within the time limited by this Act for the sending in of claims, and shall be vouched for by a bill containing the receipt of that person.

EXPENSES IN EXCESS OF MAXIMUM TO BE ILLEGAL PRACTICE.

20. (1) Subject to such exception as may be allowed in pursuance of this Act, no sum shall be paid and no expense shall be incurred by a candidate at any election or by his election agent, after the date of publication of the notice of the election in the *Gazette,* during, or after an election, on account of or in respect of the conduct or management of such election, in excess of $5,000 or of an amount equal to 10 cents for each elector on the register or list of the constituency, electoral ward or electoral district, whichever amount shall be the larger:

Provided that there shall not be included in such amount any expenditure incurred by the candidate for his personal expenses, nor the fee, if any, paid to the election agent not exceeding $500.

(2) Any candidate or election agent who knowingly acts in contravention of this section shall be guilty of an illegal practice.

CERTAIN EXPENDITURE TO BE ILLEGAL PRACTICE.

21. (1) No payment or contract for payment shall, for the purpose of promoting or procuring the election of a candidate at any election, be made —

(a)

on account of the conveyance of electors or voters to or from the poll, whether for the hiring of vehicles, vessels or animals of transport of any kind whatsoever, or for railway fares, or otherwise; or

(b)

to or with an elector or voter on account of the use of any house, land, building, or premises for the exhibition of any address, bill, notice or on account of the exhibition of any address, bill or notice.

(2)

Subject to such exception as may be allowed in pursuance of this Act, if any payment or contract for payment is knowingly made in contravention of this section either before, during, or after an election, the person making such payment or contract shall be guilty of an illegal practice, and any person receiving such payment or being a party to any such contract, knowing the same to be in contravention of this section, shall also be guilty of an illegal practice.

(3)

A person shall not let, lend, or employ for the purpose of conveyance of electors or voters to and from the poll any vehicle, vessel or animal of transport of any kind whatsoever which he keeps or uses for the purpose of letting out for hire, and if he lets, lends, or employs such vehicle, vessel or animal of transport knowing that it is intended to be used for the conveyance of electors or voters to and from the poll he shall be guilty of an illegal practice.

B.L.R.O. 1/1984

(4)

A person shall not hire, borrow or use for the purpose of conveyance of electors or voters to and from the poll any vehicle, vessel or animal of transport of any kind whatsoever which he knows the owner thereof is prohibited by subsection (3) of this section to let, lend, or employ for that purpose, and if he does so he shall be guilty of an illegal practice.

(5)

Nothing in subsection (3) or subsection (4) of this section shall prevent a vehicle, vessel or animal of transport of any kind being let to, or hired, employed, or used by an elector or voter or several electors or voters at their joint cost for the purpose of being conveyed to or from the poll.

(6)

Notwithstanding anything in the preceding provisions of this section —

(a)

where it is the ordinary business of an elector or voter as an advertising agent to exhibit for payment bills and advertisements, a payment to or contract with such elector or voter, if made in the ordinary course of business, shall not be deemed to be an illegal practice within the meaning of this section;

(b)

where electors or voters are unable at an election to reach their polling stations from their place of residence without crossing the sea or a branch or arm thereof or a river, means may be provided for conveying such electors or voters to their polling stations, or to enable them to cross the river in order to reach their polling stations, and the amount of payment for such means of conveyance may be in addition to the maximum amount of expenses allowed by this Act:

Provided always that such means of conveyance shall be made available equally to all such electors or voters who wish to avail themselves thereof.

CERTAIN EMPLOYMENT TO BE ILLEGAL.

22. (1) No person shall, for the purpose of promoting or procuring the election of a candidate at any election, be engaged or employed for payment or promise of payment for any purpose or in any capacity whatever, except for the purpose or in the capacities following —

(a) one election agent and no more;

(b) not more than one polling agent at any one time for each polling area or polling district:

Provided that where more than one polling station is provided in any polling area or polling district an additional polling agent may be employed in respect of each polling station;

(c) a reasonable number of clerks and messengers having regard to the area of the constituency, electoral ward or electoral district and the number of electors on the register or list of electors for such constituency, electoral ward or electoral district.

(2) Subject to such exception as may be allowed in pursuance of this Act, if any person is engaged or employed in contravention of this section, either before, during, or after an election, the person engaging or employing him shall be guilty of an illegal practice.

SAVING FOR CREDITORS.

23. The provisions of this Act prohibiting certain payments and contracts for payments, and the payment of any sum, and the incurring of expenses in excess of a certain maximum, shall not affect the right of any creditor, who, when the contract was made or the expense was incurred, was ignorant of the same being in contravention of this Act.

EXEMPTION FROM STAMP DUTY.

24. Any instrument made on oath or affirmation pursuant to the provisions of section 5 or 25 in any form specified in the First Schedule shall be exempt from payment of stamp duty under any written law for the time being in force relating to stamp duties.

RETURN AND DECLARATION RESPECTING ELECTION EXPENSES.

25. (1) Within 31 days after the date of publication of the result of an election in the *Gazette* the election agent of every candidate at that election shall deposit with the proper officer a true return, in this Act referred to as the "return respecting election expenses," in the Form B in the First Schedule, containing detailed statements as respects that candidate of —

(a)

all payments made by the election agent together with all the bills and receipts referred to in subsection (1) of section 18, which bills and receipts are in this Act included in the expression "return respecting election expenses" and the dates of payment of all sums for which no receipt is attached;

B.L.R.O. 1/1984

(b)

the amount of personal expenses, if any, paid by the candidate;

(c) the disputed claims so far as the election agent is aware;

(d)

all unpaid claims, if any, of which the election agent is aware in respect of which application has been made or is about to be made to an Election Judge or Judge of the High Court;

(e)

all money, securities and other valuable considerations received by or promised to the election agent from or by any candidate or any other person for the purpose of expenses incurred or to be incurred on account or in respect of the management of the election, naming every person from whom the sum may have been received or by whom such sum may have been promised, showing as to each sum whether it was received as contribution, loan, deposit or otherwise;

(f)

the amount of expenses, if any, incurred by any person authorised by the election agent under subsection (1) of section 16.

(2)

The return respecting election expenses shall be signed by the election agent and shall be accompanied by a statement made by the candidate and his election agent which shall be respectively in Forms C and D in the First Schedule and shall be on oath before the Chairman or a member of the Election Commission, a magistrate, a Commissioner for Oaths, or the Supervisor of Elections:

Provided that where the candidate has named himself as election agent under subsection (2) of section 12 such statement shall be made only in Form C of the First Schedule.

(3)

If the said return and statements are not transmitted before the expiration of the time limited for the purpose, the candidate shall not after the expiration of such time sit or vote until either such return and statements have been transmitted or until the date of the allowance of such authorised excuse for failure to transmit the same as in this Act mentioned; and if he sits or votes in contravention of this Act he shall be liable, on conviction, to a penalty of $1,000 for every day on which he so sits or votes.

(4)

If any candidate or election agent fails to comply with the requirements of subsection (1) or subsection (2) of this section he shall be guilty of an illegal practice and the provisions of this section shall be in addition to and not in derogation of the provisions of section 11.

PUBLICATION OF DEPOSIT OF RETURN ETC.

26. (1) When any return respecting election expenses and the statements made in respect thereof have been received by the proper officer, he shall, as soon as may be, cause a notice of the date on which the return and statements in question were received by him and of the time and place at which they can be inspected, to be fixed in some conspicuous place in his office and published in the *Gazette.*

(2) The proper officer shall preserve all such returns and statements with the bills and vouchers relating thereto and at all reasonable times during 6 months next after the publication in the *Gazette* of the notice mentioned in this section shall permit any person to inspect them and to make extracts therefrom on payment of a fee of $5 and shall on payment of $1 per page or part thereof, supply a copy or copies of any part thereof; and after the expiration of the said period of 6 months the said documents may be destroyed or returned to the candidate if application for their return is made by the candidate before they are destroyed.

EMPLOYERS TO ALLOW EMPLOYEES REASONABLE PERIOD FOR VOTING.

27. (1) Every employer shall, on polling day, allow to every elector in his employ a reasonable period for voting, and no employer shall make any deduction from the pay or other remuneration

of any such elector or impose upon or exact from him any penalty by reason of his absence during such period.

(2)

Any employer who, directly or indirectly, refuses, or by intimidation, undue influence, or in any other manner, interferes with the granting to any elector in his employ, of a reasonable period for voting, as in this section provided, shall be guilty of an offence: Penalty a fine of $3,000 and imprisonment for 12 months.

(3)

This section shall not extend to such categories of employees as His Majesty in Council may from time to time by notification in the *Gazette* designate.

(4)

The provisions of this section shall be binding on the Government of Brunei Darussalam.

B.L.R.O. 1/1984

LIMITATION OF POLITICAL PROPAGANDA.

28. (1) No person shall furnish or supply any musical instrument or loud speaker to any person with intent that it shall be used by any person in any way or used in or upon vessels, animals, motorcars, trucks, or other vehicles as or for the purpose of political propaganda on polling day and no person shall with any such intent use himself or use in or upon any vessel, animal, motorcar, truck, or other vehicle any such musical instrument or loud speaker on polling day.

(2)

Subject to the provisions of subsection (5) of this section no person shall furnish or supply any flag, ensign, banner, standard, poster or label to or for any person with intent that it be worn, carried or used by any person within any constituency, on polling day, as a party badge to distinguish the wearer as the supporter of any candidate, or of the political or other opinions entertained or supposed to be entertained by such candidate; and no person shall wear, carry or use any flag, ensign, banner, standard, poster or label as such badge, within any constituency, on polling day.

(3)

No person shall on polling day, within a distance of 50 yards from the limits of any polling station —

(a)

endeavour to establish the identity of any person entering a polling station;

(b)

check on any list the name of any person entering or leaving a polling station;

(c)

place any desk or table or establish any office or booth for any purpose connected with an election;

(d)

solicit or persuade or attempt to persuade any person to abstain from voting at the election, or to vote or to abstain from voting for any candidate at the election;

(e)

wait or loiter except for the purpose of gaining entry to the polling station to cast his vote;

(f)

congregate or move in any public place in any electoral ward in a group of 5 or more persons with the intention of showing support for or opposition to any candidate or political party:

Provided that nothing herein shall prevent the proper officer or any person authorised by the proper officer from carrying out his duties in relation to the conduct of any election.

(4)

Subject to the provisions of subsection (5) of this section no flag, ensign, banner, standard, poster or label shall at any time be publicly displayed as or for the purpose of political propaganda on polling day; and the proper officer shall remove or cause to be removed any such flag, ensign, banner, standard, poster or label displayed in contravention of this subsection.

(5)

Nothing contained in subsection (2) or subsection (4) of this section shall be deemed to extend to the furnishing or supplying of any rosette or favour not exceeding 7 square inches in superficial area bearing the symbol allotted to any candidate or of any label not exceeding 50 square inches in superficial area bearing such symbol or to the wearing upon the person of one such rosette or favour to the display of one such label on any vehicle or vessel.

(6)

An offence under this section shall be a seizable offence within the meaning of the Criminal Procedure Code (Chapter 7).

(7)

Any person who contravenes any of the provisions of this section shall be guilty of an offence: Penalty, a fine of $6,000 and imprisonment for 2 years.

APPOINTMENT OF CANVASSERS.

29. (1) No person shall, between the date on which the candidates for election are nominated and the time of the declaration by the returning officer of the result of the elections, on behalf of any candidate canvass for votes or address any public meeting held in the constituency, electoral ward or electoral district, as the case may be, unless he is —

(a)

not disqualified for appointment as an election agent under subsection (1) of section 13; and

(b)

in possession of a written authority, in the Form E in the First Schedule, signed by an election agent.

(2)

Every election agent shall, within 48 hours of issuing any authority under subsection (1) of this section, lodge 3 copies of such authority with the proper officer.

(3)

In this section "canvass" means soliciting on behalf of any candidate the votes of electors in any constituency, electoral ward or electoral district for or against any candidate or political party at an election by —

B.L.R.O. 1/1984 (a) visiting electors at their homes or places of work;

(b)

convening or organising or assisting in convening or organising any public meeting, procession or demonstration;

(c) interviewing members of the public; or

(d)

distributing or causing to be distributed any written or printed appeal in favour of or against any candidate or political party.

(4)

Any person who contravenes or fails to comply with any of the provisions of this section shall be guilty of an offence: Penalty, a fine of $6,000 and imprisonment for 2 years.

PUNISHMENT FOR CONVICTION FOR ILLEGAL PRACTICE.

30. (1) Every person who commits an illegal practice shall, on conviction by a magistrate, be liable to a fine of $3,000 and, subject to any specific provision to the contrary in any written law relating to any election, shall by conviction until the expiration of 5 years from such conviction become incapable of being registered or listed as an elector or of voting at any election under this Act or of being elected at any election, and if at that date he has been elected at any election, his seat shall be vacated from the date of such conviction.

(2) A prosecution for an illegal practice shall not be instituted without the sanction of the Public Prosecutor.

PART V EXCUSE FOR CORRUPT OR ILLEGAL PRACTICE

REPORT EXONERATING CANDIDATE IN CERTAIN CASES OF CORRUPT AND ILLEGAL PRACTICE BY AGENTS.

31. Where, upon the trial of an election petition respecting an election, the Election Judge reports that a candidate at such election has been guilty by his agents of the offence of treating or undue influence or of any other corrupt or illegal practice in reference to such election, and the Election Judge further reports, after giving the Attorney General an opportunity of being heard, that the candidate has proved to the Court —

(a)

that no corrupt or illegal practice was committed at such election by the candidate or his election agent and the offences mentioned in the said report were committed contrary to the orders and without the sanction or connivance of such candidate or his election agent; and

(b)

that such candidate and his election agent took all reasonable means for preventing the commission of corrupt and illegal practices at such election; and

(c)

that the offences mentioned in the said report were of a trivial, unimportant and limited character; and

(d)

that in all other respects the election was free from any corrupt or illegal practice on the part of such candidate and of his agents,

then the election of such candidate shall not, by reason of the offences mentioned in such report, be void, nor shall the candidate be subject to any incapacity under this Act.

POWER TO EXCEPT INNOCENT ACT FROM BEING ILLEGAL PRACTICE ETC.

32. Where, on application made, it is shown to an Election Judge or to a Judge of the High Court by such evidence as seems to the Judge sufficient—

(a)

that any act or omission of a candidate at any election, or of his election agent or of any other agent or person, would, by reason of being the payment of a sum or the incurring of expense in excess of any maximum amount allowed by this Act, or of being a payment, engagement, employment or contract in contravention of this Act, or of otherwise being in contravention of any of the provisions of this Act, be but for this section an illegal practice; and

(b)

that any such act or omission arose from inadvertence or from accidental miscalculations or from some other reasonable cause of a like nature, and in any case did not arise from any want of good faith,

and in the circumstances it seems to the Judge, after giving the candidates, the returning officer, and any elector within the constituency, electoral ward or electoral district an apportunity of being heard, to be just that the candidate in question and the said election and other agent and person, or any of them, should not be subject to any of the consequences under this Act of

B.L.R.O. 1/1984

the said act or omission, the Judge may make an order allowing such act or omission to be an exception from the provisions of this Act which would otherwise make the same and thereupon such candidate, agent or person shall not be subject to any of the consequences under this an illegal practice, payment, employment, or hiring Act of the said act or omission.

AUTHORISED EXCUSE FOR NON-COMPLIANCE WITH PROVISIONS AS TO RETURN AND DECLARATION RESPECTING ELECTION EXPENSES.

33. (1) Where the return and statements respecting election expenses of a candidate at an election have not been transmitted as required by this Act, or being transmitted contain some error or false statement, then—

(a)

if the candidate applies to an Election Judge or a Judge of the High Court and shows that the failure to transmit such return and declarations, or any of them, or any part thereof, or any error or false statement therein, has arisen by reason of his illness, or of the absence, death, illness, negligence or misconduct of his election agent or of any clerk or officer of such agent, or by reason of inadvertence or of any reasonable cause of a like nature, and not by reason of any want of good faith on the part of the applicant; or

(b)

if the election agent of the candidate applies to an Election Judge or a Judge of the High Court and shows that the failure to transmit the return and statements which he was required to transmit, or any part thereof, or any error or false statement therein, arose by reason of his illness, or of the death, illness, negligence or misconduct of any prior election agent of the candidate, or of the absence, death, illness or misconduct of any clerk, or officer of an election agent of the candidate, or by reason of inadvertence or of any reasonable cause of a like nature, and not by reason of any want of good faith, on the part of the applicant,

the Judge may, after such notice of the application, and on production of such evidence of the grounds stated in the application and of the good faith of the application, and otherwise, as to the Judge seems fit, and after giving the other candidates, the proper officer and any elector within the constituency, electoral ward or electoral district an opportunity of being heard, make such order for allowing an authorised excuse for the failure to transmit such return and statements, or for an error or false statement in such return and statements, as to the Judge seems just.

(2)

Where it appears to the Judge that any person being or having been an election agent has refused or failed to make such return or supply such particulars as will enable the candidate and his election agent, respectively, to comply with the provisions of this Act as to the return and statements respecting election expenses, the Judge before making an order allowing the excuse as in this section mentioned shall order such person to attend before the Judge, and shall, unless he attends and shows cause to the contrary, order him to make the return and statements, or to deliver a statement of the particulars required to be contained in the return, as to the Judge seems just, and to make or deliver the same within such time and to such person and in such manner as the Judge may direct, or may order him to be examined with respect to such particulars, and, in default of compliance with any such order, such person shall be guilty of an illegal practice.

(3)

The order may make the allowance conditional upon the making of the return and statements in a modified form or within an extended time, and upon the compliance with such other terms as to the Judge seems best calculated for carrying into effect the objects of this Act, and an order allowing an authorised excuse shall relieve the applicant for the order from any liability or consequences under this Act in respect of the matter excused by the order; and where it is proved by the candidate to the Judge that any act or omission of the election agent in relation to the return and statements respecting election expenses was without the sanction or connivance of the candidate, and that the candidate took all reasonable means for preventing such act or omission, the Judge shall relieve the candidate from the consequences of such act or omission on the part of his election agent.

(4)

The date of the order, or, if conditions and terms are to be complied with, the date at which the applicant fully complies with them, is referred to in this Act as the date of the allowance of the excuse.

PART VI GROUNDS FOR AVOIDING ELECTIONS

AVOIDANCE BY CONVICTION OF CANDIDATE.

34. The election of a candidate at any election is avoided by his conviction for any corrupt or illegal practice at such election.

B.L.R.O. 1/1984

AVOIDANCE OF ELECTION ON ELECTION PETITION.

35. The election of a candidate at any election shall be declared to be void on an election petition on any of the following grounds which may be proved to the satisfaction of the Election Judge, namely —

(a)

that general bribery, general treating or general intimidation or other misconduct or other circumstances whether similar to those before enumerated or not have so extensively prevailed that they may be reasonably supposed to have affected the result of the election;

(b)

non-compliance with the provisions of any written law relating to any election, if it appears that the election was not conducted in accordance with the principles laid down in such written law and that such non-compliance affected the result of the election;

(c)

that a corrupt practice or illegal practice was committed in connection with the election by the candidate or with his knowledge or consent, or by any agent of the candidate;

(d)

that the candidate personally engaged a person as his election agent, or as a canvasser or agent, knowing that such person had within 7 years previous to such engagement been convicted or found guilty of a corrupt practice by a magistrate or by the report of an Election Judge;

(e)

that the candidate was at the time of his election a person disqualified for election.

PART VII ELECTION PETITIONS

APPOINTMENT AND POWERS OF ELECTION JUDGE.

36. (1) Every election petition shall be tried by the Chief Justice or by a Judge of the High Court nominated by the Chief Justice for the purpose.

(2)

Witnesses shall be subpoenaed and sworn in the same manner as nearly as circumstances admit as in a trial by the High Court in the exercise of its original civil jurisdiction and shall be subject to the same penalties for the giving of false evidence.

(3)

On the trial of an election petition under this Act the Election Judge may, by order under his hand, compel the attendance of any person as a witness who appears to him to have been concerned in the election to which the petition refers, and any person refusing to obey such order shall be guilty of a contempt of Court. The Election Judge may examine any witness so compelled to attend or any person in Court, although such witness is not called and examined by any party to the petition. After the examination of a witness as aforesaid by the Election Judge, such witness may be cross-examined by or on behalf of the petitioner and respondent, or either of them.

(4)

Unless otherwise ordered by the Chief Justice, all interlocutory matters in connection with an election petition may be dealt with and decided by any Judge of the High Court.

WHO MAY PRESENT PETITION.

37. An election petition may be presented to the High Court by any one or more of the following persons, namely —

(a)

some person who voted or had a right to vote at the election to which the petition relates;

(b)

some person claiming to have had a right to be returned or elected at such election;

(c)

some person alleging himself to have been a candidate at such election.

RELIEF WHICH MAY BE CLAIMED.

38. All or any of the following reliefs to which the petitioner may be entitled may be claimed in an election petition, namely —

(a) a declaration that the election is void;

(b)

a declaration that the person was not duly elected or ought not to have been returned;

(c)

a declaration that any candidate was duly elected and ought to have been returned;

(d)

where the seat is claimed for an unsuccessful candidate on the ground that he had a majority of lawful votes, a scrutiny.

B.L.R.O. 1/1984

CERTIFICATE OF JUDGE AS TO VALIDITY OF ELECTION.

39. At the conclusion of the trial of an election petition the Election Judge shall determine whether the candidate whose return or election is complained of, or any other and what person, was duly returned or elected, or whether the election was void, and shall certify such determination to His Majesty. Upon such certificate being given, such determination shall be final; and the return shall be confirmed or altered, or His Majesty shall within one month of such determination give notice of election in the constituency, electoral ward or electoral district concerned, as the case may require, in accordance with such certificate.

REPORT OF JUDGE AS TO CORRUPT OR ILLEGAL PRACTICE.

40. (1) At the conclusion of the trial of an election petition the Election Judge shall also report to His Majesty in writing —

(a)

whether any corrupt or illegal practice has or has not been proved to have been committed by or with the knowledge and consent of any candidate at the election, or by his agent, and the nature of such corrupt or illegal practice, if any; and

(b)

the names and descriptions of all persons if any, who have been proved at the trial to have been guilty of any corrupt or illegal practice.

(2)

Before any person, not being a party to an election petition nor a candidate on behalf of whom the seat is claimed by an election petition, is reported by an Election Judge under this section, the Election Judge shall give such person an opportunity of being heard and of giving and calling evidence to show why he should not be so reported.

(3)

When an Election Judge reports that a corrupt or illegal practice has been committed by any person, that person shall be subject to the same incapacities as if at the date of the said report he had been convicted of that practice and a person shall be subject to the same incapacities if he was a candidate at the election and the Election Judge reports that such corrupt or illegal practice was committed with his knowledge and consent or by his agent.

(4)

His Majesty shall cause a copy of such report to be published in the *Gazette,* and it shall be the duty of every registering officer forthwith to peruse the report and forthwith to delete from the register or list of electors assigned to him the name of every person appearing from the report to be incapable of voting at an election.

TIME FOR PRESENTATION.

41. (1) Every election petition shall be presented within 21 days of the date of publication of the result of the election in the *Gazette*:

Provided that —

(a)

an election petition questioning the return or the election upon the ground of a corrupt practice and specifically alleging a payment of money or other act to have been made or done since the date aforesaid by the person whose election is questioned or by an agent of the person or with the privity of the person or his election agent in pursuance or in furtherance of such corrupt practice may, so far as respects such corrupt practice, be presented at any time within 28 days after the date of such payment or act;

(b)

an election petition questioning the return or the election upon an allegation of an illegal practice may, so far as respects such illegal practice, be presented within the time following, that is to say —

(i)

at any time before the expiration of 14 days immediately after the date of the publication in the *Gazette* of the notice required by section 26 as to the election expenses of the person whose election is questioned;

(ii)

if the election petition specifically alleges a payment of money or other act to have been made or done since the said date by the person whose election is questioned or by an agent of the person or with the privity of the person or of his election agent in pursuance or in furtherance of the illegal practice alleged in the petition, the petition may be presented at any time within 28 days immediately after the date of such payment or other act.

(2)

An election petition presented in due time may, for the purpose of questioning the return or the election upon an allegation of a corrupt or illegal practice, be amended with the leave of a Judge of the High Court within the time within which an election petition questioning the return or the election upon that ground may be presented.

(3)

For the purposes of this section, where there is an authorised excuse for failing to make and transmit the return and statements respecting election expenses, the date of the allowance of the excuse or, if there was a failure in 2 or more particulars and the excuse was allowed at different times, the date of the allowance of the last excuse shall be substituted for the date of the publication of the notice mentioned in subparagraph (i) of paragraph*(b)* of the proviso to subsection (1) of this section.

PROHIBITION OF DISCLOSURE OF VOTE.

42. No elector who has voted at any election shall, in any proceeding to question the election, be required to state for whom he has voted.

VOTES TO BE STRUCK OFF AT SCRUTINY.

43. (1) On a scrutiny at the trial of an election petition the following votes only shall be struck off, namely —

(a)

the vote of any person whose name was not on the register or list of electors assigned to the polling station at which the vote was recorded or who has not been authorised to vote at such station;

(b)

the vote of any person whose vote was procured by bribery, treating, or undue influence;

(c)

the vote of any person who committed or procured the commission of personation at the election;

(d)

where the election was an ordinary election, the vote of any person proved to have voted at such ordinary election in more than one constituency, electoral ward or electoral district;

(e)

Total

B.L.R.O. 1/1984

PERSONAL EXPENSES PAID BY CANDIDATE. Note 2. All payments are to be vouched for by a bill stating the particulars, except as provided by section 17 of the Election Offences Act.

Name of payee	Description of service paid for	State whether bill attached. Yes/No (*See* Note 2)	Amount $ ¢
		Total	

OTHER EXPENSES. Please *see* Note 2 above.

Description	Serial No of attached list	Amount $ ¢

Payments to agents, clerks and messengers, as listed Travelling expenses of above, as listed Travelling expenses of other persons, as listed Printing Advertising Stationery Postage, telegrams and telephone charges Hire of rooms for public meeting or as Committee rooms Licences Miscellaneous expenditure, as listed Expenses by person authorised, as listed Disputed claims, as listed Unpaid claims, as listed Total

DECLARATION

To be completed by agent

I, ... being election agent, make the above return respecting election expenses of the said candidate in the said election and certify that to the best of my belief it is complete and correct.

Signature ....

Date ....

To be completed by candidate acting as his own agent.

I, ... acting as my own election agent, make the above return respecting my election expenses at the said election and certify that to the best of my belief they are complete and correct.

Signature ....

Date ....

B.L.R.O. 1/1984

FORM C

(Section 25(2))

STATEMENT ON OATH BY CANDIDATE

I, ...

being a candidate for election in the ....
constituency/electoral ward/electoral district, do hereby solemnly affirm (or swear) that the above return of election expenses is true to the best of my knowledge and belief, and that except the expenses therein set forth, no expenses of any nature whatsoever have to my knowledge or belief been incurred in, or for the purposes of, my candidature.

Dated this .... day of ...., 20 ....

.... Candidate

Solemnly affirmed (or sworn to) before me,

....

Chairman or Member of the Election Commission Magistrate Commissioner for Oaths Supervisor of Elections

FORM D

(Section 25(2))

STATEMENT ON OATH BY AN ELECTION AGENT

I, ... being appointed election agent for .... a candidate for election in the .... constituency/electoral ward/electoral district, do hereby solemnly affirm (or swear) that the above return of election expenses is true to the best of my knowledge and belief, and that, except the expenses therein set forth, no expenses of any nature whatsoever have to my knowledge or belief been

incurred in, or for the purposes of, ...
.... candidature.

Dated this .... day of ...., 20 ....

.... Election Agent

Solemnly affirmed (or sworn to) before me,

....

Chairman or Member of the Election Commission Magistrate Commissioner for Oaths Supervisor of Elections

B.L.R.O. 1/1984

FORM E

(Section 29)

AUTHORITY UNDER SECTION 29

I, ... being the election agent of .... a candidate for election in the ....

constituency/electoral ward/electoral district, do hereby authorise .... of .... to canvass and address public meetings on behalf of the aforesaid candidate.

Dated this .... day of ...., 20 ....

.... Election Agent

SECOND SCHEDULE

(Section 45)

ELECTION PETITION RULES

Citation.

1. These Rules may be cited as the Election Petition Rules.

INTERPRETATION.

2. In these Rules, unless the context otherwise requires —

"the Act" means the Election Offences Act;

"advocate" means a person who has been registered under the Advocates Enactment 1957;

[22 of 1957]

"Judge" means the Election Judge as defined in section 2 of the Act;

"Registrar" means the Registrar of the Supreme Court and includes an Assistant Registrar.

MANNER OF PRESENTATION OF PETITION.

3. (1) The presentation of an election petition shall be made by delivering it at the office of the Registrar, and the Registrar or the officer of his department to whom the petition is delivered shall, if required, give a receipt in the following form —

Received on the .... day of ...., 20.........., at the Registry of the Supreme Court, a petition touching the election of A.B.,

.... for .... purporting to

be signed by .... (insert the names of petitioners).

C.D.,

REGISTRAR, OR OTHER OFFICER TO WHOM THE PETITION IS DELIVERED.

B.L.R.O. 1/1984

(2) There shall also be left with the petition 2 copies thereof.

CONTENTS AND FORM OF ELECTION PETITION.

4. (1) An election petition shall contain the following statements —

(a)

it shall state the right of the petitioner to petition within section 34 of the Act;

(b)

it shall state the holding and result of the election, and shall briefly state the facts and grounds relied on to sustain the prayer.

(2)

The petition shall be divided into paragraphs, each of which, as nearly as may be, shall be confined to a distinct portion of the subject, and every paragraph shall be numbered consecutively, and no costs shall be allowed for drawing or copying any petition not substantially in compliance with this Rule, unless otherwise ordered by the Court or a Judge.

(3)

The petition shall conclude with a prayer as, for instance, that some specified person should be declared duly returned or elected, or that the election should be declared void, and shall be signed by all the petitioners.

(4) The following form, or one to the like effect, shall be sufficient —

IN THE SUPREME COURT OF BRUNEI DARUSSALAM

Election for .... (state the constituency,

electoral ward or electoral district) holden on the .... day

of ...., 20.........

The petition of A., of .... (or of A.,

of .... and B., of ...., as the case may be) whose name/s is/are subscribed.

(1)

Your petitioner A. is a person who voted (or had a right to vote, as the case may be) at the above election (or claims to have had a right to be returned at the above election, or was a candidate at the above election), and your petitioner B. (here state in like manner the right of each petitioner).

(2)

And your petitioners state that the election was holden on the.......................... day of ...., 20 ...., when A.B., C.D. and

E.F. were candidates, and the Returning Officer has returned A.B. as being duly elected.

(3) AND YOUR PETITIONERS SAY THAT (HERE STATE THE FACTS AND GROUNDS ON WHICH THE PETITIONERS RELY).

Wherefore your petitioners pray that it might be determined that the said A.B. was not duly elected or returned, and that the election was void (or that the said E.F. was duly elected and ought to have been returned).

(Signed) A ....

B ....

EVIDENCE NOT TO BE STATED IN PETITION PARTICULARS.

5. Evidence need not be stated in the petition, but the Judge may, upon application in writing by a respondent, order such particulars as may be necessary to prevent surprise and unnecessary expense, and to ensure a fair and effectual trial upon such terms as to costs and otherwise as may be ordered.

WHERE MORE THAN ONE PETITION IS PRESENTED IN RELATION TO SAME ELECTION.

6. Where more petitions than one are presented relating to the same election or return, all such petitions shall be dealt with as one petition, so far as the inquiry into the same is concerned.

LIST OF VOTES OBJECTED TO WHERE SEAT CLAIMED BY UNSUCCESSFUL CANDIDATE.

7. When a petitioner claims the seat for an unsuccessful candidate, alleging that he had a majority of lawful votes, the party complaining of or defending the election or return shall, 6 days before the day appointed for trial, deliver to the Registrar, and also at the address, if any, given by the petitioners and respondent, as the case may be, a list of the votes intended to be objected to, and of the heads of objection to each such vote, and the Registrar shall allow inspection and office copies of such lists to all parties concerned; and no evidence shall be given against the validity of any vote, nor upon any head of objection not specified in the list, except by leave of

the Judge, upon such terms as to amendment of the list, postponement of the inquiry, and payment of costs, as may be ordered.

LIST OF OBJECTIONS IN RECRIMINATORY CASE.

8. The respondent in a petition complaining of an undue return and claiming the seat for some person may lead evidence to prove that the election of such person was undue, and in such case such respondent shall, 6 days before the day appointed for trial, deliver to the Registrar, and also at the address, if any, given by the petitioner, a list of the objections to the election upon which he intends to rely, and the Registrar shall allow inspection of office copies of such lists to all parties concerned; and no evidence shall be given by a respondent of any objection to the election not specified in the list, except by leave of the Judge, upon such terms as to amendments of the list, postponement of the inquiry, and payments of costs, as may be ordered.

APPOINTMENT OF ADVOCATE TO PETITIONER.

9. With the petition the petitioner or petitioners shall leave at the office of the Registrar a writing, signed by him or them, giving the name of an advocate whom he or they authorise to act as his or their advocate or stating that he or they act for himself or themselves, as the case may be, and in either case giving an address within Brunei Darussalam at which notices may be left; and if no such writing be left or address given, then all notices may be given by leaving the same at the office of the Registrar. Every such writing shall be stamped with the duty payable thereon under the law for the time being in force.

APPOINTMENT OF ADVOCATE BY RESPONDENT.

10. Any person returned may at any time, after he is returned, send or leave at the office of the Registrar a writing signed by him on his behalf, appointing an advocate to act as his advocate in case there should be a petition against him, or stating that he intends to act for himself, and in either case giving an address within Brunei Darussalam at which notices addressed to him may be left; and if no such writing be left or address given, all notices and proceedings may be given or served by leaving the same at the office of the Registrar. Every such writing shall be stamped with the duty payable thereon under the law for the time being in force.

REGISTRAR TO KEEP BOOK WITH ADDRESSES AND NAMES OF ADVOCATES.

11. The Registrar shall cause to be kept a book at his office in which shall be entered all addresses and the names of advocates given under rule 9 or 10 of these Rules which book shall be open to inspection by any person during his office hours.

SECURITY BY PETITIONER FOR COSTS ETC. OF ELECTION PETITION.

12. (1) At the time of the presentation of the petition, or within 3 days afterwards, security for the payment of all costs, charges, and expenses that may become payable by the petitioner shall be given on behalf of the petitioner.

(2)

The security shall be to an amount of not less than $3,000. If the number of charges in any petition shall exceed 3, additional security to an amount of $1,500 shall be given in respect of each charge in excess of the first 3. The security required by this Rule shall be given by a deposit of money.

(3)

If security as in this Rule provided is not given by the petitioner, no further proceedings shall be had on the petition, and the respondent may apply to the Judge for an order directing the dismissal of the petition and for the payment of the respondent's costs. The costs of hearing and deciding such application shall be paid as ordered by the Judge, and in default of such order shall form part of the general costs of the petition.

SECURITY BY DEPOSIT OF MONEY.

13. (1) The deposit of money by way of security for payment of costs, charges, and expenses payable by the petitioner shall be made by payment to the proper officer which shall be vested in and drawn upon from time to time by the Chief Justice for the purposes for which security is required by these Rules. A receipt shall be given by the proper officer for the same, which shall forthwith be left at the office of the Registrar by the petitioner.

(2) The Registrar shall file such receipt and keep a book open to the inspection of all parties concerned, in which shall be entered from time to time the amount and the petition to which it is applicable.

B.L.R.O. 1/1984

RETURN OF MONEY SO DEPOSITED.

14. (1) Money so deposited shall, if and when the same is no longer needed for securing payment of such costs, charges and expenses, be returned or otherwise disposed of as justice may require by order of the Judge.

(2)

Such order may be made after such notice of intention to apply and proof that all just claims have been satisfied or otherwise sufficiently provided for as the Judge may require.

(3)

Such order may direct payment either to the party in whose name the same is deposited or to any person entitled to receive the same.

NOTICE OF PETITION AND COPY OF PETITION TO BE SERVED ON RESPONDENT.

15. Notice of the presentation of a petition, accompanied by a copy thereof, shall, within 10 days of the presentation of the petition, be served by the petitioner on the respondent. Such service may be effected either by delivering the notice and copy aforesaid to the advocate appointed by the respondent under Rule 10 of these Rules or by posting the same in a registered letter to the address given under Rule 10 of these Rules at such time that, in the ordinary course of post, the letter would be delivered within the time above mentioned, or if no advocate has been appointed, or no such address given, by a notice published in the *Gazette* stating that such petition has been presented, and that a copy of the same may be obtained by the respondent on application at the office of the Registrar.

WHEN PETITION TO BE DEEMED AT ISSUE.

16. On the expiration of the time limited for making petitions the petition shall be deemed to be at issue.

LIST OF PETITIONS.

17. The Registrar shall make out the election petition list. In it he shall insert the names of the advocates of the petitioners and respondents appointed under Rules 9 and 10 of these Rules, respectively, and the addresses to which notices may be sent, if any. The list may be inspected at the office of the Registrar at any time during office hours, and shall be affixed for that purpose upon a notice board appropriated to proceedings under the Order, and headed ".

TIME AND PLACE OF TRIAL OF ELECTION PETITION.

18. The time and place of the trial of each election petition shall be fixed by the Judge, and not less than 14 days' notice thereof shall be given to the petitioner and respondent by letter directed to the address left by such petitioner or respondent with the Registrar, or, if no such address has been left, by notice in the *Gazette*.

POSTPONEMENT OF TRIAL.

19. The Judge may, from time to time, by order made on the application of a party to the petition, postpone the beginning of the trial to such day as he may name; and such order, when made, shall forthwith be published by the Registrar in the *Gazette*.

ADJOURNMENT AND CONTINUATION OF TRIAL.

20. No formal adjournment of the Court for the trial of an election petition shall be necessary, but the trial is to be deemed adjourned, and may be continued from day to day until the inquiry is concluded; and in the event of the Judge who begins the trial being disabled by illness or otherwise, it may be recommenced and concluded by another Judge.

WITHDRAWAL OF ELECTION PETITION.

21. (1) An election petition shall not be withdrawn without the leave of the Judge. Such leave may be given upon such terms as to the payment of costs and otherwise as the Judge may think fit.

(2)

Before leave for the withdrawal of an election petition is granted, there shall be produced affidavits, as required by this Rule, by all the parties to the petition and their advocates, and by the election agents of all the said parties who were candidates at the election:

Provided that a Judge of the Supreme Court may, on cause shown, dispense with the affidavit of any particular person if it seems to such Judge on special grounds to be just so to do.

(3)

Each affidavit shall state that, to the best of the deponent's knowledge and belief, no agreement or terms of any kind whatsoever has or have been made, and no undertaking has been entered into in relation to the withdrawal of the petition; but if any lawful agreement has been made with respect to the withdrawal of the petition, the affidavit shall set forth that

B.L.R.O. 1/1984

agreement, and shall make the foregoing statement subject to what appears from the affidavit.

(4) The affidavits of the applicant and his advocate shall further state the ground on which the petition is sought to be withdrawn.

FORM OF APPLICATION TO WITHDRAW PETITION.

22. (1) An application for leave to withdraw a petition shall be in writing signed by the petitioner or petitioners or his or their advocate or advocates. It shall state the ground on which the application is supported.

(2) The following form shall be sufficient —

(2) The abatement of a petition shall not affect the liability of the petitioner or of any other person to the payment of costs previously incurred.

APPLICATION TO BE SUBSTITUTED AS PETITIONER, ON ABATEMENT.

28. (1) Notice of abatement of a petition, by death of the petitioner or surviving petitioner, shall be given by the party or person interested in the same manner as notice of an application to withdraw a petition, and the time within which application may be made to a Judge to be substituted as a petitioner shall be one calendar month, from the day of the publication of the notice of abatement or such further time as, upon consideration of any special circumstances, the Judge may allow.

(2)

Any person who might have been a petitioner in respect of the election to which the petition relates may apply to the Judge to be substituted as a petitioner.

(3)

The Judge may, if he thinks fit, substitute as a petitioner or any such applicant who is desirous of being substituted and on whose behalf security to the same amount is given as is required in the case of a new petition.

ON DEATH, RESIGNATION OR NOTICE NOT TO OPPOSE OF RESPONDENT, THE PETITION TO CONTINUE.

29. (1) If before the trial of an election petition a respondent dies or resigns, or gives notice in writing to the Registrar that he does not intend to oppose the petition, the petition shall not be abated but shall continue whether or not any person applies to be admitted as respondent as hereinafter provided.

(2)

Notice of the fact that a respondent has died, or resigned, or that he has given notice in writing that he does not intend to oppose the petition, shall be published in the *Gazette* by the Registrar.

(3)

Any person who might have been a petitioner in respect of the election to which the petition relates may apply to the Judge to be admitted as a respondent to oppose the petition within 10 days after such notice has been published in the *Gazette* or such further time as the Judge may allow.

(4)

The manner and time of the respondent's giving notice to the Registrar that he does not intend to oppose the petition, shall be by leaving notice thereof in writing at the office of the Registrar, signed by the respondent not less than 6 days before the day appointed for trial, exclusive of the day of leaving such notice.

B.L.R.O. 1/1984

RESPONDENT NOT OPPOSING PETITION NOT TO APPEAR AS PARTY.

30. A respondent who has given notice of his intention not to oppose a petition shall not be allowed to appear or act as a party against such petition in any proceedings thereon.

COUNTERMANDING NOTICE OF TRIAL WHERE PETITION ABATED ETC.

31. After receiving the petitioner's application for leave to withdraw or notice of the respondent's intention not to oppose, or of the abatement of the petition by death, or of the happening of any of the events mentioned in rule 29 of these Rules, if such notice be received after notice of trial shall have been given, and before the trial has commenced, the Registrar shall forthwith countermand the notice of trial. The countermand shall be given in the same manner, as near as may be, as the notice of trial.

COSTS.

32. All costs of and incidental to the presentation of a petition and to the proceedings consequent thereon shall be defrayed by the parties to the petition in such manner and in such proportions as the Judge may determine, regard being had to the disallowance of any costs which may, in the opinion of the Judge, have been caused by vexatious conduct, unfounded allegations, or unfounded objections, on the part either of the petitioner or the respondent and regard being had to the discouragement of any needless expense by throwing the burden of defraying the same on the parties by whom it has been caused, whether such parties are or are not on the whole successful.

TAXATION AND RECOVERY OF COSTS.

33. (1) Costs shall be taxed by the Registrar upon the order by which the costs are payable in the same manner as costs are taxed in the Supreme Court, but subject to such express directions, either general or specific, as the Judge may give; and costs when taxed may be recovered in the same manner as the costs of an action at law.

(2)

The Judge may direct that the whole or any part of any moneys deposited by way of security under the provisions of Rules 12 and 13 of these Rules may be applied in the payment of taxed costs.

(3)

The office fees payable for inspection, office copies and other proceedings under these Rules shall be such as may be prescribed by the Chief Justice.

NOTICE OF APPOINTMENT OF ADVOCATE.

34. An advocate shall, immediately upon his appointment as such, leave written notice thereof at the office of the Registrar.

SERVICE OF NOTICE ON ADVOCATES.

35. Service of notices and proceedings upon such advocates shall be sufficient for all purposes.

B.L.R.O. 1/1984

BRUNEI GOVERNMENT COMPOSITION

THE PRIME MINISTER'S OFFICE

The Prime Minister's Office was established on 1st January 1984 on the resumption of full independence and sovereignty of Brunei Darussalam, and the announcement by His Majesty The Sultan and Yang Di-Pertuan of Brunei Darussalam of the setting up of a ministerial form of government and the creation of the post of Prime Minister. His Majesty Sultan Haji Hassanal Bolkiah Mu'izzaddin Waddaulah, the Sultan and Yang Di-Pertuan of Brunei Darussalam himself took up the post of Prime Minster since 1984.

In 1986, the post of Speical Adviser to His Majesty the Sultan and Yang Di-Pertuan of Brunei Darussalam in the Prime Minister's Office was created. Pehin Dato Haji Isa was appointed as Special Adviser and he was also appointed as Minister of Home Affairs. The post of Special Adviser is of ministerial rank and is equivalent to a full Cabinet Minister position.

The offices of the Prime Minister's Office are located at Istana Nurul Iman and the Secretariat Building in the capital.

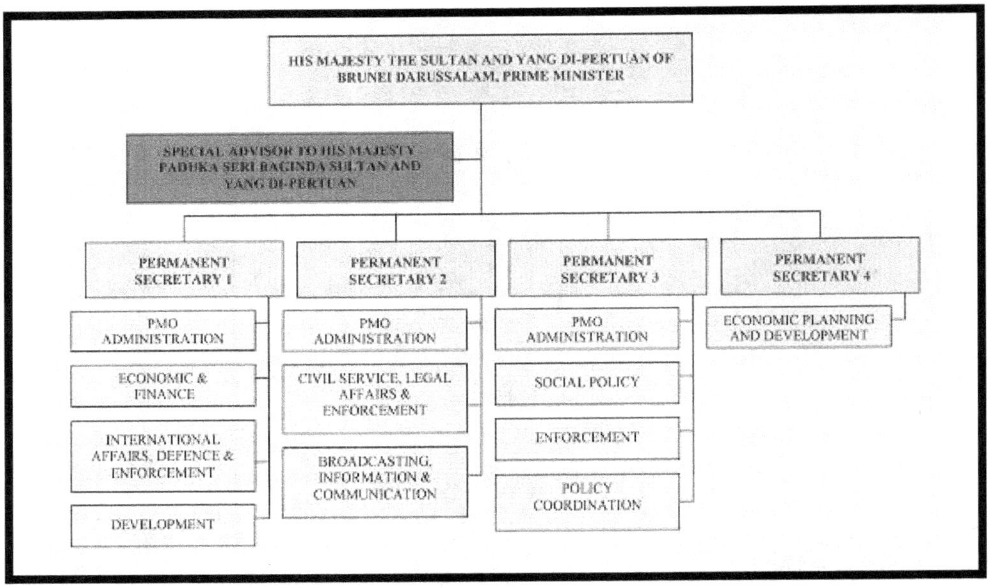

MISSION

As the main agency in Government, The Prime Minister's Office's mission is to provide authoritative and purposeful guidance and leadership to the machinery of Government, in line with national goals and aspirations as outlined by His Majesty The Sultan and Yang Di-Pertuan of Brunei Darussalam.

ROLE AND FUNCTION

The Prime Minister's Office is the central coordinating body for all Government Ministries and Agencies as it relates to national policies and the implementation of those policies.

The Prime Minister's Office is also the central agency in the management and administration of the Government and the Civil Service. Its function includes the setting of civil service policies, administrative procedures and guidelines, as well as the management of the implementation of those rules.

The Prime Minister's Office is directly responsible for the following functions:

- The maintenance of law and order
- Internal security
- Council of Cabinet Ministers and Privy Council meetings
- National ceremonies and protocol
- Government audit
- Management and regulation of the hydrocarbon industry
- Enforcement against corruption and drug abuse
- Regulation of the broadcasting industry
- Information and the media
- Government transport pool

The Ministry also provides administrative and other support services to the Office of His Majesty The Sultan and the Office of the Special Adviser to His Majesty The Sultan in the Prime Minister's Office.

MINISTERS & OFFICIALS

HIS MAJESTY SULTAN HAJI HASSANAL BOLKIAH MU'IZZADDIN WADDAULAH, SULTAN AND YANG DI-PERTUAN OF BRUNEI DARUSSALAM

THE PRIME MINISTER
MINISTER OF DEFENCE
MINISTER OF FINANCE

His Majesty Sultan Haji Hassanal Bolkiah Mu'izzaddin Waddaulah, Sultan and Yang Di-Pertuan of Brunei Darussalam, is the 29th of his line, which dates back to the fourteenth century.

Being the eldest son, His Majesty was made Crown Prince in 1961 and acceded to the Throne on 5th October 1967 following the voluntary abdication the previous day of his father, then His Highness Sultan Haji Omar Ali Saifuddien Sa'adul Khairi Waddien.

His Majesty the Sultan was crowned on 1st August 1968 in pomp and pageantry befitting Brunei Darussalam's ancient customs and traditions.

His Majesty was born on 15th July 1946 at Istana Darussalam (Darussalam Palace) in the capital, Brunei Town (now Bandar Seri Begawan). He received his early education in the form of private tuition at Istana Darul Hana (Darul Hana Palace) and attended top institutions in then Brunei and Malaya (now Brunei Darussalam and Peninsular Malaysia respectively) before furthering his studies in the United Kingdom where he later qualified for admission as Officer Cadet at Sandhurst Royal Military Academy and was commissioned as Captain in 1967. He left Sandhurst in October of the same year to succeed to the throne.

Besides being the Sultan and Ruler, His Majesty Sultan Haji Hassanal Bolkiah is concurrently the Prime Minister, the Defence Minister and Finance Minister as well as the Head of Islamic Religious Faith and Royal Custom and Tradition. Being a working monarch, he is involved in the Conduct of State Affairs, internally as well as internationally.

Like his illustrious father, who is fondly remembered as the Architect of Modern Brunei, His Majesty is a caring monarch and tirelessly works for the continued well-being of his people. In addition to the usual day-to-day administration of the Government and receiving foreign dignitaries in audiences, His Majesty is constantly on the move, visiting government departments and related institutions, security forces on military manoeuvres, and villages, including remote parts of the State. This brings him very close to the people, who love and revere him.

The promotion and strengthening of relations with the outside world also receive the attention of His Majesty, who has travelled widely in Southeast Asia, West Asia, Europe and the United States. He addressed the United Nations General Assembly on Brunei Darussalam's admission to the world body in September 1984 and again in 1994 and 1995.

His Majesty takes a great interest in sports, including polo in which he has distinguished himself in matches against international sides both within and outside the state.

His Majesty is married to to Her Majesty Raja Isteri Pengiran Anak Hajjah Saleha and Her Royal Highness Pengiran Isteri Hajjah Mariam. He has ten children ó four princes and six princesses.

His Majesty's official residence is the Istana Nurul Iman, which is also the country's centre of administration.

THE HONOURABLE. PEHIN DATO HAJI ISA BIN PEHIN DATO HAJI IBRAHIM

SPECIAL ADVISER TO HIS MAJESTY THE SULTAN AND YANG DI-PERTUAN OF BRUNEI DARUSSALAM

(Yang Berhormat Pehin Orang Kaya Laila Setia Bakti Di-Raja Dato Laila Utama Haji Awang Isa bin Pehin Datu Perdana Manteri Dato Laila Utama Haji Awang Ibrahim)

Born in Brunei Darussalam in 1935. Married to Datin Seri Utama Hajjah Rosnah binti Abdullah (Seri Laila Pengiring Di-Raja) and has five children: two sons and three daughters.

QUALIFICATIONS AND APPOINTMENTS

July 1961	B.A. Honours (Law), University of Southampton, England
February 1962	Barrister-at-Law, Middle Temple, London
March 1962	Joined Government service as Assistant Counsel and Deputy Public Prosecutor in the Legal Department
February 1963	Secretary to Brunei Delegation at negotiations on merger with Malaysia
September 1965	Appointed Assistant Attorney General
January 1968	Appointed Deputy Attorney General. On a number of occasions, also acted as Attorney General during the absence of the Attorney General
October 1970	Appointed Deputy Menteri Besar (Deputy Chief Minister)
October 1971	Appointed to the post of General Adviser to His Majesty the Sultan and Yang Di-Pertuan of Brunei Darussalam
October 1986 to the present	Appointed Special Adviser to His Majesty the Sultan and Yang Di-Pertuan of Brunei Darussalam in the Prime Minister's Office and Minister of Home Affairs

Honours and Decorations

- The Most Esteemed Family Order Laila Utama (D.K.)
- The Most Honourable Order of Seri Paduka Mahkota Brunei 1st Class (S.P.M.B.)
- The Most Blessed Order of Setia Negara Brunei 2nd Class (D.S.N.B.)
- Sultan Hassanal Bolkiah Medal (P.H.B.S.)
- Pingat Bakti Laila Ikhlas (P.B.L.I.)
- Meritorious Service Medal (P.J.K.)

PEHIN ORANG KAYA SERI UTAMA DATO SERI PADUKA AWANG HAJI YAHYA BIN BEGAWAN MUDIM DATO PADUKA HAJI BAKAR

PERMANENT SECRETARY I

PERSONAL DATA

Date of Birth : 4 May 1954
Spouse: Datin Dayang Norlina binti Dato Haji Abu Bakar
Children: 5 children: 2 sons and 3 daughters

ACADEMIC QUALIFICATIONS

1. B.A. (Hons) Economics (United Kingdom);
2. M.A. International Law and Diplomacy (United States); and,
3. Diploma in Education (Singapore).

Working Experience

1979 - 1983: Education Officer;
1983 - 1987: Administrative Officer at the Ministry of Foreign Affairs;
1987 - 1989: Deputy Director-General ASEAN, Ministry of Foreign Affairs;
1989 - 1990: Director, Economics Department, Ministry of Foreign Affairs;
1990 - 1992: Private and Confidential Secretary to His Royal Highness Prince Mohamed Bolkiah, Minister of Foreign Affairs;
1992 - Sept 1997: Senior Administrative Officer, Office of His Majesty the Sultan and Yang Di-Pertuan of Brunei Darussalam;

1 Oct 1997 to the present	: Permanent Secretary at the Prime Minister's Office;
7 July 1999 - 9 May 2004	: Also appointed as Director of the Anti Corruption Bureau in addition to the appointment as Permanent Secretary at the Prime Minister's Office

Other Positions Held In Government and Government Agencies

1. A member of the Brunei Oil and Gas Authority (BOGA) from 1 September 1998 to the present.
2. Deputy Chairman of the Board of Directors of the Brunei Investment Agency (BIA) from 16 July 1998 to the present.
3. Acting Chairman of the Board of Directors of the Brunei Investment Agency (BIA) from 22 November 2004 to the present.
4. Deputy Chairman of the Board of Directors of the Royal Brunei Airlines (RBA) Company sendirian Berhad from 7 September 1998 to the present.
5. Deputy Chairman of the Board of Directors of Brunei Shell Petroleum (BSP) Company Sendiran Berhad forom 5 September 1998 to the present.

6. Deputy Chaiman of the Board of Directors of the Brunei Liquefied Natural Gas (BLNG) Company Sendiran Berhad form 5 September 1998 to 30 July 1999.
7. Acting Chaiman of the Board of Directors of the Brunei Shell Marketing (BSM) Company Sendirian Berhad from 5 September 1998 to 30 July 1999.
8. Acting Chairman of the Board of Directors of the Brunei Shell Tanker (BST) Company Sendiran Berhad from 5 September 1998 to 30 July 1999.
9. Acting Chairman of the Board of Directors of the Brunei Gas Carriers (BGC) Company Sendirian Berhad from 5 September 1998 to 30 July 1999.
10. A member of the Board of Directors of the Semaun Holding Company Sendirian Berhad.
11. A member of the Board of Directors of the Semaunprim Company Sendirian Berhad.
12. A member of the Board of Directors of SEIWA Enterprise Sendirian Berhad.
13. A member of the Board of Directors of SEAGRO Sendirian Berhad.
14. A member of the Board of Directors of SEMAUN SEAFOOD Sendirian Berhad.

Honours and Decorations

1. Conferred the title of Pehin Orang Kaya Seri Utama on the 11 July 1996;
2. Conferred with the following Decorations and Honours:

a. The Most Honourable Order of Seri Paduka Mahkota of Brunei - First Class (SPMB) - July 1998 (carries the title Dato Seri Paduka)

b. The Most Blessed Order of Setia Negara Brunei - Second Class (DSNB) - July 1995 (Carries the title of Dato Setia);

c. The Most Honourable Order of Seri Paduka Mahkota Brunei - Third Class (SMB) - July 1994;

d. Pingat Indah Kerja Baik (PIKB) - 1989;

e. Pingat Jasa Kebaktian (PJK) - 15/2/1999;

f. Honorary Commander of the Royal Victorian Order (CVO) - 1992; and

g. Honorary Commandeur De La Legion D'Houneur - 1997.

Hobbies and Sports : Reading, Badminton.

Address :

Prime Minister's Office
Istana Nurul Iman
Bandar Seri Begawan BA1000

DIVISIONS

Corporate Affairs Division

- The Corporate Affairs Division is responsible for the general office management and day-to-day administration of the Prime Minister's Office. This includes the administration of its human resources and finance.
- The Division also provides the public relations services for the Prime Minister's Office. This includes the issuance of Government Circulars and PMO Press and News Releases.
- The Division is also responsible for the management of the Government VIP Transport Pool.

Enforcement Division

- The Enforcement Division is responsible for the development and coordination of policies relating to national security and the maintenance of law and order. This responsibility includes providing policy direction and advice to law enforcement agencies.

Economic and Finance Division

- The Economic and Finance Division is responsible for overseeing the policy relating to the country's economy and finance as well as the implementation and coordination of such Government policies as they affect the country's economy and finance.
- The responsibility of this Division includes the monitoring of the management of certain Government agencies and Government related agencies such as the Prime Minister's Corporation and the Petroleum Unit.

Public Service Division

- The Public Service Division is responsible for the management and formulation of civil service policy and policy directives for the civil service.

- The Division is also responsible for the implementation of civil service programmes in areas of human resource management and public sector reform programmes in order to achieve a productive, efficient and excellent civil service.

Development Division

- The Development Division is responsible for policy coordination in areas that relate to the national physical infrastructure. It is also responsible for monitoring the development and implementation of the National Development Plans, as well as political and other issues that relate to the plans.

- The Division is also responsible for monitoring the development and implementation of the national education system and human resource issues in Brunei Darussalam.

- The Division is also tasked with coordinating specific areas or issues such as the National Housing Schemes, public utilities and industrial standards.

Broadcasting and Information Division

- The Broadcasting and Information Division is responsible for the planning and development of policy in areas of broadcasting and information. This responsibility includes the monitoring and regulating of the local broadcasting and electronic media industries as well as regional broadcasting development and the national information infrastructure.

- The Division is also responsible for the accreditation of foreign journalists and media visiting Brunei Darussalam to conduct news/media coverage.

- In addition, this Division also issues Broadcasting Licences to firms broadcasting satellite television and radio transmissions in Brunei Darussalam.

International Affairs Division

- The International Afffairs Division of the Prime Minister's Office is responsible for coordinating the handling of policy issues and Brunei Darussalam's country positions in the international arena in line with the directives of His Majesty The Sultan and Yang Di-Pertuan of Brunei Darussalam as Head of State and Prime Minister. This responsibility includes the monitoring of international and regional developments and the country's response thereto as well as its various government agencies.

- The Division is also charged with handling congratulatory messages to heads of states from His Majesty the Sultan and Yang Di-Pertuan of Brunei Darussalam as Head of State and Prime Minister .

Social Policy Division

- The Social Policy Division is responsible for monitoring policy development and policy coordination in areas such as health care, welfare, religious affairs and state traditions and customs.

- The Division is also concerned with the coordination of specific social and other issues that concern society.

Policy Coordination and Implementation Division

- The Policy Coordination and Implementation Division is responsible for monitoring and coordinating the implementation of policies, development programmes and projects in line with His Majesty's speeches and expressed wishes.

DEPARTMENTS

In 1984, the Prime Minister's Office had 10 departments within its purview. At present, there are 17 departments, namely

- Adat Istiadat Negara (Royal Custom and Traditions)
- Audit
- Narcotics Control Bureau
- Information
- Royal Brunei Police Force
- Anti-Corruption Bureau
- Councils of State
- Radio Television Brunei
- Internal Security
- Public Service
- Management Services
- Petroleum Unit
- Public Service Commission
- State Mufti
- Judiciary
- Attorney General's Chambers
- Government Printer

ADAT ISTIADAT NEGARA (ROYAL CUSTOM AND TRADITIONS)

Established On 1 July, 1954 as the department which was known as The Adat Istiadat Negara, Religious and Public Welfare Department which was placed in the main Office of The State Secretary Building (now known as The Secretariat Building). The establishment was approved by the general order of His Majesty the Maulana Al-Sultan Omar Ali Saifuddien Sa'adul Khairi Waddien (now known as Al-Marhum Sultan Haji Omar Ali Saifuddien Sa'adul Khairi Waddien) who appointed Pengiran Pemancha Sahibul Ra'e Wal Mashuarah Pengiran Muda Haji Mohamed Alam as the Adat Istiadat, Religious and Public Welfare Officer.

By 29 September, 1959 with the establishment of Religious Department, the former was known as The Adat Istiadat and Public Welfare Department. In 1962, Public Welfare Department formed it's own department and this made The Adat Istiadat Department run individually under the former head. In 1968 The Adat

Istiadat Department moved to the Lapau Building.

Since first established, The Adat Istiadat Department has been given priority to direct access to His Majesty Sultan and Yang Di-Pertuan of Negara Brunei Darussalam on matters concerning the conferment of state honours on individuals.

AUDIT DEPARTMENT

Profile of Auditor General

Name	**Dato Paduka Haji Abdul Kani bin Haji Mohd Salleh**
Appointment as Auditor General	Acting Auditor General from 23 November 1996 to 1 June 1997, and confirmed as Auditor General on 2 June 1997
Qualification	BSc (Mechanical Engineering) MSc (Petroleum Reservoir) - Imperial College of Science & Technology, London ACGI (Associate of the City and Guilds Institute of London
Work Experience	Production Engineer, Reservoir Engineer (Brunei Shell, 1975 - 1982) Director of Petroleum Unit (1983 - 1992) Special Duties Officer (Prime Minister's Office, 1992 - 1996)

Appointment of Auditor General

	The Constitution of Brunei Darussalam Sec. 66:
66(1)	The Auditor General is appointed by His Majesty the Sultan and Yang DiPertuan of Negara Brunei Darussalam.
66(3)	The Auditor General of Brunei Darussalam may at any time resign his office, but shall not be removed from his office except in the like grounds and in the like manner as a member of the Public Service Commission.
	[The constitution of Brunei Darussalam Sec. 71(b)
	A member of the Public Service Commission shall only be removed from his office for inability to perform the functions of his office (whether arising from

	infirmity of body or mind or any other cause) or for misbehaviour, and shall not be so removed unless his case has been investigated by a person who holds or has held high judicial office in Brunei Darussalam or in any part of the Commonwealth, nominated for that purpose by His Majesty the Sultan and Yang DiPertuan, and that person has recommended that he should be removed.]

Audit Reports

The constitution of Brunei Darussalam Section 68 and Audit Act Chapter 152, Setion 9:

9(7) The Auditor General may at any time submit a report to His Majesty the Sultan and Yang DiPertuan

THE NARCOTICS CONTROL BUREAU

The Narcotics Control Bureau is a government department under the Prime Minister's Office. It was set up on 1st October 1988 specifically to take over the responsibilities of enforcing relevant drug laws in Brunei Darussalam from the Royal Brunei Police Force and the Preventive Drug Education activities from the Anti Drug Unit which was under the purview of the Ministry of Education.

The first Director was Dato Seri Laila Jasa Haji Ahmad bin Dato Paduka Matnor, who was then succeeded by Awang Haji Momin bin Haji Sawal on 1st November 1992.

The first office was in Jalan Sumbiling, Bandar Seri Begawan and later moved to Jalan Rakis Berakas. In May 1995, the office moved to Jalan Tungku Gadong. The department has branches in Kuala Belait and Tutong.

BRUNEI INFORMATION SERVICE

Brunei Information Service was the original designated name for the Information Department, when it was mooted on April 1st, 1952.

It started with a staff of 16 including an Assistant Information Officer, Pengiran Mohd Yusof bin Pengiran Abd Rahman (now known as Yang Amat Mulia Pengiran Setia Negara Pengiran Hj Mohd Yusof) as head of the department.

In the early period, the Brunei Information Service provided entertainment and information with the screening of films in Malay and English obtained from the Central Office of Information, London. Apart from these, films on Medical and Health were shown throughout the State. In 1954, 4 documentary films were produced locally, namely His Majesty Birthday Celebration, Ear Piercing Ceremony of the Royal Princess, Prophet Mohamad S.A.W. birthday celebration and landing of the first aircraft at Berakas Airport.

It also supplied photographs for use by local newspapers. Some photographs were also meant for display at the Information Reading Room largely patronised by schoolchildren from rural areas.

In providing service to the public, cars equipped with public addressing system were used to inform the public on such matters as healthy food, football matches and school sports day.

The Information Branch in the Belait District and the Information Reading Room were established in 1954.

In 1956, the first issue of Pelita Brunei, the official government newspaper was published fortnightly in cyclostyle form.

The Information Reading Room was established in Pekan Bangar, Temburong District in 1957, and in Tutong District the following year.

With the establishment of Radio Brunei Service in 1957, Information Service gave the public subsidy to buy radios by monthly instalments for one year. In 1958, the Information Service sold 1,048 sets of radio throughout the State.

In February, 1959 Pelita Brunei after going through several changes started the use of printing machines for the first time.

In March 1960, a monthly English Language publication entitled "Brunei (The Abode of Peace)" was published containing events of the month. It has a circulation of 500 copies for overseas distribution.

In 1961, Brunei Information Service and Radio Brunei Service were merged and later known as Broadcasting and Information Department.

The Broadcasting and Information Department were separated into two entities in June 1975, whereby Information was designated as Information Division and was put under the jurisdiction of the State Secretariat Office.

The status of the Information Division was later upgraded and it become the Information Department in 1983. The Information Department was under the jurisdiction of the Ministry of Culture, Youth and Sport as of 1st January 1984.

The Information Department and Radio Television Brunei were merged and later known as Broadcasting and Information Department on 1st December 1985.

On 20th October 1986, the Broadcasting and Information Department was under the wing of the Prime Minister's Office.

However, on 1st March 1991, the Broadcasting and Information Department was separated to two departments, and Information become the Information Department and it is under the charge of the Prime Minister's Office.

POLICE DEPARTMENT

Mission

To maintain law and order in accordance with the powers conferred by any written law of the land in the most professional manner.

Targets & Objectives

- To minimise the number of transgression against the law.
- To maximise the detection of criminal activities and the conviction of criminals.
- Ready to respond against public and societal needs.
- Immediate restoration of public order and safety following disruptive incidents.
- To enhance police professionalism through proper training of officers and personnel.
- To increase community involvement in fighting crime and transgression of national laws.
- To project a friendly, caring and approachable image of the institution.
- To maximise educational programmes for the general public relating to traffic rules and regulations.
- To maintain and carry all resolutions passed and adopted by the ASEANAPOL Conference and the INTERPOL General Assembly.
- To maintain good liaison with other law enforcement agencies and Government Departments.

Strategies

- Upgrading of qualification
- Sense of commitment
- Dedication
- High moral values
- High degree of professionalism
- Knowledgeable
- Discipline
- Rights to be trained

Administrative Modernisation

- Review of salary structures / allowances
- Review of terms and conditions of employment

- Revision of training modules
- Restructuring of badges of rank
- Personnel Information System
- Paperless bureaucracy
- Empowerment
- Career Planning System
- Dynamic Recruitment Policy
- Use of e-mail

ANTI-CORRUPTION BUREAU OFFICES

Anti-Corruption Bureau
Old Airport Road
Berakas BB 3510
Brunei Darussalam
Tel: 02-383575 / 02-383197

Anti-Corruption Bureau
Kuala Belait Branch
Jalan Sungai Pandan
Kuala Belait KA 1931
Negara Brunei Darussalam
Tel: 03-331560

Head Office

02-382395 (Direct line) or 08-810436 (Mobile)

Kuala Belait Branch

03-331513 (Direct line) or 08-813643 (Mobile)

Please forward your question/ suggestion to us at the above addresses/ telephone numbers or send to our e-mail address:

info_bmr@mail.gov.bn

COUNSILS OF STATE

As stipulated in the 1959 Constitution of Brunei Darussalam, there shall be three Councils which are handled by this Department namely:-

a. The Privy Council - Section 5(1);
b. The Executive/Ministers' Council - Section 10; and
c. The Legislative Council - Section 23.

a. Structure of the Privy Council

The establishment of the Council is in accordance with the requirement of Section 5(1) of 1959 Constitution of Brunei Darussalam, whose members consist of:

i. Ex-Officio Members i.e the Wazirs and 11 Cabinet Ministers; and
ii. Appointed Members.

Their tenure of membership is only during the pleasure of His Majesty Paduka Seri Baginda Sultan and Yang Di-Pertuan who presides at meetings of the Privy Council.

b. The Council of Ministers

The Council of Ministers is established in accordance with Section 10 of the 1959 Constitution. The existing membership is as follows:

1. Prime Minister
2. Minister of Defence
3. Minister of Finance
4. Minister of Foreign Affairs
5. Minister of Home Affairs
6. Minister of Education
7. Minister of Industry and Primary Resources
8. Minister of Religious Affairs
9. Minister of Development
10. Minister of Culture, Youth and Sports
11. Minister of Health
12. Minister of Communications

The Council of Cabinet Ministers meet regularly and is presided over by His Majesty Paduka Seri Baginda Sultan and Yang Di-Pertuan.

c. The Legislative Council

The Legislative Council is established in accordance with Section 23 of the 1959 Constitution of Brunei Darussalam and its Members shall be appointed in accordance with Section 24. Until today the Legislative Council is not reconstituted following its dissolution in 1984 in view of the Section relating to its formation being suspended.

MEMBERS OF THE COUNCIL OF CABINET MINISTERS

Chairman

His Majesty,
Paduka Seri Baginda Sultan Haji Hassanal Bolkiah Mu'izzaddin Waddaulah

ibni Al-Marhum Sultan Haji Omar 'Ali Saifuddien Sa'adul Khairi Waddien, Sultan dan Yang Di-Pertuan Negara Brunei Darussalam, Prime Minister, Minister of Defence, Minister of Finance, Brunei Darussalam

1. Duli Yang Teramat Mulia,
   Paduka Seri Pengiran Perdana Wazir Sahibul Himmah Wal-Waqar Pengiran Muda Mohamed Bolkiah ibni Al-Marhum Sultan Haji Omar 'Ali Saifuddien Sa'adul Khairi Waddien, DKMB., DK., PHBS., PBLI., PJK.,
   Minister of Foreign Affairs,
   Brunei Darussalam

2. Yang Berhormat,
   Pehin Orang Kaya Laila Setia Bakti Diraja
   Dato Laila Utama Haji Awang Isa bin Pehin Datu
   Perdana Manteri Dato Laila Utama Haji Awang Ibrahim,
   DK., SPMB., DSNB., PHBS., PBLI., PJK.,
   Special Adviser to His Majesty The Sultan and Yang Di-Pertuan in the Prime Minister's Office and Minister of Home Affairs,
   Brunei Darussalam.

3. Yang Berhormat,
   Pehin Orang Kaya Laila Wijaya Dato Seri Setia
   Haji Awang Abdul Aziz bin Begawan Pehin
   Udana Khatib Dato Seri Paduka Haji Awang Umar,
   PSNB., DPMB., SLJ., PJK.,
   Minister of Education and Acting Minister of Health,
   Brunei Darussalam.

4. Yang Berhormat,
   Pehin Orang Kaya Setia Pahlawan Dato Seri
   Setia Haji Awang Abdul Rahman bin Dato Setia
   Haji Mohamed Taib,
   PSNB., SLJ., PHBS, PJK.,
   Minister of Industry and Primary Resources,
   Brunei Darussalam.

5. Yang Berhormat,
   Pehin Jawatan Luar Pekerma Raja Dato Seri Utama
   Dr. Ustaz Haji Awang Mohd. Zain bin Haji
   Serudin, DK, PSSUB., DSLJ., PHBS., PJK.,
   Minister of Religious Affairs,
   Brunei Darussalam.

6. Yang Amat Mulia,
   Pengiran Indera Wijaya Pengiran Dr. Haji Ismail
   bin Pengiran Haji Damit, PSNB., SPMB., DSLJ., PJK.,

Minister of Development,
Brunei Darussalam.

7. Yang Berhormat,
Pehin Orang Kaya Digadong Seri Lela Dato Seri
Paduka Haji Awang Hussein bin Pehin Orang Kaya
Digadong Seri Diraja Dato Laila Utama Haji
Awang Mohd. Yusof, SPMB., DSNB., PHBS., PJK.,
Minister of Culture, Youth and Sports,
Brunei Darussalam.

8. Yang Berhormat,
Pehin Orang Kaya Amar Pahlawan Dato Seri Setia
Awang Haji Zakaria bin Datu Mahawangsa Haji
Sulaiman, PSNB., DSLJ., PHBS., PJK.,
Minister of Communications,
Brunei Darussalam.

ANTI CORRAPTION BUREAU

A Brief History of The ACB

On January 1, 1982, the Government of His Majesty the Sultan and Yang Di Pertuan of Brunei Darussalam had enforced the Emergency (Prevention of Corruption) Act, which was subsequently in 1984 known as the Prevention of Corruption Act (Chapter 131). For the purpose of enforcing the said enactment, an independent body was established called the Anti-Corruption Bureau (ACB) on February 1, 1982.

Under the provision of Section 3 of the Act, His Majesty the Sultan and Yang Di Pertuan of Brunei Darussalam shall appoint a Director who will be responsible for the direction and administration of the Bureau. The act also stated that the Director of ACB is not subject to any other person apart from His Majesty the Sultan and Yang Di Pertuan of Brunei Darussalam.

The Prevention of Corruption Act provides specific powers to the ACB for the purpose of investigating into complaints against corruption. The Act also provides power for ACB to investigate into certain offences under the Penal Code and offences under other written laws, provided such offences were disclosed during the course of ACB investigation into offences under the Prevention of Corruption Act.

A SYNOPSIS OF THE PREVENTION OF CORRUPTION ACT

Part I
Preliminary

1.		Citation and commencement.
2.	(a)-(h)	Interpretation:-. agent, bureau, Director, gratification, officer of the bureau, prescribed offences, principal, public body.
Part II		
3.	(1)-(5)	Appoinment of Director and officers of the ACB.
4.	(1)-(2)	Officers of the Bureau are deemed to be Public Servants.
Part III		
5.	(a)-(b) (i)-(ii)	Punishment of corruption, include solicitation, inducement, agree to give, promise to give gratification.
6.	(a)-(c)	Punishment for corrupt transaction involving agent / agents.
7.		Increase in maximum penalty in certain cases.
8.	(1)-(2)	Acceptor of gratification deemed to be guilty notwithstanding that the purpose for which the gratification was given / accepted was not carried out.
9.	(a)-(b)	Corruptly cause or procure the withdrawal of tenders.
10.		Bribery involving members of the legislature.
11.	(a)-(d)	Bribery of members of the public body.
12.	(1)-(2) (a)-(b)	Offences for possession of unexplained property or maintaining a standard of living above that which is commensurate with his past or present emoluments.
13.	(a)-(b)	Abatement of offences.
14.		Attempts to commit the offence.
15.		Offence of conspiracy to commit offences under the Prevention of Corruption Act. (PCA).
16.		Legal obligation of public officer to whom a gratification is given or offered to report such incident failing which, he shall be liable to a fine not exceeding $500.00 or six months imprisonment or both.
17.		When penalty to be imposed in addition to other punishment.
Part IV		
Powers Of Investigation		
18.	(1)-(3)	Power of making an arrest without warrant.
19.	(a)-(c)	Powers of Investigation.

20.	(1)(a)-(b) (2)(a)-(b)	Powers of search and to obtain assistance.
21.	(1)-(3)	Further powers of search and sizeure.
22.		Legal Obligation for members of the public to give information.
23.	(1)(a)-(b) (2)-(5)	Special powers of investigation. Inspection into shares, bank accounts, investment accounts, safe deposit box, bank statement. The offence of hindering the provision of the act.
24.	(1)-(3)	Legal Advisers and privileged information.
25.		Presumption of corruption in certain cases.
26.		Evidence of custom, as inadmissable.
27.	(1)(a)-(b) (2)	Evidence of pecuniary resources or property.
28.		Evidence of accomplice.
29.	(1)-(3)	Examination of offenders
30.	(1)-(3)	Protection for informers. Informers shall be protected from having their identity being disclosed unless such information were subsequently deemed by the court to be false and malicious in nature.
Part VI		
Prosecution And Trial of Offences.		
31.	(1)(2)(3)	Prosecution of offences.
32.	(1)(2)	The Magistrate Court has jurisdiction to try offences under this act.
Part VII		
Miscellaneous		
33.		Frivolous, false or groundless complaints to be reported to the Public Prosector. Where at the close of a legal proceeding, the magistrate has discovered that such had occurred, he shall cause a report to be transmitted to the Public Prosecutor for his appropriate action.
34.	(a)(b)	Offences of making false, misleading report to the Director and officers of the Anti- Corruption Bureau.
35.		Offences to disclose the identity of person being investigated or the result of such investigation.
36.	(1)(2)	Alternative convictions and ammendments of particulars in the preferred charges against the accused person.
37.		Liability of the citizens of Brunei Darussalam for offences committed overseas.

38.		Offences under this Act are deemed to be seizeable offences.
39.	(1)-(2)	The principal may recover any amount of secret gifts of which was the gratification given by the agent.
40.		Application Order. The Retrospective effect of this Act. Where an offence under this Act was committed before the commencement of the act shall be liable for prosecution, and where there are conviction the offender shall be sentenced accordingly.

RADIO TV BUREAU

The management of RTB is headed by a director, assisted by a deputy director and a group of senior officers heading various divisions namely Engineering; Administration; Programmes; News; Current Affairs & Sports; Enterprise; Research & Development and Public & International Relations.

Its operational budget including cost of manpower is more than $30 million Brunei dollars.

Organisation Chart

DIRECTOR

Deputy Director					
|	|	|	|	|	|
Head of Engineering	Head of Administration/ Finance	Head of News Current Affairs and Sports	Head of Programmes	Head of Research & Development	Head of Radio

BRUNEI INTERNAL SECURITY DEPARTMENT (BISD)

Brunei Internal Security Department (BISD) was set up on 1st August 1993 and was fully operational on 1st November 1993. BISD is one of the departments under the Prime Minister's Office with the main office located at Tumasek Plaza while three branch offices are located in Kuala Belait, Tutong and Temburong.

BISD's goal is to give an early warning to the Government of any imminent threats. By doing so the Government hopefully would be able to take necessary precautions either to avoid or reduce the harm caused by such threats.

TASKS

- To identify the various threats and their sources.

- To collect information.
- To assess the information.

BISD's role is monitoring and reporting to the Government on internal security issues. For BISD, 'security' means the protection from harm caused by:

- **Espionage :** Espionage is defined as an "attempt to acquire government classified information illegally in order to assist a foreign power or government or to further a subversive aim". A subversive aim means either to undermine or embarrass the Government or to pass on damaging information to a foreign country.
- Politically motivated violence.
- **Sabotage** : sabotage is defined as "an act (or an ommission), intended to cause physical damage to plants, buildings, equipment or other targets, whether civil or military, in order to assist a foreign power to further a political aim".
- **Terrorism :** that is the use of violence and intimidation in the furtherance of a political aim.
- **Promotion of a racial and religious violence**

BRANCHES	ADDRESSES	TELEPHONE
BISD HQ	Tumasek Plaza, Jln Tutong, BSB BA1910 Negara Brunei Darussalam	673-2-242780
Tutong District	No.22, PWD Rumah Kerajaan Sungai Basung, Tutong TA1541 Negara Brunei Darussalam	673-4-222074
Belait District	No 90, Simpang 27 Jln Maulana, Kuala Belait KA2931 Negara Brunei Darussalam	673-3-340308
Temburong District	No.99, Rumah Kelas 'B' PWD, Pekan Bangar Baru PA 1751 Negara Brunei Darussalam	673-5-221872

PUBLIC SERVICE DEPARTMENT

1st July 1971	Established as a section in the office of the State Secretary and headed by an establishment officer. The main function of the section was to handle and manage matters pertaining to the administration of the Public Service personnel.
1st January 1976	The section was upgraded as a full fledge department, headed by the Director of Establishment.

1st January 1984	When Brunei Darussalam gained her independence, the Establishment Department was then placed under the Prime Minister's Office.
March 1992	The department reviewed its organisational structure to better serve the needs of the public services.
1st May 1993	The Establishment Department was renamed as the Public Service Department and its head was upgraded to the Status of the Director General.

CORE FUNCTIONS

i. Planning

Formulating, planning and coordinating Human Resource policies and needs in line with the aspirations of the Public Service and the Nation.

ii. Development

Providing an efficient, effective and competent human resource to serve the needs of the Public Service.

iii. Personnel Management Support

Formulating, administering and advising the implementation of policies, strategies, rules and regulations relating to human resource management in the Public Service.

MANAGEMENT SERVICE

This department is set up to help the Government to enhance the effectiveness, efficiency and performance of service delivery to the public by the civil service. This is achieved by providing quality consultancy/advisory service, research and support services.

Vision
To become an institution of quality and excellence with the thrust to be efficient, responsive, innovative and accountable.

Mission
To enhance effectiveness, efficiency and performance of service delivery to the public by providing quality consultancy / advisory services, research and support services to the civil service.

Objectives

- To reduce government expenditure;
- Enhance the quality of service delivery;
- Enhance management performance, efficiency and effectiveness;
- Enhance quality and productivity; and
- Monitoring the implementation of client's charter

Main Role / Function

- Change-agent / Prime-mover
- Management Consultant
- Facilitator
- Advisor

Modus Operandi

- Permanent Secretary of Prime Minister's Office.
- Ministries' / Departments' requests.
- Requests / directions of Civil Service Review Committee and other Committees where MSD acts as secretary / secretariat.
- Department's own initatives.

Division / Scope of Work

The Department is divided into 4 divisions as follows :

1. **Management Policy Division**
   To study and formulate management policies and programmes towards improvement and innovation with the objective to enhance efficiency, productivity and effectiveness of the whole civil service.
2. **Organisational Development Division**
   To study and review organisation to ensure that it can function efficiently and effectively towards achieving its set goals and objectives.
3. **Management System Development Division**
   To study, review and develop programmes / strategies / projects / pertaining to productivity / systems / processes / procedures towards enhancing performance and productivity of the civil service.
4. **Administration Division**
   Handling administrative, staffs welfare and financial matters as well as provide assistance to the various divisions on the departmental administrative matters.

Membership

The Department is also members in the following bodies :

- Commonwealth Association for Public Administration and Management (CAPAM);
- ASEAN Conference on Civil Service Matters (ACCSM);
- Civil Service Review Committee (CSR);
- General Orders Review Committee;
- Civil Service Day;
    - Civil Service Excellence Award
    - Ad Hoc Committee on Public Administrations
    - Performance Appraisal Research committee in the public service
    - Human Resource Development Committee

History

1st January 1982	Management Services Unit was formed as a unit in the Establishment Department.
1st September 1986	Management Services Unit was separated from the Establishment Department and were placed in the Prime Minister's Office as one of the divisions within the Ministry itself.
1st January 1990	The tasks and responsibilities of the Government Security Department of the Ministry of Home Affairs were transferred to the Management Services Unit of the Prime Minister's Office. Since then, Management Services Unit of the Prime Minister's Office was upgraded to become a full pledged department later known as Management Services and Government Security Department.
1st August 1993	Internal Security Department was formed simultaneously, the responsibilities and functions of the Government Security Unit of the Management Services and Government Security Department was incorporated into the newly-formed department. In line with such development, Management Services and Government Security Department has changed its name to Management Services Department of the Prime Minister's Office.

Contact

Management Services Department
Block C
Audit Department
Petroleum's Unit and Management Services
Departments's Building
Jalan Menteri Besar
Bandar Seri Begawan BB3910
Negara Brunei Darussalam

Tel : 673-02-382064 / 382065 / 382066
Facsimile : 673-02-382062
Email : msd@brunet.bn
Website address : www.msd.gov.bn

Publications

Over the years, the Department has managed to publish the following guides, pamphlets and operational manuals for the benefit of the civil service staffs.

- A guide on Filing System;
- A Book entitled "Usaha Memperkembangkan Perkhidmatan Awam: Satu Tinjauan";
- A guide on Courtesy: "Panduan Ke arah Penerapan Budaya Bersopan Santun";
- Guidelines on Civil Service Excellence Award (in the process of printing);
- A compilation of Civil Service Excellence Award Projects 1993 & 1994;
- A compilation of Civil Service Excellence Award Projects 1995, 1996 & 1997;
- A guide on Negara Brunei Darussalam's Civil Service Performance Appraisal Systems;
- Civil Service Vision in the 21st Century;
- A guide on Client's Charter;
- Recovery System "Tekad Pemedulian Orang Ramai", Management Services Department;
- Guidelines on drafting the ACCSM Country Paper;
- Guidelines on drafting the ACCSM Position Paper;
- Guidelines on drafting the ACCSM Technical Paper;
- Guidelines on drafting the ACCSM Project Proposal;
- Guidelines on drafting the ACCSM Report;
- Guidelines on drafting the Working Paper to be submitted to the Civil Service Review Committee;
- Guidelines on drafting minute of the Civil Service Review Committee.

THE PETROLEUM UNIT

The Petroleum Unit, established on 15th June 1982, was initially under the State Secretariat and was known as the Oil Unit. Since its establishment, the Petroleum Unit has been entrusted with increasing responsibilities in its work scope. The Petroleum Unit is headed by a Director and assisted by a Deputy Director. At present there are just under 100 personnel in the Petroleum Unit, of whom more than half are graduate officers from various disciplines, e.g., engineering, finance, economics, legal, human resource management, etc.

On 1st January 1993, an important milestone was reached in Brunei's oil and gas history when the Brunei Oil and Gas Authority (BOGA) was created. BOGA's role is to advise and provide recommendations to His Majesty the

Sultan and Yang Di-Pertuan of Negara Brunei Darussalam on all matters pertaining to oil and gas including policies and their implementations. Currently BOGA is chaired by Yang Berhormat Pehin Orang Kaya Setia Pahlawan Dato Seri Setia Awang Haji Abdul Rahman bin Dato Setia Awang Mohd Taib. The Petroleum Unit is the Secretariat to BOGA with the Director of the Petroleum Unit appointed as its Chief Executive Officer and main spokesperson.

Enquiries

The Petroleum Unit welcomes enquiries relating to the petroleum activities and opportunities in Brunei Darussalam. Enquiries must be made in writing to the Director of the Petroleum Unit at the following postal address:

The Petroleum Unit
Office of the Prime Minister
Bahirah Building
Jalan Menteri Besar
Brunei Darussalam BB3910.

Telephone: 673-2-387 102
Facsimile: 673-2-383 004
E-Mail: brupet@brunet.bn

Mission

To ensure that all natural resources - especially oil, natural gas and coal are prudently exploited for the benefit of the nation.

Aims

- Continually develop an organisation with up to date knowledge and expertise in technical and management skills
- Oversee that oil and gas production is prudently exercised so that reserve life will be prolonged whilst concurrently promoting the development of downstream industries
- Fix the price level for Brunei Darussalam's crude oil
- Encourage International Oil Companies to invest in Brunei Darussalam
- Update petroleum laws and mining agreements
- Ensure Brunei oil and gas prices are comparable with world market prices

- Promote the commitments and involvement of Bruneians at all levels of oil and gas related activities
- Ensure that all oil companies adhere to internationally accepted standard on technical, accounting and health, safety and environment matters

DOMESTIC & INTERNATIONAL INVOLVEMENT

Domestic

- Responsible for all matters relating to the relationship between the Government and existing and potential concessionaires, and for ensuring that all activities carried out are within the terms and conditions agreed
- Ensure that all oil and gas activities follow current internationally accepted standards
- Oversee budget spending and work programmes of concessionaires are in accordance with agreed terms and conditions, and productions are carried out cost-effectively
- Advise and update government representatives in the Board of Directors of Brunei Shell Companies of important development in the said group of companies
- Function as the Secretariat for the Committee to review the draft of Brunei Production Sharing Contract
- Carry out specific tasks as required by the Government, e.g., involvement in Brunei Gas Carriers Sendirian Berhad, a joint-venture company set up to build and own a LNG Ship, and scheduled to come into service with Brunei LNG Sendirian Berhad in mid 2002

International

- Represent Brunei Darussalam as a Member of ASEAN Council of Petroleum (ASCOPE). Other ASCOPE members are Petronas (Malaysia), Pertamina (Indonesia), PNOC (Philippines), PTT (Thailand), SPC (Singapore) and Petro-Vietnam (Vietnam).
- Represent the Government in meetings and negotiations between Brunei LNG Sdn. Bhd. and Japanese buyers, and between BLNG and South Korean Buyers.
- Participate and represent the Government in international Petroleum Industry-related meetings.

OIL & GAS ACTIVITIES & OPPORTUNITIES

UPSTREAM ACTIVITIES

Concession Areas

The Petroleum Unit, on behalf of the Government of His Majesty the Sultan and Yang Di-Pertuan of Brunei Darussalam, controls and oversees all activities that are carried out by concessionaires in relation to their concessions. At present, a total area of 11,000 square kilometres is being held by two concessionaires.

One of the concessionaires, Brunei Shell Petroleum, is a company jointly owned by the Government of His Majesty the Sultan and Yang Di-Pertuan of Negara Brunei Darussalam and Royal Dutch Shell.

Conservation Policy

Beginning 1981, Brunei Darussalam introduced a conservation policy whereby production was gradually reduced from a peak of 261,000 barrel per day (bpd) to 150,000 bpd. The said conservation level was reached in 1988.

Export Destinations

Brunei crude oil is exported to various countries including several ASEAN countries, e.g., Indonesia, Singapore and Thailand. In year 2004, Thailand is the main export destination for Brunei Darussalam crude oil, i.e., 31.38% from the overall export. This is followed by Japan (17.73%), South Korea (14.66%), U.S.A (10.75%), Australia (8.75%), India (6.24%), Singapore (5.25 %), New Zealand (2.25 %), China (2.12 %) and Indonesia (0.86%).

Open Areas

There are currently more than 38,229 sq. km. of open areas available for future exploration activities. These areas, divided into blocks, include the Brunei Muara, Tutong, Temburong, rural area of Belait District and several areas of Brunei water up to 200 nautical miles within the Brunei Exclusive Economic Zone.

DOWNSTREAM ACTIVITIES

Oil Refinery

The Seria Oil Refinery, operated by Brunei Shell Petroleum and situated at the oil town of Seria in the Belait District, has a production capacity of 10 000 bpd each for its Crude Distillation Unit (CDU) and Reformer unit. This refinery produces unleaded motor gasoline, gasoil, Jet A1, and Kerosene.

LNG Plant

Natural gas produced from Brunei oil fields is exported as liquefied natural gas (LNG) to three buyers in Japan namely Tokyo Gas, Tokyo Electric, and Osaka Gas and one buyer from South Korea, Korea gas Corporation. The LNG is processed at Brunei LNG Sdn. Bhd. Plant at Lumut, Seria. In year 2004, LNG exports amounted to 192 'B-Class' cargoes where 88.48% are exported to Japan and the rest (11.52%) are exported to South Korea.

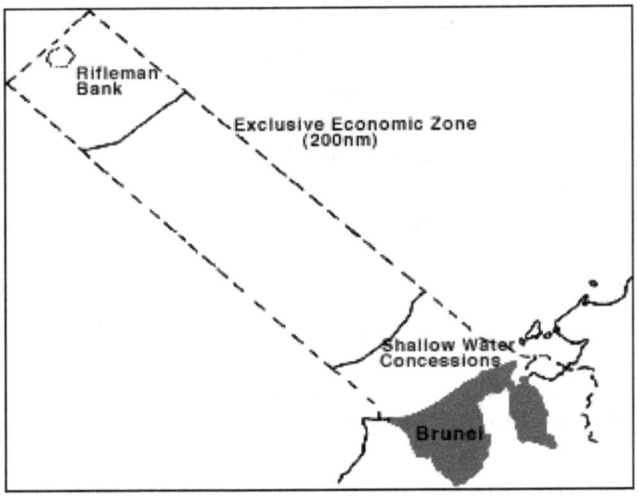

Brunei Export Oriented Refinery

The Government of His Majesty the Sultan and Yang Di-Pertuan of Negara Brunei Darussalam, through the Petroleum Unit, is actively promoting the setting up of export oriented oil refineries in the country. Several studies, made under Memorandum of Understanding between His Majesty Government and international consortiums are currently being carried out to study the feasibility of producing petrochemical by-products for exports to other countries in the region.

PUBLIC SERVICE COMMISSION (PSC)

Public Service Commission (PSC) is an independent body formed on 1st January, 1962, in accordance with Section 71(1) of Brunei Constitution 1959.

MISSION

TOWARDS EXCELLENCE AND FAIRNESS IN THE PUBLIC SERVICE.

JURISDICTION

The Public Service Commission is responsible to submit to His Majesty Paduka Seri Baginda Sultan and Yang Di-Pertuan of Brunei Darussalam matters on the appointments, transfers, promotions, dismissal or disciplinary action of the Public Service officers within its jurisdiction and in accordance with General Orders.

MEMBERS OF PSC

The Chairman, Deputy Chairman, six Members and a Secretary are appointed by His Majesty Paduka Seri Baginda Sultan and Yang Di-Pertuan of Brunei Darussalam.

OBJECTIVE

The objective of the public service commission is to provide and ensure that the public service has the right number and quality of staff to meet the developmental needs of Brunei Darussalam by providing efficient, effective and impartial services.

ORGANISATIONAL SRUCTURE OF PSC

Public Service Commission is assisted by a secretariat consisting a Secretary and more than 130 officers and staff. The secretariat is also responsible for the Public Officers' In-Service Training committee.

Effective from 1st January 1997, His Majesty Paduka Seri Baginda Sultan and Yang Di-Pertuan of Brunei Darussalam consented the PSC new organisational (Personnel) structure.

PSC Organisational Chart

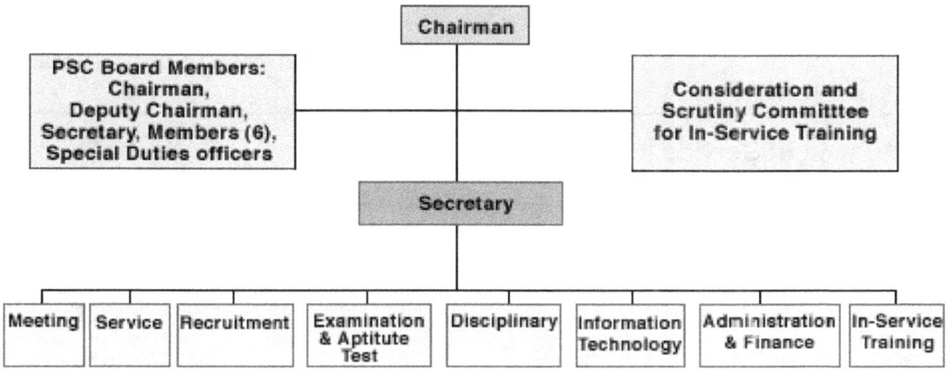

CONTACT

Extension to Sections: Tel: 673-2-381961

Any enquiries regarding:

JOB APPLICATION, please contact

Recruitment Section,
2nd Floor
Tel No: 673-02-381961 ext. 588
Fax No: 673-02-382160

EXAMINATIONS / TESTS, please contact

Examination and Test Section,
2nd Floor
Tel No: 673-02-381961 ext. 561

CORRESPONDENCE

Please address to:

Secretary of the Public Service Commission
Old Airport
Bandar Seri Begawan BB3510
Negara Brunei Darussalam

E-MAIL
Secretary PSC: sectspa@brunet.bn
Recruitment Section: blpspa@brunet.bn

FAX NO: 673-2-382772

SERVICE SECTION		
NO.	DECISION	TIME OF COMPLETION (w.e.f the receipt of full-details from PSD)
1.	Continuation of Service (month to month / Contract)	2 - 3 weeks
2.	Acting Appointment	2 - 3 weeks
3.	Re-engagement after retirement	2 - 3 weeks
4.	Re-engagement after marriage	2 - 3 weeks
5.	Confirmation of Appointment	2 - 3 weeks
6.	Extension of probationary period	2 - 3 weeks
7.	Changes in the terms of appointment	2 - 3 weeks
8.	Appeal on salary	4 - 6 weeks
9.	Promotion	4 - 8 weeks
10.	Appointment on 'Open Vote' service	4 - 8 weeks

RECRUITMENT SECTION (APPLICATION FOR POST)			
NO.	SUBJECT	DECISION	DURATION FOR REPLY BY PSC
1.	Advertisement Regulation 7(a)	Not succesful for test / interview	4 weeks after closing date
2.	Advertisement Regulation 38(a) and 38(b)	Not succesful for test / interview	3 weeks after receipt from Department / Ministry
3.	Scholarship Student	Not succesful for test / interview	2 weeks - 2 months after receipt of recommendation from PSD
	As in Nos (1) & (2) above	Not sucessful after test	2 - 3 weeks after the test date
	As in Nos (1), (2) & (3) above	Not successful after interview	4 weeks - 3 months after the last date of local / overseas interview
	As in Nos (1), (2) & (3) above	Succesful	4 weeks to 3 months after the last date of local / overseas interview

DISCIPLINARY SECTION	
SUBJECT	TIME OF COMPLETION BY PSC
Decision on recommendation for disciplinary action	1 - 3 months after receipt of necessary information and recommendation from PSD

IN-SERVICE TRAINING SECTION	
SUBJECT	TIME OF COMPLETION BY PSC
Decision on recommendation for an officer to undergo in-service training	1 month after receipt of necessary information and recommendation from PSD

MINISTRY OF DEVELOPMENT

The Ministry of Development has been entrusted the task of providing the necessary foundation for the continuous growth of the nation while still upholding the basic tenets of a Malay Islamic Monarchy. Thus in its efforts to serve the society of Brunei Darussalam, it upholds the sovereignty of the Monarchy and practises Islamic values and Malay culture.

In addition, the Ministry also aligns itself with the economic direction outlined for the country through the promotion of the construction industry as a viable alternative economic sector to the oil and gas industries and assisting local entrepreneurs to achieve success in their business endeavours. This thrust will eventually bear fruit in the formation of a strong Bruneian business entity that can lead the country into the next millennium as an international force to reckon with.

In carrying out its role, the Ministry equips itself with the latest cutting-edge technology and resources. It strives to raise the skills and expertise of the local workforce through constant training and upgrading. With the latest equipment and highly efficient human resources, greater levels of productivity and quality can be achieved.

While promoting constant development in the country, environmental conservation is not forsaken. In fact, it is one of the principles to which the Ministry adheres in any development project it undertakes. The environment is one of the vital assets of the country which must be religiously preserved.

The Ministry consists of 6 units and 13 departments which provide a wide range of services ranging from training of human resource to laying down basic infrastructure such as roads, drainage and sewerage facilities and providing utilities services. In line with its motto which clearly expresses its discipline and commitment, the officers and staff of the Ministry of Development are always ready to provide the highest quality of service and consumer satisfaction to the public.

THE INVESTMENT INCENTIVES ACT (CAP. 97)

The Act which is administered by the Economic Development Board offers incentives in the form of tax exemption under the following headings:

Incentives for Expansion of Established Enterprises

The Economic Development Board may declare any industry to be an Approved Industry and Products if the Board is satisfied that:

1. The increased manufacture of the product would be of economic benefit to Brunei Darussalam.
2. It is expedient in the public interest to do so.

Any company intending to incur new capital expenditure for the purpose of the manufacture or increased manufacture of an Approved Product may apply to the Economic Development Board for an Expansion Certificate.

To qualify for an Expansion Certificate, the company must incur new capital expenditure in the purchase of productive equipment exceeding B$1 million or not less than B$100,000 and will result in an increase of not less than 30% in value at original cost of all the productive equipment of the company. The productive equipment is intended to increase the production or profitability.

An approved expanding company can be given tax exemption up to a period of five years subject to certain conditions.

The tax exemption period are as follows:

New Capital Expenditure		Tax Exemption Period
Up to B$250,000		3 years
More than B$250,000 5 years		3 years

Incentives for Foreign Loans

.	There is a 20% withholding tax for interest paid to non-resident lenders. However the government may grant tax exemption for any "approved foreign loan" if 1. The loan is utilised for the purchase of productive equipment; 2. The credit facilities are obtained through financial agreement with the foreign lending company; 3. The amount of loan is not less than B$200,000

Any limited company which have been granted Pioneer Certificate is given the following incentives:

- **Exemption from Corporate Tax**
  The 30% corporate tax is exempted for a pioneer company for a basic period of two to five years depending on the level of fixed capital expenditure. The exemption commences on the first day of production

  The tax exemption period are as follows:

Fixed Capital Expenditure	Tax Exemption Period
Less than B$250,000	2 years
B$250,000 but less than B$500,000	3 years

B$500,000 but less than B$1 million	4 years
B$ 1 million or over	5 years

Tax exemption may be extended up to three additional years in certain circumstances.

- **Exemption from Taxes on Imported Capital Goods**
  A pioneer company is also exempted from customs duty on plant, machinery and equipment to be installed in the pioneer factory.
- **Examption from Taxes on Imported Raw Materials**
  A pioneer company is exempted from paying import duties on raw materials not available or produced in Brunei Darussalam intended for the production of the pioneer products.

The following industries have been declared by the Economic Development Board as Pioneer Industries and Products.

	INDUSTRY	PRODUCTS
1.	Cement Finish Mill	Cement.
2.	Aluminium Wall Tile	Aluminium wall tiles and other decorative tiles.
3.	Rolling Mill Plant	Manufacturing / fabricating iron and steel, steel bars, angle iron, U-channel etc.
4.	Shipyard	Ship repair and maintenance.
5.	Textile	Various types of clothing.
6.	Furniture	Wooden, rattan, knock-down furniture.
7.	Glass	Sheet glass; scientific, laboratory and industrial glassware; optical and photographic glass; lighting and decorative glassware; glass products for houses and automobiles.
8.	Ceramic and Potteries	Tiles, sanitaryware, chinaware, stoneware, potteryware, porcelainware.
9.	Woodbase	Plywood and wooden construction elements.
10.	Plastic and Synthetic Rubber	PVC tubing, pipes, plastic bottles, containers, various types of medical and surgical and household rubber products.
11.	Gas	Various types of industrial gas.
12.	Sheet Metal-Forming	Roofing, metal furniture, walling, fencing, roof trusses, frames, fitting and fixtures, ducting, containers for storage and transport, other related building materials.

MANUFACTURE OF ELECTRICAL INDUSTRIAL MACHINERY & APPARATUS

The manufacture, renovation of electric motor, generators and complete turbine-generator and engine generator sets, transformers, switch gear and switchboard apparatus, rectifiers, other electrical transmission and distribution equipment, electrical industrial control devices such as motor starters and controllers, electro-magnetic clutches and brakes, electrical welding apparatus and other electrical industrial apparatus.

Pioneer Certificates have already been granted to companies in the areas of aircraft catering service, industrial chemical, shipyard, textile and canning, bottling and packaging.

The granting of Pioneer Certificate is not limited to a single company for a specific pioneer industry. Other companies who wish to apply for a Pioneer Certificate in a similar pioneer industry could be considered by the Economic Development Board.

The Economic Development Board would also consider any application for Pioneer Status from investors for industries which are not in the list, provided the following requirements are met:

1. The industry is one which has not been previously carried out in Brunei Darussalam on a commercial scale suitable to the economic requirements or development of Brunei Darussalam.
2. There are favourable prospects of further developing the industry to provide for exports or there are insufficient facilities in Brunei Darussalam to carry on the industry on a suitable commercial scale.
3. It is expedient in the public interest to encourage the development, including development for export, and establishment of the industry in Brunei Darussalam.

DEVELOPMENT BANK OF BRUNEI BERHAD

DBB is absolutely your ideal banking partner if you are thinking to venture into the following businesses:-

- Manufacturing and processing industries
- Fisheries, forestry, plantation and mining
- Tourism
- Construction
- Urban development
- Shipping, transportation and other related service industries etc

Type of financial packages

- Medium and long term loans
- Short term working capital
- Letters of Credit and Trust Receipts
- Overdraft
- Banker's Guarantee
- Demand Loan Line

Interest rate
The Choice is yours ...!

Subject to your repayment period, DBB can even offer you the minimum prevailing market prime rate. You have the option to choose from the range of interest rates available and simply let us know the rate that you prefer. Remember, the interest rates are as low as the prime rate (6.5% p.a.) and up to 3.0% p.a. (annual reducing) above the prevailing prime rate.

Security
All loans extended by DBB shall be fully secured by either one or more of the following:
- Mortgage on loan and property
- First charge on fixed assets and property to be financed
- Project shareholder(s) and director(s) of the company as guarantor of the loan
- Acceptable security(s) may be required on exceptional cases.

Documents
To ensure prompt evaluation and approval, the following information should be made available:
- Borrower's background
- Corporate and Business profile
- Project description/Cash flow
- Proof of approved contracts/tenders from relevant authorities (if any)
- Project costs and etc.

For further information, please contact:

Development Bank of Brunei Berhad
First Floor, RBA Plaza, Jalan Sultan,
Bandar Seri Begawan BS 8811, Brunei Darussalam
P.O.Box 3080,
Bandar Seri Begawan BS 8671, Brunei Darussalam
Tel: 673-2-233 430(10 lines)
Fax: 672-2-233 429

PRODUCTS & SERVICES

Suppliers of Locally Produced Construction Materials Ordinary Portland Cement

Butra Djajanti Cement Sdn. Bhd.
- The only cement manufacturer in Brunei Darussalam which started full commercial productin in 1996. It has an accredited laboratory enabling the company to test cement conforming to BS12: 1996.

Burnt Clay Bricks

Andulau Brickworks Co.
Hup Soon Brickworks and Ceramic Sdn. Bhd.
Jerudong Brickworks and Trading Sdn. Bhd.
M/s Soon Huat Bricks Manufacturing
PYP Holdings Sdn. Bhd.
Swee Brickworks Sdn. Bhd.
Syarikat Pengeluaran Batu-Bata
Teck Leong Brickworks Co.
Tong Bun Fa General Contractor and Bricks Factory

Cement Suppliers

Bee Huat Building Materials Company
Bian Hoe Sdn. Bhd.
Brusima Sdn. Bhd.
Butra Djajat Cement Sdn. Bhd.
Hock Hin Trading Company
Hong Leong Timber Trading Co.
Low San Hardwares Sdn. Bhd.
Risons General Supplier Sdn. Bhd.

LIST OF PREFERRED INDUSTRIES, ASSOCIATED ACTIVITIES AND PRODUCTS

Manufacture of Silica Products

1. Processing and manufacturing of silica products

Manufacture of Clay Products

1. Ceramic products
2. Pottery

Manufacture of Metal Products

1. Metal products processing and manufacturing
2. Metal containers for storage and transport
3. Wire products (exc. electric)
4. Nails, screws, nuts, bolts, rivets and similar parts of iron / steel / copper
5. Tools for use manually or by machines
6. Sanitary, plumbing, heating, lighting fixtures and fittings

Manufacture of Non-Metal Products

1. Lime, cement and fabricated building materials
2. Refractory construction material
3. Mineral manufacturing

Manufacture of Apparel Products

1. Apparel products

Manufacture of Textile Mill Products

1. Synthetic and regenerated (artificial) fibres
2. Floor covering, tapestries etc.
3. Materials of rubber
4. Plastic material, regenerated cellulose and artificial resins

Manufacture of Leather products

1. Footwear
2. Other leather products

Manufacture of Electrical and Electronic Machineries / Equipment / Apparatus

1. Electrical power machinery and switch gear
2. Electrical apparatus for medical purposes and radiological apparatus
3. Telecommunication apparatus
4. Domestic electrical equipment
5. Equipment for distributing electricity

Printing Industry

1. Printed matter
2. Signs and advertising

Manufacture of Chemical Products

1. Pigments, paints, varnishes, and related materials
2. Chemical materials and other chemical products
3. Fertiliser
4. Medicinal and pharmaceutical products
5. Essential oils, perfumes and flavour materials
6. Soaps, cleansing and polishing compounds
7. Inorganic chemicals, element oxides and halogen salts

Shipyards

1. Maintenance and repair

Other Manufactured Goods

1. Perambulators, toys, games and sporting goods
2. Jewellery and goldsmith / silversmith wares
3. Travel goods, handbags and similar articles

THE MINISTRY OF FOREIGN AFFAIRS

The Ministry of Foreign Affairs was formally established upon the resumption of Brunei Darussalam's full independence on 1 January 1984. His Royal Highness

Prince Mohamed Bolkiah was appointed as the Minister of Foreign Affairs of Brunei Darussalam.

The process of setting up the Ministry, however, began way back in early 1979 with the establishment of the Diplomatic Service Department. Its main function was to gradually take over the responsibility of handling Brunei Darussalam's external affairs. Brunei Darussalam then has three missions overseas, namely Brunei Darussalam Commission in Kuala Lumpur, London and Singapore. All these missions were upgraded to High Commission in 1984.

The Ministry of Foreign Affairs can be reached at the following address :-

Ministry of Foreign Affairs
Jalan Subok
Bandar Seri Begawan BD 2710
Brunei Darussalam
Tel: (673) 2 261177
Fax: (673) 2 262904

OBJECTIVES

To promote Brunei Darussalam's national interests :-

- ***Maintain its sovereignty, independence and territorial integrity.***
- ***Enhance the prosperity and economic and social well being of the country.***
- ***preserve the political, cultural and religious identity of the country.***

To help promote regional and global peace, security, stability and prosperity.

GUIDING PRINCIPLES

- ***Mutual respect for the territorial integrity, sovereignty, independence and national identity of all nations.***
- ***Recognition of the equality of all nations large and small.***
- ***Non-interference in each others internal affairs.***
- ***Peaceful settlement of disputes.***
- ***Cooperation for mutual benefits.***

DEPARTMENTS

ADMINISTRATION DEPARTMENT

Tel No. **(673) 2 261105**
Fax No. **(673) 2 262209**
E-Mail **dadmin@brunet.bn**

DIRECTOR	Haji Ishaaq Haji Abdullah
DEPUTY DIRECTOR (ACTING)	Haji Abdul Karim Haji Abdul Wahab
FUNCTIONS	
▪ To provide logistics and general services required by the Ministry and Brunei Darussalam missions abroad. ▪ To increase productivity and develop expertise through Human Resource Planning. ▪ To enhance the welfare of the staff working within the Ministry and abroad.	

MULTILATERAL ECONOMICS DEPARTMENT

Tel No **(673) 2 262486**
Fax No **(673) 2 262480**
E-Mail **dme@brunet.bn**

Director
Haji Shofry bin Haji Abdul Ghafor
E-mail: shofry_ghafor@mfa.gov.bn
Deputy Director
Pg. Basmillah bte Pg. Haji Abbas
E-mail: basmillah_abas@mfa.gov.bn

Mission Statement
The Department of Multilateral Economics was established in April 1997 and has the following roles and objectives :- • To oversee & coordinate Brunei Darussalam's involvement in regional and multilateral economic organisations that Brunei is a member. • To participate in various regional and international meetings in promoting Brunei Darussalam's interests. • To monitors various international trade & financial issues
Our Work
Brunei Darussalam is a member of the following regional & international multilateral economic organisations. DME coordinates Brunei Darussalam's participation in these organizations.

POLICY PLANNING DEPARTMENT

Tel No (673) 2 262213
Fax No (673) 2 262207
E-Mail dpolicy@brunet.bn

DIRECTOR	Dr. Haji Emran bin Haji Bahar
DEPUTY DIRECTOR (ACTING)	Pg. Haji Alihashim bin Pg. Haji Yussof

F U N C T I O N S :-

- To formulate and submit policy recommendations on international affairs. These involves:
  - i. an overall Brunei Darussalam Foreign Policy: i.e. Current status and its projection in the short, medium and long term.
  - ii. Specific Brunei Darussalam policy on issues or events.
- To act as a leading and coordinating agency in Brunei Darussalam for political and security cooperation in the region, and on all matters pertaining to the ARF, ZOPFAN, SEANWFZ, ASEAN-SOM, TAC.
- To complement the work of other departments in the Ministry of Foreign Affairs especially in areas where Brunei Darussalam has direct interests such as:
  - i. Maritime and border issues
  - ii. South China Sea issues
  - iii. UNCLOS
- To promote Brunei Darussalam policy through public information.
- To look at matters that do not fall under the purview of other departments in the Ministry of Foreign Affairs. These involves :
  - i. New issues.
  - ii. Regional and international political cooperation where Brunei Darussalam is a member.
  - iii. Establishment of diplomatic relations.
- To service the offices of the Minister of Foreign Affairs and Permanent Secretaries.

POLITICAL I DEPARTMENT

Tel No (673) 2 262235
Fax No (673) 2 262078
E-Mail polmfa@brunet.bn

DIRECTOR	Hjh Maimunah Dato Paduka Hj Elias

DEPUTY DIRECTOR	Emaleen Abdul Rahman Teo
F U N C T I O N S :-	
• To facilitate and maintain bilateral and diplomatic relations between Brunei Darussalam and the various countries in the Asia Pacific region. • To keep abreast of political issues within the Asia Pacific region which are of interest to Brunei Darussalam and to formulate policies relating to them. • To act as a focal point in pursuing Brunei Darussalam's national interests bilaterally with countries in the Asia-Pacific region.	
AREAS OF COVERAGE :-	
SOUTH EAST ASIA • Cambodia • Indonesia • Laos • Malaysia • Myanmar	• Philippines • Singapore • Thailand • Vietnam
PACIFIC • Australia • Kingdom of Tonga • Marshall Island • New Zealand • Papua New Guinea • Republic of Kiribati	• Republic of Fiji • Republic of Nauru • Republic of Palau • Solomon Islands • Western Samoa
NORTH EAST ASIA • Japan • Republic of Korea	• People's Republic of China • Mongolia

POLITICAL II DEPARTMENT

Tel No (673) 2 261423

Fax No (673) 2 262477

E-Mail 2dpol@brunet.bn

DIRECTOR	Haji Abdul Ghafar bin Haji Ismail
DEPUTY DIRECTOR	Magdalene Teo Chee Siong
F U N C T I O N S :-	
• Manage all aspects of bilateral relations with countries under its coverage.	

<table>
<tr><td>

- To focus and review ways to enhancing our relations with priority countries.
- To address issue of importance to Brunei Darussalam.
- To monitor and assess political, social, cultural and economic developments of importance to the international community especially those that may affect Brunei Darussalam.
- To support our mission abroad and maintain close coordination with them.

To coordinate and consult with other ministries/department.
</td></tr>
<tr><td>AREAS OF COVERAGE :-</td></tr>
<tr><td>Europe, Russia and Central Asian States
North & South America
Middle East
South Asia
Africa</td></tr>
</table>

PROTOCOL AND CONSULAR AFFAIRS DEPARTMENT

Tel No (673) 2 262345

Fax No (673) 2 261740

E-Mail dprocon@brunet.bn

<table>
<tr><td>DIRECTOR</td><td>Zainidi Haji Sidup</td></tr>
<tr><td>ACTING DEPUTY DIRECTOR (Protocol)</td><td>Awg. Haji Salleh bin Abdul Hamid</td></tr>
<tr><td>ACTING DEPUTY DIRECTOR (Consular)</td><td>Rakiah bte Haji Abdul Lamit</td></tr>
<tr><td colspan="2">F U N C T I O N S :-</td></tr>
<tr><td>• Protocol Section</td><td>Visits

Co-ordinate all States and official overseas visits of His Majesty Paduka Seri Baginda Sultan and Yang Di-Pertuan of Brunei Darussalam;
Co-ordinate all States and official visits of Foreign Head of States / Governments to Brunei Darussalam.

Ceremonial

Co-ordinate and handle the preparations for the</td></tr>
</table>

	Presentations of Credentials of Foreign Ambassadors or High Commissioners to Brunei Darussalam; Prepare the Letter of Credence for Brunei Darussalam Ambassadors/ High Commissioners to our overseas missions; Co-ordinate audiences and courtesy calls for VVIP and Head of Missions; Co-ordinate National Day reception for Foreign Embassies and High Commissions based in Brunei Darussalam; Handle all official messages from foreign missions and Brunei Darussalam missions.
• Consular Affairs Section	To provide protection to Brunei Darussalam's citizens and its interest overseas in accordance with the provisions of Article 5 in the Vienna Convention on Consular Relations 1961; To provide and administer Diplomatic Privileges to Foreign Diplomats in accordance with the Vienna Convention on Diplomatic Relations (1961) and for other matters connected therewith.

IMPORTANT GOVERNMENT CONTACTS

Prime Minister's Office
E-Mail: PRO@jpm.gov.bn
Telephone: 673 - 2 - 229988
Fax: 673 - 2 - 241717
Telex: BU2727
Address:
Prime Minister's Office
Istana Nurul Iman
Bandar Seri Begawan BA1000

Audit Department
Prime Minister's Office
Jalan Menteri Besar
Bandar Seri Begawan BB 39 10
Brunei Darussalam
Telephone: (02) 380576
Facsimile: (02) 380679
E-mail: jabaudbd@brunet.bn

Information Department
Prime Minister's Office
Berakas Old Airport
Bandar Seri Begawan
BB 3510
Brunei Darussalam.
E-mail:- pelita@brunet.bn
Fax: 673 2 381004
Tel: 673 2 380527

Narcotics Control Bureau
Prime Minister's Office
Jalan Tungku Gadong
Bandar Seri Begawan BE 2110
Tel No: 02-448877 / 422479 / 422480 / 422481
Fax No: 02-422477
E-mail: ncb@brunet.bn

One-Stop Agency
The Ministry of Industry and Primary Resources
Bandar Seri Begawan 1220
Brunei Darussalam

Telefax: (02) 244811
Telex: MIPRS BU 2111
Cable: MIPRS BRUNEI

Head Policy and Administration Division
Ministry of Industry and Primary Resources
Jalan Menteri Besar, Bandar Seri Begawan 1220
Brunei Darussalam
Tel: (02) 382822

Secretary of Public Service Commission
Old Airport
Bandar Seri Begawan BB 3510
Tel No: 02-381961
E-mail: bplspa@brunet.bn

Semaun Holdings Sdn Bhd
Unit 2.02, Block D, 2nd Floor
Yayasan Sultan Haji Hassanal Bolkiah Complex
Jalan Pretty
Bandar Seri Begawan BS8711
Brunei Darussalam
E-mail address: semaun@brunet.bn

Department of Agriculture
Ministry of Industry & Primary Resources
BB3510
Brunei Darussalam
Telephone: + 673 2 380144
Fax: + 673 2 382226
Telex: PERT BU 2456

Land Transport Department
KM 6, Jalan Gadong,
Beribi BE1110,
Brunei Darussalam.
Tel : (673-2) 451979
Fax : (673-2) 424775
Email : latis@brunet.bn

JUDICIARY BRANCH OF THE GOVERNMENT

THE SUPREME COURT OF BRUNEI DARUSSALAM

The Supreme Court of Brunei Darussalam was established in 1963 after the dissolution of the joint Sarawak, North Borneo and Brunei Supreme Court. The Supreme Court Building has been sited at various places including Kuala Belait. It has occupied a portion of old Secretariat building and the old Lapau building.

In 1978 the Government organised an architectural competition for the design of the new Supreme Court Building. The panel of assessors for the competition consisted of the following members:

- The Chief Justice - Dato Setia Sir Geoffrey Briggs.
- The Attorney General - Yang Amat Mulia Pengiran Laila Kanun Diraja Pengiran Haji Bahrin bin Pengiran Haji Abbas.
- The Chairman of Public Service Commission - Yang Dimuliakan Pehin Orang Kaya Digadong Seri Lela Dato Laila Utama Haji Awang Abdul Rahman.
- The Director of Public Works - Dato Paduka Haji Talib Derwish.

The site selected for the building is bounded by Sungai Kedayan to the east and Jalan Tutong to the north. The construction of the building commenced in February 1981 and was completed in 1983. The building has a floor area of 96,500 square feet and was built at cost of B$20 million.

The department is responsible for the administration of Justice through the Intermediate Court, High Court and Court of Appeal, and the Magistrates' Court which sit at Bandar Seri Begawan, Kuala Belait, Tutong and Temburong.

All courts hear both criminal and civil cases, with the majority of cases coming before the Magistrates' Courts. Those outside the limits of their jurisdiction being are by the Intermediate Court and the High Court. Appeals from the Magistrates' Courts are heard by the High Court. From the Intermediate Court and the High Court, appeals go to the Court of Appeal. Court of Appeal is the Highest Appellate Court for criminal cases. In civil cases, an appeal is referred to the Judicial Committee of Her Majesty's Privy Council in London if all parties agree to do so before the hearing of the appeal in the Brunei Court of Appeal.

In addition to the usual civil and criminal jurisdiction the courts deal with cases of bankruptcy and companies winding up. The Judiciary also deals with applications for Grants of Probate and Letters of Administration of deceased's person's estates. A further function of the judiciary is the administration of the admission of advocates and solicitors, who wish to practise in Brunei Darussalam, under the Legal Profession Act, and the issuance of annual Practising Certificates.

JUDGES

Arrangements were made with Hong Kong Government for Judges of the Supreme Court of Hong Kong to sit as Judges of the Supreme Court of Brunei Darussalam. The practice was for Judges of the Supreme Court of Hong Kong to be appointed as Judicial Commissioners of the Supreme Court of Brunei Darussalam for a period of three years. This long standing judicial arrangement with Hong Kong was officially ended in 1993. However, we have continued to rely on the services of retired Hong Kong judges to fill appointments in the Brunei Supreme Court.

It was also the practice for the Chief Justice of Hong Kong to be appointed as the Chief Justice of Brunei Darussalam. However, with effect from 15th March, 1988 the former Chief Justice of Hong Kong Dato Seri Paduka Sir Denys Tudor Emil Roberts, KCMG., SPMB., on his retirement as Chief Justice of Hong Kong continues to be Chief Justice of Brunei Darussalam. The Chief Justice of Hong Kong Dato Seri Paduka Sir Yang Ti Liang, KBE., SPMB., was appointed on 24 May 1988 as President of Court of Appeal. He was President of Court of Appeal until 16 May 1993. 0n 17 May 1993 a retired Hong Kong Court of Appeal Judge Dato Kutlu Tekin Fuad, CBE., was appointed as President of Court of Appeal.

The Chief Justice, the President of the Court of Appeal and other Supreme Court Judges are appointed until the age of 65 years or such later time as His Majesty may approve.

Chief Justice
Justice Mohamed Saied
(appointed 1st August, 2001)

President of the Court of Appeal
Sir Allan Huggins Armstrong
(appointed on 18 September , 2000)

Whilst the Chief Justice is the head of the judiciary, the day to day administration o is headed by the Chief Registrar. The Chief Registrar is also appointed as Intermediate Court Judge, Probate Officer, Official Receiver, Magistrate and Sheriff. As Chief Registrar he deals with interlocutory applications in chambers on civil matters before trial in the High Court. As Probate Officers he grants Probate and Letters of Administration in non-contentious matters. As Official Receiver, he deals with cases of bankruptcy and companies' winding up.

The Chief Registrar is also responsible for the administration of the Judiciary in relation to judicial staff, building maintenance, office equipment and facilities, etc.

In performing his various duties the Chief Registrar is assisted by the Deputy Chief Registrar, the Senior Registrars, Registrars, the Chief Magistrate, the Senior Magistrates and Magistrates. In order to assist the Chief Registrar, they are also appointed as Deputy Official Receiver and Deputy Probate Officer. The Chief Magistrate, Senior Magistrates and Magistrates are also appointed as Registrars of the Supreme Court for the same reason. In order to assist the Magistrates, the Chief Registrar, Deputy Chief Registrar, Senior Registrars and Registrars are also appointed as Magistrates.

The Chief Magistrate, Senior Magistrates, Magistrates, Senior Registrars and Registrars of the Supreme Court are also appointed as Marriage Registrars. The Marriage Registrar solemnizes and registers civil marriages.

Chief Justice of the Supreme Court since 1979

Dato Seri Paduka Sir Denys Tudor Emil Roberts, KCMG., SPMB.,
(appointed on 18 June, 1979 - 30 July 2001)
Justice Mohamed Saied
(appointed on 1 August 2001)

Chief Registrar of Supreme Court since 1950's
Mr. Tan Yam Thong
(1951-1960)
Mr. Charlie Foo Chee Tung
(1/3/1973-5/1/1981)
Dato Mohd. Ali bin Salleh
(6/1/1981-30/6/1986)
Mr. Mohamed Saied
(1/7/1986-28/6/1987)
Mr. Edward Timothy Starbuck Woolley
(29/6/1987-1/2/1989)
Dato Paduka Kifrawi bin Dato Paduka Haji Kifli
(1/1/1991 to 23/6/1998)
Datin Paduka Hayati binti POKSDSP Haji Mohd. Salleh
(24/6/1998 to 31/12/2000)
Pg Hjh Zabaidah binti Pg Hj Kamaludin
(1/1/2001 to 28/7/2001)

Awang Hairol Arni Hj Abd Majid (Acting)
(28/7/2001 to date)

Chief Magistrate
Awang Haji Mohd. Ali bin Daud
(1976-16/6/1977)
Awang Ivan Leong Onn Khong
(01/05/1978-04/11/1979)
Awang Robert Adrien Augustin
(05/11/1979-31/01/1989)
Datin Paduka Hayati binti POKSDSP Hj. Mohd. Salleh
(01/02/1989 - 30/06/1991)
Awang Steven Chong Wan Oon
(01/07/91-31/12/1997)
Awang Hairolani bin Haji Abd. Majid
(01/02/1999 - to date)

HIGH COURT

JURISDICTION

The High Court hears appeals against the judgments of the Magistrates Courts. The High Court has unlimited original civil and criminal jurisdiction. The court hears civil and criminal cases, which the Intermediate Court and Magistrate Courts have no jurisdiction to hear.

Most of the criminal cases heard by the High Court are as follows:-

1. Murder/culpable homicide not amounting to murder.
2. Possession of fire arms.
3. Trafficking controlled drugs.
4. Gang Robbery.
5. Rape

Judges of The High Court

Chief Justice:
Justice Mohammad Saied

Judges:

Justice Datin Paduka Hayati binti Pehin Orang Kaya Shahbandar Dato Seri Paduka Awang Haji Mohd. Salleh.
Justice Steven Chong Wan Oon.

Registrars of the High Court

Chief Registrar (Acting):
Awang Hairol Arni Hj Abd Majid

Deputy Chief Registrar:
Dayang Lim Siew Yen.

Senior Registrar:
Dayangku Hajah Hanani binti Pg Hj Metusain

Registrars:
Awang Fathan bin Haji Anuar
Dayang Ramzidah binti Pehin Datu Kesuma Diraja Hj Abdul Rahman

MAGISTRATES' COURTS

Jurisdiction of Magistrates' Courts

(1) The High Court, the Intermediate Courts and the Magistrates' Courts hear criminal and civil cases. The majority of cases are heard by the Magistrates' Courts, those which are outside the limit of their jurisdiction are heard by the High Court and the Intermediate Courts. The Magistrates' Courts are situated at Bandar Seri Begawan, Kuala Belait, Tutong and Temburong.

(2) The Subordinate Courts Act (Chapter 6) which came into force on the 1st day of January, 1983 established the Magistrates' Courts as the Subordinate Courts of Brunei Darussalam, replacing the Magistrates' Courts of the First, Second and Third Class which were formerly established under the Courts Enactment of 1952.

(3) (a) A court of a Magistrate exercising criminal jurisdiction has the jurisdiction and powers conferred on it by the Subordinate Courts Act and Criminal Procedure Code (Chapter 7) and any other written law.

(b) The most common criminal cases heard by the Magistrates' Courts are as follows:-

1. Theft
2. Criminal breach of trust
3. Cheating
4. Handling stolen goods
5. Mischief
6. Criminal trespass
7. Criminal intimidation
8. Causing hurt
9. Possession and consumption of controlled drugs.
10. Corruption cases
11. Immigration cases

12. Customs and Excise cases
13. Offences under the Road Traffic Acts
14. Municipal cases
15. Fisheries cases
16. Forestry cases

(c) A notice under the Criminal Procedure Code (Chapter 7) provides that Magistrates have power to impose imprisonment not exceeding 7 years or a fine of B$10,000.00 and whipping.

However, the power to impose punishment is subject to the provisions of any written law, which may give special jurisdiction to a Magistrates' Court. For example, the Prevention of Corruption Act and the Misuse of Drugs Act give special jurisdiction to a Magistrate Court to impose imprisonment and fine which are higher from those provided by the Criminal Procedure Code.

(4) A Court of a Magistrate has jurisdiction to hear civil cases where the amount claimed or the value of the subject matter in dispute does not exceed B$30,000.00. As provided by the Subordinate Courts Act, the Chief Justice, with the approval of His Majesty The Sultan and Yang Di-Pertuan of Brunei Darussalam, has increased the limit in the case of Magistrate, sc that the amount or value must not exceed B$30,000.00 and in the case of a Senior Magistrate/Senior Registrar Supreme Court/Chief Magistrate/Deputy Chief Registrar Supreme Court/Chief Registrar not exceeding B$50,000.00.

Chief Magistrate:
Awang Hairolarni bin Haji Abdul Majid

Senior Magistrate:
Dayangku Rostaina binti Pengiran Haji Duraman

Magistrates:
Awang Abdullah Soefri bin Dato Paduka Hj Abidin
Awang Ridzlan bin Hj Ibrahim
Awang Radin Safiee bin Radin Mas Basiuni
Awang Mohammad Faisal bin Pehin Dato Kefli

Senior Registrar of Subordinate Court:
Awang Haji Ali Hassan bin Haji Hitam.

Registrar of Subordinate Court:
Dayang Maimun bte Tajaah.

INTERMEDIATE COURT

JURISDICTION

The court has no jurisdiction to hear cases punishable with death or power to impose imprisonment exceeding 20 years. The court has jurisdiction to hear civil cases where the amount claimed, or value of the subject matter in dispute does not exceed B$100,000.00.

The criminal cases usually heard by the Intermediate Court are as follows:-

1. Criminal breach of trust.
2. House trespass.
3. Robbery.
4. Rape.
5. Causing grievous hurt
6. Arson
7. Trafficking in controlled drugs.

Intermediate Court Judges:

Awang Hairolarni bin Haji Majid. (Acting)
Dayang Lim Siew Yen (Acting)

COURT OF APPEAL

JURISDICTION

The Court of Appeal is the highest Appellate Court. It deals with appeal cases from the High Court and the Intermediate Court, both in Civil and Criminal cases.

It has only two sessions per year which are normally held in April and November. It consist of the President and two Justices of Appeal.

President Court of Appeal:
Sir Alan Armstrong Huggins

Judges of the Court of Appeal:
Sir Alan Armstrong Huggins
Sir Derek Cons
William James Silke
Dato Paduka Kutlu Tekin Fuad

THE ATTORNEY GENERAL

The Attorney General is the principal legal adviser to the Government of His Majesty the Sultan and Yang Di-Pertuan. He is assisted by the Solicitor General and counsel in advising the Government and representing the Government in civil and criminal cases. The Attorney General is also responsible for the drafting of legislation. In carrying out the task of drafting the Attorney General's

Chambers work closely with other Government Ministries and Departments.

The Attorney General is vested with the power under the Constitution to institute, proceed and discontinue once instituted any criminal proceedings. All criminal prosecutions are instituted in the name of the Public Prosecutor. In carrying out this duty, the Attorney General is not subject to the direction or control of any other person or authority. He is assisted by Deputy Public Prosecutors in the conduct of criminal trials held in the Supreme Court and the Subordinate Courts.

In addition, the Public Prosecutor and his Deputies also advise, and direct prosecution undertaken by the police and other law enforcement Departments including rendering advice in their investigations.

Apart from carrying out the above duties, the Attorney General's Chambers also provides service to the public by maintaining the following Registries:

REGISTRY	RELEVANT ACT
Companies	Companies Act (Cap. 39)
Business Names	Business Names Act (Cap. 92)
Trade Marks	Trade Marks Act (Cap. 98)
Bills of Sales	Bills of Sales Act (Cap. 70)
Marriages	Marriages Act (Cap. 76)

TRAVEL TO BRUNEI

US STATE DEPARTMENT SUGGESTIONS

COUNTRY DESCRIPTION: Brunei (known formally as the State of Brunei Darussalam) is a small Islamic Sultanate on the north coast of the island of Borneo. The capital, Bandar Seri Begawan, is the only major city. Tourist facilities are good, and generally available.

ENTRY REQUIREMENTS: For information about entry requirements, travelers may consult the Consular Section of the Embassy of the State of Brunei Darussalam, Suite 300, 2600 Virginia Ave., N.W. Washington, D.C. 20037; tel. (202) 342-0159.

MEDICAL FACILITIES: Adequate public and private hospitals and medical services are available in Brunei. Medical care clinics do not require deposits usually, but insist upon payment in full at time of treatment, and may require proof of ability to pay prior to treating or discharging a foreigner. U.S. medical insurance is not always valid outside the United States, and may not be accepted by health providers in Brunei. Travelers may wish to check with their health insurance providers regarding whether their U.S. policy applies overseas. The Medicare/ Medicaid program does not provide payment of medical services outside the United States. Supplemental medical insurance with specific overseas coverage, including provision for medical evacuation may be useful. Travel agents or insurance providers often have information about such programs. Useful information on medical emergencies abroad is provided in the Department of State, Bureau of Consular Affairs' brochure *Medical Information for Americans Traveling Abroad*, available via our home page and autofax service. For additional health information, the international travelers hotline of the Centers for Disease Control and Prevention may be reached at 1-877-FYI-TRIP (1-877-394-8747), via the CDC autofax service at 1-888-CDC-FAXX (1-888-232-3299), or via the CDC home page on the Internet: http://www.cdc.gov.

INFORMATION ON CRIME: The crime rate in Brunei is low, and violent crime is rare. The loss or theft abroad of a U.S. passport should be reported immediately to the local police and to the U.S. Embassy. Useful information on guarding valuables and protecting personal security while traveling abroad is provided in the Department of State pamphlet, *A Safe Trip Abroad.* It is available from the Superintendent of Documents, U.S. Government Printing Office, Washington, D.C. 20402 or via the Internet at http://www.access.gpo.gov /su_docs.

CRIMINAL PENALTIES: While in a foreign country, a U.S. citizen is subject to that country's laws and regulations, which sometimes differ significantly from those in the United States and do not afford the protections available to the individual under U.S. law. Penalties for breaking the law can be more severe than in the United States for similar offenses. Persons violating the law, even unknowingly, may be expelled, arrested or imprisoned. The trafficking in and the illegal importation of controlled drugs are very serious offenses in Brunei. Brunei has a mandatory death penalty for many narcotics offenses. Under the current law, possession of heroin and morphine derivatives of more than 15 grams, and cannabis of more than 20 grams, carries the death sentence. Possession of lesser amounts carries a minimum twenty-year jail term and caning.

AVIATION OVERSIGHT: The U.S. Federal Aviation Administration (FAA) has assessed the Government of Brunei's Civil Aviation Authority as Category 1 - in compliance with international aviation safety standards for oversight of Brunei's air carrier operations. For further information, travelers may contact the Department of Transportation within the U.S. at 1-800-322-7873, or visit the FAA's Internet website at http://www.faa.gov/avr/iasa/index.htm. The U.S. Department of Defense (DOD) separately assesses some foreign air carriers for suitability as official providers of air services. For information regarding the DOD policy on specific carriers, travelers may contact DOD at 618-256-4801.

ROAD SAFETY: Roads are generally good and most vehicles are new and well-maintained. However, vehicular accidents are now one of the leading causes of death in Brunei. Possibly due to excessive speed, tropical torrential rains, or driver carelessness, Brunei suffers a very high traffic accident rate.

CUSTOMS INFORMATION: More detailed information concerning regulations and procedures governing items that may be brought into Brunei is available from the Embassy of the State of Brunei Darussalam in the United States.

Registration/Embassy Location: U.S. citizens living in or visiting Brunei are encouraged to register in person or via telephone with the U.S. Embassy in Bandar Seri Begawan and to obtain updated information on travel and security within the country. The U.S Embassy is located on the third floor, Teck Guan Plaza, Jalan Sultan, in the capital city of Bandar Seri Begawan. The mailing address is American Embassy PSC 470 (BSB), FPO AP, 96534; the telephone number is (673)(2) 229-670; the fax number is (673) (2) 225-293.

Brunei-Muara

On her state visit to Brunei in September of 1998, Her Majesty Queen Elizabeth II of Britain made a tour of the Kampung Ayer in the capital a part of her busy itinerary. Made up of numerous communities, and home to some 30,000 people, the Kampung Ayer ("Villages on Water") is certainly the most well-known of all attractions in the country.

Kampung Ayer has been around for a very long time. When Antonio Pigafetta visited the country in the mid-16th century; Kampung Ayer was already a well-established, "home to some 25,000 families," according to Pigafetta. It was the hub for governance, business and social life in Brunei at that time.

The Kampung Ayer of today retains many of its old-world features described by Pigafetta. Only now, its daily well being is overlooked by the chiefs of the many villages in the area. The Kampung has almost all the amenities available in other communities, such as schools, shops and mosques. The houses there are usually well equipped with the latest in modern technology.

For as low as $1, boatmen will ferry passengers along the breadth and length of the Brunei river.

River cruises aboard ferryboats can start at both ends of the Brunei river, one at the Muara side, at the Queen Elizabeth jetty (named after the reigning British queen after her first Brunei visit in 1972), and others at the various river boat taxi stations in the heart of town.

The journey from the other end of the river starts at Kota Batu, the 16th century capital. The upstream journey during the 10 miles per hour cruise passes an ancient landmark, the tomb of Brunei's fifth ruler, Sultan Bolkiah, the Singing Captain, under whose reign Brunei was a dominant power in the 15th century.

On one bank of the Brunei river is a newer relic, a British warship used dur-ing World War II, sheltered from the elements.

The ferry moves on to Kampong Ayer, the Venice of the East. During the 18th century, here lived the fisher-men, blacksmiths, kris (native sword) makers, brass artisans, nipa palm mat makers, pearl and oyster collectors, traders and goldsmiths.

A new Kampong Ayer has risen, settlements of concrete houses with glass windowpanes, and connected by cement bridges instead of the rickety, wooden catwalks.

Overlooking the old Kampong Ayer is the House of Twelve Roofs (Bum-bungan Dua Belas), built in 1906 and formerly the official home of the British resident. In the Kota Batu area on Jalan Residency is the Arts and Handicrafts Centre, where traditional arts and crafts have been revived.

But Kampung Ayer is only one of the many charms of Brunei that intrigue visitors to the country.

The Sultan Omar Ali Saifuddien Mosque in the heart of Bandar Seri Begawan continues to attract visitors fascinated by its majestic presence, and its role in the spiritual development of the Muslim citizens of the country. The mosque is practically synonymous with Brunei in general, and with the capital in particular.

Situated very close to the mosque is the public library with its attractive mural depicting Brunei's lifestyles in the 60s. The mural was done by one of Brunei's foremost artist, Pg Dato Hj Asmalee, formerly the director of Welfare, Youth and Sports, but now the country's ambassador to a neighbour-ing country.

Another landmark of the capital is the Yayasan Sultan Hj Hassanal Bolkiah commercial complex, across the road from the Sultan Omar Ah Saifuddien mosque. The newly estab-lished complex is the prime shopping centre in Brunei - four storeys of some of the premier big-name retailers in the region! There're outlets bran-dishing branded clothing, fast food, video games, books and many more. There's a supermarket in the Yayasan's west wing, and a food court on the east.

The Royal Regalia Building is a new addition to the attractions found in the capital. Within easy walking distance of all the hotels in the capital centre, the Royal Regalia Building houses artifacts used in royal cere-monies in the country. Foremost among the displays are the Royal Chariot, the gold and silver ceremonial armoury and the jewel-encrusted crowns used in coronation ceremonies.

Entrance is free, and visitors are expected to take off their shoes before entering. Opening hours are from 8.3Oam to 5.00pm daily except for Fridays, the Building opens from 9.00am until II.30am, and in the afternoon, from 2.30pm till 5.00pm.

Located next to the Royal Regalia Building is the Brunei History Centre. Drop by the centre and learn all about the genealogy and history of the sultans of Brunei, and members of the royal family. There is an exhibition area open to the public from 7.45 am to 12.I5pm, and I.30pm to 4.3Opm daily except for Fridays.

Across the road from the Brunei Hotel, is what is known throughout Borneo as the 'tamu.' A 'tamu' is a congregation of vendors selling farm produce and general items. If you are lucky, you can find valuable bargains among the potpourri of metalware and handicraft hawked by some peddlers.

The main Chinese temple in the country lies within sight of the 'tamu.' Its elaborately designed roof and loud red color of its outer walls make the temple stand out from among the more staid schemes of nearby buildings.

A visit during one of the many festivals that is observed at this sanctum of Taoist beliefs would be a celebration of colors, spectacle and smell. Another place of worship that should not be missed by visitors to Brunei is the Church of St Andrew's. The church, possibly the oldest in Brunei, is designed like an English country parish, complete with bells in the let fry. It lies within walking distance of the Royal Regalia Building.

If you are staying in a hotel or Bandar Seri Begawan, why not pay the nightly foodstalls a visit? The stalls are located at a site in front of Sheraton Hotel, and serve a wide variety of hawker fare cheap! A dollar worth of the fried noodles is enough to fill you up.

Check out the local burgers. They're as delicious as those you'll find in established fast food outlets. Or try out 'Roti John'-the Malay version of the Big Mac. Ask for 'goreng pisang' (banana fritters), 'begedil' (potato balls), or 'popiah' (meat rolls), in your jaunts to the sweetmeat stalls.

Outside the capital center, a worthwhile place to visit is the Jame' Asr Hassanil Bolkiah Mosque in Kiarong, about six kilometers away. This is a beautiful sanctuary for communication with God, a personal bequest from His Majesty the Sultan of Brunei himself for the people of the country.

More than just a place of worship, the Jame' Asr is also a center for learning. Classes teaching Islamic religious principles and practices are held there regularly, as do religious lectures. And every Friday morning, the lobbies of its vast edifice are filled with children studying the Quran.

A visit to the mosque is usually part of the itinerary of package tours to Brunei, but if not, visitors can make the necessary arrangement with local tour operators. Visitors wishing to come inside the mosque need to report to the officers on duty, at the security counter on the ground floor.

Further on, you will find the Jerudong Park Playground. Situated some 20 kms to the west of the capital, JP as it is popularly called, is a must-go place for visitors to the country. It has been described as "Brunei's first high-tech wonderland for people of all ages."

There are many amusement rides at the Jerudong Park Playground to cater to everyone's need.

For those who like to live life on the edge, you would be pleased to know that JP has THREE (that's right, three) roller coasters, each with different degrees of thrills (or insanity factors if you want).

'Pusing Lagi' takes riders up a crest almost six storeys high, and then takes them down a steep incline, before twisting and turning at breakneck speed, so much so you will regret the 'Roti John' you just had.

'Boomerang' is for people who would rather go for diabolical twists and turns, while 'Pony Express' is a ride for those newly-initiated to roller-coasters.

Other popular rides include the 'Condor', a very fast merry-go-round that takes you up some five stores high, the 'Aladdin' (a mechanical 'flying carpet'), 'Flashdance' (no dancing experience required), and the wildly swinging 'Pirate Ship'.

There is also a bumper car arena, only for children and youngsters though, a video arcade and tracks for skateboarding and carting. For those who prefer something more sedate, also available are a 'Merry-Go-Round', certainly the most beautiful this side of London, and the 'Simulator Tour' (virtual reality rides into the fantastic and the exotic). Try the up-tower rides, where you are taken up a tower 15 stores high, and given a superb view of the park, and the surrounding area.

Situated next to the playground is the 20-acre Jerudong Park Gardens, which is well-known for its concert class auditorium. This was where Michael Jackson had his performances some years back, drawing a record 60,000 people to a colorful extravaganza the first time he performed.

Whitney Houston was another megastar who has had performed here, as well as Stevie ("I Just Called To Say I Love You) Wonder and the wonderful Seal ("Kissed By A Rose").

And if all that running and riding gives you an appetite, there's good food to be found in the eating area next to the parking lot. Almost anything you could crave for is available, ranging from the local hawker spreads to international fast food fare. If you're not doing anything on a Friday morning or late afternoon, take the no.55 purple bus to the end of its line at Jerudong Beach. Jerudong Beach on Fridays, especially around 9.00-

10.00am, is a hive of activity as fishermen start landing their catch and customers rush to avail themselves of the freshest fish possible. The people you'll get to meet there are among the friendliest in the country, easy with the smile and always ready for the idle chatter.

But the place is more than just an informal fish market. Local fruits hang prominently from many of the stalls, and food stalls sell take-outs to cater to hungry visitors. Swim in the calm, waveless waters of the man-made cove, or try your luck fishing, if that is what you want to do. Just go around people watching.

And if you need to go back to town, just board the purple bus to make the return journey.

The Bukit Shabbandar Forest Park is just the place to put those hiking legs to use. About ten minutes drive from the Jerudong Park Playground, the park is hectares upon hectares of greenery, dissected by tracks and paths for hiking, jogging and biking. While hiking, you can partake the wonders of the local forests - the rich diversity of its plant life, the exquisite charms and colors of the insects and reptiles that live within, and the symphony in the singing of the birds. Bukit Shahbandar Forest Park is just one of the 11 forest reserves in the country. To the east of Bandar Seri Begawan, about 6 kms into the Kota Batu area, visitors will find the Brunei Museum exhibits artifacts that archive the history of Negara Brunei Darussalam, both ancient and the relatively recent.

Well made cannons and kettles with their dragon motifs and elaborate patterns recall the glory days of the country -when Brunei was an important political and mercantile power in the region with territories that stretched that stretched all the way from Luzon Island in the Philippines to the whole western Borneo island.

There are exhibits which depict the traditional lifestyles of the various communities in the country, plus displays on the local flora and fauna. The exhibit by the local petroleum company Brunei Shell, illustrates the history on the discovery of oil in the country, and the commodity's significant role in economy of Brunei.

The Museum is open every day except Mondays from 9.00am till 5.00pm. On Fridays however, there is a scheduled prayer break from 11.30am until 2.30pm.

And situated downhill of the Brunei Museum is the Malay Technology Museum, which, as its name implies, houses the technological tools utilised by the Malays in ancient times.

A government booklet describes it as offering the "the visitor an intriguing insight into the lifestyle of the people of Brunei in by-gone eras". The Technology Museum is open daily, except Tuesdays, from 9.00 am till 5.00 pm. with a 3-hour midday prayer break on Fridays. Entrance is free.

There is an "Asean Square" in Persiaran Damuan which is located on a stretch between Jalan Tutong and the bank of the Brunei River about 4.5km from the capital. The "Asean

Square" has on permanent display the work of a chosen sculptor themed Harmony in Diversity from each of the Asean member countries.

HOLIDAYS

Brunei Darussalam's vision is to promote the country as a unique tourist destination and gateway to tourism excellence in South East Asia. The objectives are to create international awareness of Brunei Darussalam as a holiday destination; to maximize earings of foreign exchange and make tourism as one of the main contributor to GDP. In addition, it will create employment opportunities.

The country offers a wide variety of attractive places to be visited and experienced. The rainforest and National Parks are rich in flora and fauna. Its most magnificent mosques, water village (traditional and historic houses on stilts), rich culture and Jerudong Theme Park are among the uniqueness of Brunei Darussalam.

The government is now actively promoting tourism as an important part of its economic diversification. It would like to see a target of 1 million-visitor arrival by the year 2000. From January to August 1999, the statistic recorded 405,532 visitors visited Brunei Darussalam.

National Day Celebration

The nation celebrates this joyous occasion on the 23rd of February and the people usually prepare themselves two months beforehand. Schoolchildren, private sector representatives and civil servants work hand-in-hand rehearsing their part in flash card displays and other colourful crowd formations. In addition mass prayers and reading of Surah Yaasin are held at mosques throughout the country.

Fasting Month (Ramadhan)

Ramadhan is a holy month for all Muslims. This marks the beginning of the period of fasting - abstinence from food, drink and other material comforts from dawn to dusk. During this month, religious activities are held at mosques and *suraus* throughout the country

Hari Raya Aidilfitri

Hari Raya is a time for celebration after the end of the fasting month of Ramadhan. In the early part of the first day, prayers are held at every mosque in the country. Families get together to seek forgiveness from the elders and loved ones. You will see Bruneians decked-out in their traditional garb visiting relatives and friends.

Special festive dishes are made especially for Hari Raya including satay (beef, chicken or mutton kebabs), ketupat or lontong (rice cakes in coconut or banana leaves), rendang (spicy marinated beef) and other tantalizing cuisines. In these auspicious occassion Istana Nurul Iman was open to the public as well as to visitors for 3 days.

This provides the nation and other visitors the opportunity to meet His Majesty and other members of the Royal Family, in order to wish them a Selamat Hari Raya Aidilfitri.

Royal Brunei Armed Forces Day

31st of May marks the commemoration of the Royal Brunei Armed Forces formation day. The occassion is celebrated with military parades, artillery displays, parachuting and exhibitions.

Hari Raya Aidiladha

This is also known as Hari Raya Korban. Sacrifices of goats and cows are practiced to commemorate the Islamic historical event of Prophet Ibrahim S.A.W. The meat is then distributed among relatives, friends and the less fortunates.

His Majesty the Sultan's Birthday

This is one of the most important events in the national calendar with activities and festivities taking place nationwide. Celebrated on 15th July, this event begins with mass prayer throughout the country. On this occassion, His Majesty the Sultan delivers a 'titah' or royal address followed by investiture ceremony held at the Istana Nurul Iman. The event is also marked with gatherings at the four districts where His Majesty meets and gets together with his subjects.

Birthday of the Prophet Muhammad

In Brunei Darussalam, this occasion is known as the Mauludin Nabi S.A.W. Muslims throughout the country honour this event. Readings from the Holy Koran - the Muslim Holy Book, and an address on Islam from officials of the Ministry of Religious Affairs marks the beginning of this auspicious occasion. His Majesty the Sultan also gives a royal address and with other members of the Royal family, leads a procession on foot through the main streets of Bandar Seri Begawan. Religious functions, lectures and other activities are also held to celebrate this important occasion nationwide.

Chinese New Year

Celebrated by the Chinese community, this festival lasts for two weeks. It begins with a reunion dinner on the eve of the Lunar New Year to encourage closer rapport between family members. For the next two week, families visit one another bringing with them oranges to symbolize longevity and good fortune. Traditional cookies and food are aplenty during this festivity. Unmarried young people and children will receive 'angpow' or little red packets with money inside, a symbolic gesture of good luck, wealth and health.

Christmas Day

Throughout the world, 25th of December marks Christmas day, a significant day for all Christians. Christmas is nevertheless a joyous and colourful celebration enjoyed by Christians throughout the country.

Teachers' Day

Teachers' Day is celebrated on every 23rd September in recognition of the good deeds of the teachers to the community, religion and the country. It is celebrated in commemoration of the birthday of the late Sultan Haji Omar 'Ali Saifuddien Saadul Khairi Waddien, the 28th Sultan of Brunei for his contribution in the field of education including religious education. On this occassion, three awards are given away namely, Meritorious Teacher's Award, Outstanding Teacher's Award and *"Guru Tua"* Award.

Public Service Day

The date 29th September is observed as the Public Service Day with the objective to uphold the aspiration of the Government of His Majesty the Sultan and Yang Di-Pertuan of Brunei Darussalam towards creating an efficient, clean, sincere and honest public service. The Public Service Day commemorates the promulgation of the first written Constitution in Brunei Darussalam. The Public Service Day is celebrated with the presentation of the meritorious service award to Ministries and Government Departments.

PUBLIC HOLIDAYS

1 January	New Year's Day
8 January	* Hari Raya Aidilfitri
5 February	Chinese New Year
23 February	National Day
16 Mac	* Hari Raya Aidiladha
6 April	Muslim Holy Month of Hijiriah
31 May	Royal Brunei Armed Forces Day
15 Jun	The Birthday of Prophet Muhammad S.A.W.
15 July	The Birthday of His Majesty Sultan Haji Hassanal Bolkiah Mu'izzaddin Waddaulah, Sultan and Yang Di-Pertuan of Brunei Darussalam
25 October	* Israk Mikraj
27 November	* First Day of Ramadhan (Muslim fasting month)
13 December	Anniversary of The Revelation of the Quran
25 December	Christmas
27 December	* Hari Raya Aidilfitri

BUSINESS CUSTOMS

Customs & Traditions:	Brunei Darussalam possess a long heritage of traditions and customs, behavioural traits and forms of address. Muslims observe religious rites and rituals, which is woven into the lifestyle of Bruneian Malays.

	Breach of Malay conduct can be liable to prosecution in Islamic courts.
Social Protocol for non-Muslims:	It is customary for Bruneians to eat with their fingers rather than use forks and spoons. Always use the right hand when eating. It is polite to accept even just a little food and drink when offered. When refusing anything that is being offered, it is polite to touch the plate lightly with the right hand . As the left hand is considered unclean, one should use one's right hand to give and receive things. Bruneians sit on the floor, especially when there's a fairly large gathering of people. It is considered feminine to sit on the floor with a woman's legs tucked to one side, and equally polite for men to sit with folded legs crossed at the ankles. It's rude for anyone to sit on the floor with the legs stretched out in front, especially if someone is sitting in front. It is considered impolite to eat or drink while walking about in public except at picnics or fairs. During the Islamic fasting (Puasa) month, Muslims do not take any food from sunrise to sundown. It would be inconsiderate to eat and drink in their presence during this period. It is not customary for Muslims to shake hands with members of the opposite sex. Public display of affection such as kissing and hugging are seen to be in bad taste. Casual physical contact with the opposite sex will make Muslims feel uncomfortable. In the relationship between sexes, Islam enforces strict legislation. If a non-Muslim is found in the company of a Muslim of the opposite sex in a secluded place rather than where there are a lot of people, he/she could be persecuted. If you are found committing 'khalwat' that is seen in a compromising position with a person of the opposite sex who is a Muslim, you could be deported. When walking in front of people, especially the elderly and those senior in rank or position, it is a gesture of courtesy and respect for one to bend down slightly, as if one is bowing, except this time side way to the person or persons in front of whom one is passing. One of the arms should be positioned straight downwards along the side of the body. Leaning on a table with someone seated on it especially if he/she is an official or colleague in an office is considered rude.

	Resting one's feet on the table or chair is seen as overbearing. So is sitting on the table while speaking to another person who is seated behind it. To touch or pat someone, including children, on the head is regarded as extremely disrespectful. The polite way of beckoning at someone is by using all four fingers of the right hand with the palm down and motioning them towards yourself. It is considered extremely impolite to beckon at someone with the index finger.

SUPPLEMENTS

IMPORTANT LAWS OF BRUNEI

ACT / ORDER	CHAPTER / NOTIFICATION NO.	DATE OF COMMENCEMENT	STATUS
ADMIRALTY JURISDICTION ACT [2000 Ed.]	CAP. 179	01-10-1996	
ADOPTION OF CHILDREN ORDER 2001	S 16/2001	26-03-2001	
AGRICULTURAL PESTS AND NOXIOUS PLANTS ACT [1984 Ed.]	CAP. 43	01-08-1971	
AIR NAVIGATION ACT [1984 Ed., Amended by S 21/97, S 41/00, S 42/00, Repealed by S 63/06 - Civil Aviation Order]	CAP. 113	01-03-1978	REPEALED w.e.f. 20-05-06
AIRPORT PASSENGER SERVICE CHARGE ACT [2000 Ed.]	CAP. 188	01-05-1999	
ANTI-TERRORISM (FINANCIAL AND OTHER MEASURES) ACT [2008 Ed.]	CAP. 197	14-06-2002	
ANTIQUITIES AND TREASURE TROVE ACT [2002 Ed.]	CAP. 31	01-01-1967	
APPLICATION OF LAWS ACT [2009 Ed.]	CAP. 2	25-04-1951	
ARBITRATION ACT [1999 Ed.]	CAP. 173	24-04-1994	
ARBITRATION ORDER, 2009	S 34/2009		not yet in force
ARMS AND EXPLOSIVES ACT [2002 Ed.]	CAP. 58	08-04-1927	
ASIAN DEVELOPMENT BANK ACT [2009 Ed.]	CAP. 201	25-04-2006	
AUDIT ACT [1986 Ed., Amended by S 39/03]	CAP. 152	01-01-1960	
AUTHORITY FOR INFO-COMMUNICATIONS TECHNOLOGY INDUSTRY OF BRUNEI DARUSSALAM ORDER 2001 [Amended by S 13/03, S 35/03]	S 39/2001	01-01-2003	
BANISHMENT ACT [1984 Ed.]	CAP. 20	31-12-1918	
BANKERS' BOOKS (EVIDENCE) ACT [1984 Ed., Amended by S 29/93, Repealed by S 13/06]	CAP. 107	17-04-1939	REPEALED w.e.f. 12-02-06
BANKING ACT [2002 Ed., Repealed by S 45/06 - Banking Order]	CAP. 95	01-01-1957	REPEALED w.e.f. 04-03-06
BANKING ORDER, 2006	S 45/2006	04-03-2006	
BANKRUPTCY ACT [1984 Ed., Amended	CAP. 67	01-01-1957	

by S 12/96, S 52/00]			
BILLS OF EXCHANGE ACT [1999 Ed.]	CAP. 172	03-05-1994	
BILLS OF SALE ACT [1984 Ed.]	CAP. 70	16-01-1958	
BIOLOGICAL WEAPONS ACT [1984 Ed.]	CAP. 87	11-04-1975	
BIRTHS AND DEATHS REGISTRATION ACT [1984 Ed.]	CAP. 79	01-01-1923	
BISHOP OF BORNEO (INCORPORATION) ACT [1984 Ed.]	CAP. 88	25-04-1951	
BRETTON WOODS AGREEMENT ACT [2000 Ed.]	CAP. 176	30-09-1995	
BROADCASTING ACT [2000 Ed., Corrigendum S 41/07]	CAP. 180	15-03-1997	
BRUNEI ECONOMIC DEVELOPMENT BOARD ACT [2003 Ed., Amended by S 11/03]	CAP. 104	11-04-1975	
BRUNEI FISHERY LIMITS ACT [1984 Ed., Amended by S 25/09]	CAP. 130	01-01-1983	
BRUNEI INVESTMENT AGENCY ACT [2002 Ed., Amended by S 14/03, S 64/04, S 15/08, S 78/08]	CAP. 137	01-07-1983	
BRUNEI MALAY SILVERSMITHS GUILD (INCORPORATION) ACT [1984 Ed.]	CAP. 115	15-07-1959	
BRUNEI NATIONAL ARCHIVES ACT [1984 Ed.]	CAP. 116	01-08-1981	
BRUNEI NATIONAL PETROLEUM COMPANY SENDIRIAN BERHAD ORDER 2002 [Amended by S 6/2003, S 12/2003]	S 6/2002	05-01-2002	
BRUNEI NATIONALITY ACT [2002 Ed., Amended by S 55/2002]	CAP. 15	01-01-1962	
BUFFALOES ACT [1984 Ed.]	CAP. 59	01-01-1909	
BURIAL GROUNDS ACT [1984 Ed.]	CAP. 49	01-01-1932	
BUSINESS NAMES ACT [1984 Ed., Amended by S 30/88]	CAP. 92	01-03-1958	
CENSORSHIP OF FILMS AND PUBLIC ENTERTAINMENTS ACT [2002 Ed.]	CAP. 69	21-08-1962	
CENSUS ACT [2003 Ed.]	CAP. 78	07-06-1947	
CENTRE FOR STRATEGIC AND POLICY STUDIES ORDER, 2006	S 64/2006	01-07-2006	
CHILD CARE CENTRES ORDER 2006	S 37/06	04-03-2006	
CHILDREN AND YOUNG PERSONS ORDER, 2006 [Corrigendum S 24/06, Amended by S 60/08]	S 9/2006		not yet in force
CHILDREN ORDER 2000 [Amended by S 84/00, S 48/03]	S 64/2000	01-09-2000	

CHINESE MARRIAGE ACT [1984 Ed., Amended by S 44/89]	CAP. 126	31-07-1955	
CIVIL AVIATION ORDER, 2006	S 63/2006	20-05-2006	
COIN (IMPORT AND EXPORT) ACT [1984 Ed.]	CAP. 33	01-01-1909	
COMMISSIONS OF ENQUIRY ACT [1984 Ed., Amended by S 35/05]]	CAP. 9	28-04-1962	
COMMISSIONERS FOR OATHS ACT [1999 Ed.]	CAP. 169	26-08-1993	
COMMON GAMING HOUSES ACT [2002 Ed., Amended by S 20/08]	CAP. 28	01-01-1921	
COMPANIES ACT [1984 Ed., Amended by S 26/98, S 23/99, S 69/01, S 10/03, S 45/06, S 96/08]	CAP. 39	01-01-1957	
COMPULSORY EDUCATION ORDER, 2007	S 56/2007	24-11-2007	
COMPUTER MISUSE ACT [2007 Ed.]	CAP. 194	21-06-2000	
CONSTITUTION OF BRUNEI DARUSSALAM [2004 Ed., Amended by S 14/06] Article 8A, 9(2), 9(4), 9(5) - suspended by S 15/06 w.e.f. 21/02/06	CONST. I	29-09-1959	
CONSTITUTION [FINANCIAL PROCEDURE] ORDER [2004 Ed., Amended by S 14/08, S 36/08]	CONST. III	01-01-1960	
CONSULAR RELATIONS ACT [1984 Ed.]	CAP. 118	01-01-1984	
CONTINENTAL SHELF PROCLAMATION [1984 Ed.]	SUP. II		
CONTRACTS ACT [1984 Ed., Amended by S 60/02]	CAP. 106	17-04-1939	
CO-OPERATIVE SOCIETIES ACT [1984 Ed.]	CAP. 84	01-07-1975	
COPYRIGHT ORDER 1999	S 14/2000	01-05-2000	
CRIMINAL CONDUCT (RECOVERY OF PROCEEDS) ORDER 2000 [Amended by S 30/07]	S 52/2000	01-07-2000	
CRIMINAL LAW (PREVENTIVE DETENTION) ACT [2008 Ed.]	CAP. 150	26-11-1984	
CRIMINAL PROCEDURE CODE [2001 Ed., Amended by S 63/02, GN 273/02, S 62/04, S 32/05, S 6/06, S 9/06, S 4/07]	CAP. 7	01-05-1952	S 6/06 & S 9/06 not yet in force
CRIMINALS REGISTRATION ORDER, 2008	S 42/2008	01-04-2008	
CURRENCY ACT [1984 Ed., Repealed by S 16/04 - Currency and Monetary Order]	CAP. 32	Please refer Act	REPEALED w.e.f. 01-02-04

CURRENCY AND MONETARY ORDER 2004 [Corrigendum S 71/04; Amended by S 59/05, S 39/07]	S 16/2004	01-02-2004	
CUSTOMS ACT [1984 Ed., Amended by S 23/89, S 82/00, S 52/01, S 39/06, Repealed by S 39/06 - Customs Order]	CAP. 36	01-01-1955	REPEALED w.e.f. 04-03-06
CUSTOMS ORDER, 2006 [Amended by S 98/08]	S 39/06	04-03-2006	
DANA PENGIRAN MUDA MAHKOTA AL-MUHTADEE BILLAH FOR ORPHANS ACT [2000 Ed.]	CAP. 185	25-08-1998	
DEBTORS ACT [2008 Ed.]	CAP. 195	16-10-2000	
DEFAMATION ACT [2000 Ed.]	CAP. 192	17-08-1999	
DESCRIPTION OF LAND (SURVEY PLANS) ACT [1984 Ed.]	CAP. 101	03-09-1962	
DEVELOPMENT FUND ACT [1984 Ed.]	CAP. 136	01-01-1960	
DIPLOMATIC PRIVILEGES (EXTENSION) ACT [1984 Ed.]	CAP. 85	02-12-1949	
DIPLOMATIC PRIVILEGES (VIENNA CONVENTION) ACT [1984 Ed.]	CAP. 117	01-09-1982	
DISAFFECTED AND DANGEROUS PERSONS ACT [1984 Ed.]	CAP. 111	29-07-1953	
DISASTER MANAGEMENT ORDER 2006	S 26/06	01-08-2006	
DISSOLUTION OF MARRIAGE ACT [1999 Ed.]	CAP. 165	29-04-1992	
DISTRESS ACT [2009 Ed.]	CAP. 199	16-10-2000	
DOGS ACT [1984 Ed., Amended by S 14/90]	CAP. 60	17-04-1939	
DRUG TRAFFICKING (RECOVERY OF PROCEEDS) ACT [2000 Ed., Amended by S 29/07]	CAP. 178	30-03-1996	
EDUCATION ORDER 2003 [Amended by S 86/06]	S 59/2003	20-12-2003	
EDUCATION (BRUNEI BOARD OF EXAMINATIONS) ACT [1984 Ed.]	CAP. 56	01-01-1975	
EDUCATION (NON-GOVERNMENT SCHOOLS) ACT [1984 Ed., Repealed by S 59/03 - Education Order]	CAP. 55	01-01-1953	REPEALED w.e.f. 20-12-03
ELECTION OFFENCES ACT [1984 Ed.]	CAP. 26	28-04-1962	
ELECTRICITY ACT [2003 Ed. Amended by S 68/05]	CAP. 71	05-03-1973	
ELECTRONIC TRANSACTION ACT [2008 Ed.]	CAP. 196	01-05-2001	except Part X
EMBLEMS AND NAMES (PREVENTION OF IMPROPER USE) ACT [1984 Ed.]	CAP. 94	18-01-1968	

EMERGENCY REGULATIONS ACT [1984 Ed.]	CAP. 21	21-02-1933	
EMPLOYMENT AGENCIES ORDER, 2004	S 84/2004	20-12-2004	
EMPLOYMENT INFORMATION ACT [1984 Ed.]	CAP. 99	15-05-1974	
EVIDENCE ACT [2002 Ed., Amended by S 1/06, S 13/06]	CAP. 108	17-04-1939	
EXCHANGE CONTROL ACT [1984 Ed., Repealed by S 70/00]	CAP. 141	01-01-1957	REPEALED w.e.f. 01-07-00
EXCISE ACT [1984 Ed., Repealed by S 40/06 - Excise Order]	CAP. 37	01-01-1925	REPEALED w.e.f. 04-03-06
EXCISE ORDER 2006	S 40/06	04-03-2006	
EXCLUSIVE ECONOMIC ZONE, Proclamation of	S 4/94	20-07-1993	
EXTRADITION (MALAYSIA AND SINGAPORE) ACT [1999 Ed.]	CAP. 154	19-05-84 [S] 01-11-83 [M]	
EXTRADITION ACT [1984 Ed., Repealed by S 10/06 - Extradition Order]	CAP. 8	09-12-1915	REPEALED w.e.f. 07-02-06
EXTRADITION ORDER 2006	S 10/06	07-02-2006	
FATAL ACCIDENTS AND PERSONAL INJURIES ACT [1999 Ed.]	CAP. 160	01-02-1991	
FINANCE COMPANIES ACT [2003 Ed., Amended by S 41/06]	CAP. 89	01-08-1973	
FINGERPRINTS ENACTMENT [Repealed by S 42/08 - Criminals Registration Order, 2008]	17 of 1956	01-01-1957	REPEALED w.e.f. 01-04-08
FIRE SERVICES ACT [2002 Ed., Amended by S 79/06] now become FIRE AND RESCUE w.e.f. 1/8/2006	CAP. 82	04-08-1966	
FISHERIES ACT [1984 Ed., Amended by S 20/02, Repealed by S 25/09 - Fisheries Order, 2009]	CAP. 61	05-03-1973	REPEALED w.e.f. 30-05-09
FISHERIES ORDER, 2009	S 25/2009	30-05-2009	
FOREST ACT [2002 Ed., Amended by S 47/07]	CAP. 46	30-10-1934	
GENEVA AND RED CROSS ACT [1984 Ed.]	CAP. 86	12-12-1938	
GENEVA CONVENTION ORDER, 2005	S 40/2005		not yet in force
GUARDIANSHIP OF INFANTS ACT [2000 Ed.]	CAP. 191	01-08-1999	

GURKHA RESERVE UNIT ACT [1984 Ed.]	CAP. 135	09-05-1981	
HALAL CERTIFICATE AND HALAL LABEL ORDER, 2005 [Amended by S 75/08]	S 39/2005	01-08-2008	
HALAL MEAT ACT [2000 Ed., Amended by GN 274/02]	CAP. 183	17-04-1999	
HIJACKING AND PROTECTION OF AIRCRAFT ORDER 2000	S 41/2000	24-05-2000	
HIRE PURCHASE ORDER, 2006	S 44/06	04-03-2006	
IMMIGRATION ACT [2006 Ed., Amended by S 34/07]	CAP. 17	01-07-1958	
INCOME TAX ACT [2003 Ed., Amended by S 51/08, S 52/08, S 13/09]	CAP. 35	31-12-1949	
INCOME TAX (PETROLEUM) ACT [2004 Ed.]	CAP. 119	18-12-1963	
INDUSTRIAL CO-ORDINATION ORDER 2001	S 44/2001	01-06-2001	
INDUSTRIAL DESIGNS ORDER 1999	S 7/2000	01-05-2000	
INFECTIOUS DISEASES ORDER 2003 [Amended by S 27/06]	S 34/2003	08-05-2003	
INSURANCE ORDER, 2006 [Amended by S 88/06, S 28/07, S 54/07]	S 48/2006	04-03-2006	
INTERMEDIATE COURTS ACT [1999 Ed., Amended by S 57/04, S 74/04, S 80/06]	CAP. 162	01-07-1991	
INTERNAL SECURITY ACT [2008 Ed.]	CAP. 133	01-04-1983	
INTERNATIONAL ARBITRATION ORDER, 2009	S 35/2009		not yet in force
INTERNATIONAL BANKING ORDER 2000 [Amended by S 9/01]	S 53/2000	01-07-2000	
INTERNATIONAL BUSINESS COMPANIES ORDER 2000 [Amended by S 37/03]	S 56/2000	01-07-2000	
INTERNATIONAL INSURANCE AND TAKAFUL ORDER 2002	S 43/2002	01-07-2002	
INTERNATIONAL LIMITED PARTNERSHIP ORDER 2000 [Amended by S 7/01]	S 45/2000	01-07-2000	
INTERNATIONAL TRUSTS ORDER 2000	S 55/2000	01-07-2000	
INTERNATIONALLY PROTECTED PERSONS ACT [1984 Ed.]	CAP. 16	08-07-1995	
INTERPRETATION AND GENERAL CLAUSES ACT [2006 Ed.]	CAP. 4	29-09-1959	
INTOXICATING SUBSTANCES ACT [1999 Ed., Amended by S 58/07]	CAP. 161	01-05-1992	

NATIONAL BANK OF BRUNEI BERHAD; NATIONAL FINANCE SENDIRIAN BERHAD ACT [1999 Ed.]	CAP. 156	19-11-1986	
NATIONAL REGISTRATION ACT [2002 Ed.]	CAP. 19	01-03-1965	
NEWSPAPERS ACT [2002 Ed., Amended by S 36/05, S 86/08]	CAP. 105	01-01-1959	
NORTH BORNEO (DEFINITION BOUNDARIES) ORDER IN COUNCIL 1958 [1984 Ed.]	Sup. III		
NURSES REGISTRATION ACT [1984 Ed.]	CAP. 140	01-01-1968	
OATHS AND AFFIRMATIONS ACT [2001 Ed.]	CAP. 3	08-09-1958	
OFFENDERS (PROBATION AND COMMUNITY SERVICE) ORDER, 2006 [Amended by S 80/08]	S 6/2006		not yet in force
OFFICIAL SECRETS ACT [1988 Ed., Amended by S 52/05]	CAP. 153	02-01-1940	
OLD AGE AND DISABILITY PENSIONS ACT [1984 Ed., Amended by GN 273/02, GN 649/03, S 38/08]	CAP. 18	01-01-1955	
PASSPORTS ACT [1984 Ed., Amended by S 6/86, S 2/00, S 44/03, S 24/04, S 54/05, S 33/07]	CAP. 146	14-12-1983	
PATENTS ORDER, 1999	S 42/99		not yet in force
PAWNBROKERS ACT [1984 Ed., Repealed by S 41/05 - Pawnbrokers Order]	CAP. 63	01-01-1920	REPEALED w.e.f. 01-08-05
PAWNBROKERS ORDER 2002 [Amended by S 41/05]	S 60/2002	01-08-2005	
PENAL CODE [2001 Ed.]	CAP. 22	01-05-1952	
PENSIONS ACT [1984 Ed., Amended S 23/87, S 37/08]	CAP. 38	01-03-1959	
PERBADANAN TABUNG AMANAH ISLAM BRUNEI ACT [1999 Ed., Amended by S 15/03, S 29/04]	CAP. 163	29-09-1991	
PERSATUAN BULAN SABIT MERAH NEGARA BRUNEI DARUSSALAM (INCORPORATION) ACT [1999 Ed., Amended by S 40/05]	CAP. 159	28-11-1999	S 40/05 not yet in force
PETROLEUM MINING ACT [2002 Ed.]	CAP. 44	18-11-1963	
PETROLEUM (PIPE-LINES) ACT [1984 Ed.]	CAP. 45	04-03-1920	
PHARMACISTS REGISTRATION ORDER 2001	S 21/2001	01-07-2001	

POISONS ACT [1984 Ed., Amended by S 16/96, S 28/01]	CAP. 114	01-07-1957	
PORTS ACT [1984 Ed., Amended by S 17/88, S 26/02, S 18/05]	CAP. 144	01-01-1986	
POST OFFICE ACT [1984 Ed., Amended by S 17/97]	CAP. 52	01-05-1988	
POWERS OF ATTORNEY ACT [2002 Ed.]	CAP. 13	01-01-1922	
PRESERVATION OF BOOKS ACT [1984 Ed.]	CAP. 125	18-01-1967	
PREVENTION OF CORRUPTION ACT [2002 Ed.]	CAP. 131	01-01-1982	
PREVENTION OF POLLUTION OF THE SEA ORDER, 2005	S 18/2005	28-03-2005	
PRICE CONTROL ACT [2002 Ed.]	CAP. 142	13-03-1974	
PRIME MINISTER'S INCORPORATION ORDER 1984 [Amended the Constitution (Mentri Besar Incorporation) Order 1960 (S 55/60)]	S 5/84	01-01-1984	
PRISONS ACT [1984 Ed., Amended by S 12/89]	CAP. 51	01-07-1979	
PROBATE AND ADMINISTRATION ACT [1984 Ed.]	CAP. 11	01-02-1956	
PROTECTED AREAS AND PROTECTED PLACES ACT [1984 Ed.]	CAP. 147	01-12-1983	
PUBLIC ENTERTAINMENT ACT [2000 Ed.]	CAP. 181	01-06-1997	
PUBLIC HEALTH (FOOD) ACT [2000 Ed., Amended by S 73/00, S 64/02]	CAP. 182	01-01-2001	
PUBLIC OFFICERS (LIABILITIES) ACT [1984 Ed., Repealed by S 40/00]	CAP. 80	25-02-1929	REPEALED w.e.f. 24-05-00
PUBLIC ORDER ACT [2002 Ed., Amended by S 33/05]	CAP. 148	01-11-1983	
PUBLIC SERVICE COMMISSION ACT [1984 Ed.]	CAP. 83	01-01-1983	
QUARANTINE AND PREVENTION OF DISEASE ACT [1984 Ed., Repealed by S 34/03 - Infectious Diseases Order]	CAP. 47	09-08-1934	REPEALED w.e.f. 08-05-03
RECIPROCAL ENFORCEMENT OF FOREIGN JUDGMENTS ACT [2000 Ed.]	CAP. 177	27-03-1996	
REGISTERED AGENTS AND TRUSTEES LICENSING ORDER 2000	S 54/2000	01-07-2000	
REGISTRATION OF ADOPTIONS ACT [1984 Ed., Amended by S 15/01]	CAP. 123	01-01-1962	
REGISTRATION OF GUESTS ACT [1984 Ed.]	CAP. 122	01-07-1974	
REGISTRATION OF MARRIAGES ACT	CAP. 124	01-01-1962	

[2002 Ed.]			
RELIGIOUS COUNCIL AND KADIS COURTS ACT [1984 Ed., Amended by S 1/88, S 31/90, S 37/98, S 12/00, S 24/03, S 17/05, S 26/05]	CAP. 77	01-02-1956	
ROAD TRAFFIC ACT [2007 Ed., Amended by S 39/04, S 59/08]	CAP. 68	01-01-1956	S 39/04 not yet in force
ROYAL BRUNEI ARMED FORCES ACT [1984 Ed., Amended by S 2/06]	CAP. 149	01-01-1984	
ROYAL BRUNEI POLICE FORCE ACT [1984 Ed.]	CAP. 50	31-12-1983	
ROYAL ORDERS AND DECORATIONS [1984 Ed.]	Sup. V		
RUBBER DEALERS ACT [1984 Ed.]	CAP. 64	01-01-1921	
SALE OF GOODS ACT [1999 Ed.]	CAP. 170	03-05-1994	
SARAWAK (DEFINITION OF BOUNDARIES) ORDER IN COUNCIL 1958 [1984 Ed.]	Sup. IV		
SEAMEN'S UNEMPLOYMENT INDEMNITY ACT [1984 Ed.]	CAP. 75	02-10-1939	
SECOND-HAND DEALERS ACT [1984 Ed.]	CAP. 65	01-01-1934	
SECURITIES ORDER 2001 [Amended by S 33/02, S 43/05]	S 31/2001	01-03-2001	
SECURITY AGENCIES ACT [2000 Ed.]	CAP. 187	01-06-2000	
SEDITION ACT [1984 Ed., Amended by S 34/05]	CAP. 24	06-04-1948	
SMALL CLAIMS TRIBUNALS ORDER, 2006	S 81/2006		not yet in force
SOCIETIES ACT [1984 Ed., Repealed by S 1/05 - Societies Order]	CAP. 66	04-10-1948	REPEALED w.e.f. 04-01-05
SOCIETIES ORDER, 2005	S 1/2005	04-01-2005	
SPECIFIC RELIEF ACT [1984 Ed., Amended by S 59/04]	CAP. 109	17-04-1939	
STAMP ACT [2003 Ed.]	CAP. 34	01-01-1909	
STATISTICS ACT [1984 Ed.]	CAP. 81	01-08-1977	
STATUTORY DECLARATION ACT [1984 Ed.]	CAP. 12	11-01-1951	
STATUTORY FUNDS APPROPRIATION ENACTMENT 1959 [Amended by S 63/63, 7 of 1966, 19 of 1967, 4 of 1975, S 50/76, S 49/76, S 110/79, S 12/82, S 13/82, S 42/84, S 13/86, S 22/93, S 22/03, S 39/08]	9 of 1959	01-01-1960	

SUBORDINATE COURTS ACT [2001 Ed., Amended by S 56/04, S 73/04, S 9/06, S 60/08]	CAP. 6	01-01-1983	S 9/06 and S60/08 not yet in force
SUBSCRIPTION CONTROL ACT [1984 Ed.]	CAP. 91	15-12-1953	
SUCCESSION AND REGENCY PROCLAMATION 1959 [2004 Ed., Amended by S 16/06, S 78/06]	CONST. II	29-09-1959	
SUMMONSES AND WARRANTS (SPECIAL PROVISIONS) ACT [1999 Ed.]	CAP. 155	19-05-84 [S] 01-11-83 [M]	
SUNGAI LIANG AUTHORITY ACT [2009 Ed.]	CAP. 200	06-04-2007	
SUPREME COURT ACT [2001 Ed., Amended by S 55/04, S 61/04, S 72/04]	CAP. 5	16-09-1963	
SUPREME COURT (APPEALS TO PRIVY COUNCIL) ACT [1999 Ed., Amended by S 45/05]	CAP. 158	01-02-1990	
SUSTAINABILITY FUND ORDER, 2008	S 36/2008	11-03-2008	
SYARIAH COURTS ACT [2000 Ed., Amended by S 17/05]	CAP. 184	26-03-2001	
SYARIAH COURTS CIVIL PROCEDURE ORDER, 2005 [available in Malay text only] - PERINTAH ACARA MAL MAHKAMAH-MAHKAMAH SYARIAH, 2005	S 26/2005	06-04-2005	
SYARIAH COURTS EVIDENCE ORDER, 2001	S 63/2001	15-10-2001 except s.5	
SYARIAH FINANCIAL SUPERVISORY BOARD ORDER, 2006 [Amended by S 65/07]	S 5/2006	17-01-2006	
TABUNG AMANAH PEKERJA ACT [1999 Ed., Amended by S 9/99, S 9/00, S 16/03, S 2/07]	CAP. 167	01-01-1993	
TAKAFUL ORDER, 2008	S 100/2008	30-09-2008	
TELECOMMUNICATIONS ACT [1984 Ed. Repealed by S 38/01 - Telecommunication Order]	CAP. 54	01-12-1974	REPEALED w.e.f. 01-04-06
TELECOMMUNICATIONS ORDER 2001	S 38/2001	01-04-2006	
TELECOMMUNICATION SUCCESSOR COMPANY ORDER 2001 [Corrigendum S 25/06]	S 37/2001	01-04-2006	
TERRITORIAL WATERS OF BRUNEI ACT [2002 Ed.]	CAP. 138	10-02-1983	
TOBACCO ORDER 2005	S 49/2005	01-06-2008	

TOKYO CONVENTION ACT [2008 Ed.]	CAP. 198	24-05-2000	
TOWN AND COUNTRY PLANNING (DEVELOPMENT CONTROL) ACT [1984 Ed.]	CAP. 143	19-09-1972	
TRADE DISPUTES ACT [1984 Ed.]	CAP. 129	21-01-1962	
TRADE MARKS ACT [2000 Ed.]	CAP. 98	01-06-2000	
TRADE UNIONS ACT [1984 Ed.]	CAP. 128	20-01-1962	
TRAFFICKING AND SMUGGLING OF PERSONS ORDER, 2004	S 82/2004	20-12-2004	
TRANSFER OF FUNCTIONS OF THE MINISTER OF LAW ACT [2000 Ed.]	CAP. 186	16-09-1998	
TRAVEL AGENTS ACT [1984 Ed.]	CAP. 103	01-01-1982	
TREATY OF FRIENDSHIP AND CO-OPERATION [1984 Ed.]	SUP. I		
TRESPASS ON ROYAL PROPERTY ACT [1984 Ed.]	CAP. 23	01-01-1918	
UNDESIRABLE PUBLICATIONS ACT [1984 Ed., Amended by S 60/07]	CAP. 25	01-12-1986	
UNFAIR CONTRACTS TERMS ACT [1999 Ed.]	CAP. 171	18-06-1994	
UNIVERSITI BRUNEI DARUSSALAM ACT [1999 Ed., Amended by S 22/00, S 17/03, S 84/06]	CAP. 157	01-07-1988	
UNIVERSITI ISLAM SULTAN SHARIF ALI ORDER, 2008	S 71/2008	14-08-2008	
UNLAWFUL CARNAL KNOWLEDGE ACT [1984 Ed.]	CAP. 29	15-01-1938	
VALUERS AND ESTATE AGENTS ORDER, 2009	S 30/2009	01-07-2009	
VETERINARY SURGEONS ORDER, 2005	S 30/2005	02-06-2008	
VICAR APOSTOLIC OF KUCHING (INCORPORATION) ACT [1984 Ed.]	CAP. 110	11-08-1973	
WATER SUPPLY ACT [1984 Ed.]	CAP. 121	01-01-1968	
WEIGHTS AND MEASURES ACT [1986 Ed.]	CAP. 151	01-01-1987	
WILD FAUNA AND FLORA ORDER, 2007	S 77/2007	31-12-2007	
WILD LIFE PROTECTION ACT [1984 Ed.]	CAP. 102	01-08-1981	
WILLS ACT [2000 Ed.]	CAP. 193	21-10-1999	
WOMEN AND GIRLS PROTECTION ACT [1984 Ed., Amended by GN 649/03]	CAP. 120	19-04-1973	
WORKMEN'S COMPENSATION ACT [1984 Ed., Amended by GN 273/02]	CAP. 74	01-04-1957	
YAYASAN SULTAN HAJI HASSANAL BOLKIAH ACT [2008 Ed.]	CAP. 166	05-10-1992	

STRATEGIC GOVERNMENT CONTACT IN BRUNEY

Prime Minister's Office
E-Mail: PRO@jpm.gov.bn
Telephone: 673 - 2 - 229988
Fax: 673 - 2 - 241717
Telex: BU2727
Address:
Prime Minister's Office
Istana Nurul Iman
Bandar Seri Begawan BA1000

Audit Department
Prime Minister's Office
Jalan Menteri Besar
Bandar Seri Begawan BB 39 10
Brunei Darussalam
Telephone: (02) 380576
Facsimile: (02) 380679
E-mail: jabaudbd@brunet.bn

Information Department
Prime Minister's Office
Berakas Old Airport
Bandar Seri Begawan
BB 3510
Brunei Darussalam.
E-mail:- pelita@brunet.bn
Fax: 673 2 381004
Tel: 673 2 380527

Narcotics Control Bureau
Prime Minister's Office
Jalan Tungku Gadong
Bandar Seri Begawan BE 2110
Tel No: 02-448877 / 422479 / 422480 / 422481
Fax No: 02-422477
E-mail: ncb@brunet.bn

One-Stop Agency
The Ministry of Industry and Primary Resources
Bandar Seri Begawan 1220
Brunei Darussalam
Telefax: (02) 244811
Telex: MIPRS BU 2111
Cable: MIPRS BRUNEI

Head Policy and Administration Division
Ministry of Industry and Primary Resources
Jalan Menteri Besar, Bandar Seri Begawan 1220
Brunei Darussalam
Tel: (02) 382822

Secretary of Public Service Commission
Old Airport
Bandar Seri Begawan BB 3510
Tel No: 02-381961
E-mail: bplspa@brunet.bn

Semaun Holdings Sdn Bhd
Unit 2.02, Block D, 2nd Floor
Yayasan Sultan Haji Hassanal Bolkiah Complex
Jalan Pretty
Bandar Seri Begawan BS8711
Brunei Darussalam
E-mail address: semaun@brunet.bn

Department of Agriculture
Ministry of Industry & Primary Resources
BB3510
Brunei Darussalam
Telephone: + 673 2 380144
Fax: + 673 2 382226
Telex: PERT BU 2456

Land Transport Department
KM 6, Jalan Gadong,
Beribi BE1110,
Brunei Darussalam.
Tel : (673-2) 451979
Fax : (673-2) 424775
Email : latis@brunet.bn

FOREIGN MISSIONS

AUSTRALIA

Australian High Commission
(His Excellency Mr. Neal Patrick Davis - High Commissioner)
4th flr Teck Guan Plaza, Jln Sultan
Bandar Seri Begawan BS8811
Brunei Darussalam
or
P.O. Box 2990
Bandar Seri Begawan, BS8675
Brunei Darussalam
Tel: 673 2 229435/6
Fax: 673 2 221652

AUSTRIA

Austrian Consulate General
No. 5 Taman Jubli, Spg 75,
Jalan Subok,
Bandar Seri Begawan BD2717
Brunei Darussalam
or
P.O. Box 1303,
Bandar Seri Begawan, BS8672
Brunei Darussalam
Tel : 673 2 261083
Email: austroko@brunet.bn

BANGLADESH

High Commission of People's Republic of Bangladesh
(His Excellency Mr. Muhammad Mumtaz Hussain - High Commissioner)
AAR Villa, House No. 5,
Simpang 308, Jalan Lambak Kanan,
Berakas, BB1714
Brunei Darussalam
Tel: 673 2 394716
Fax: 673 2 394715

BELGIUM

Consulate of Belgium
2nd Floor, 146 Jln Pemancha
Bandar Seri Begawan BS8711
Brunei Darussalam
or
P.O.Box 65,
Bandar Seri Begawan, BS8670
Brunei Darussalam
Tel: 673 2 222298
Fax: 673 2 220895

BRITAIN

British High Commission
(His Excellency Mr. Stuart Laing - High Commissioner)
Unit 2.01, Block D of Yayasan Sultan Hassanal Bolkiah
Bandar Seri Begawan BS8711
Brunei Darussalam
or
P.O.Box 2197
Bandar Seri Begawan, BS8674
Brunei Darussalam
Tel: 673 2 222231
Fax: 673 2 226001

CAMBODIA

Royal Embassy of Cambodia
(His Highness Prince Sisowath Phandaravong - Ambassador)
No. 8, Simpang 845
Kampong Tasek Meradun, Jalan Tutong, BF1520
Brunei Darussalam
Tel: 673 2 650046
Fax: 673 2 650646

CANADA

High Commission of Canada
(His Excellency Mr. Neil Reeder - High Commissioner)
Suite 51 - 52, Britannia House, Jalan Cator
Bandar Seri Begawan, BS8811
Brunei Darussalam
Tel: 673 2 220043
Fax: 673 2 220040

CHINA

Embassy of People's Republic of China
(His Excellency Mr. Wang Jianli - Ambassador)
No. 1, 3 & 5, Simpang 462
Kampong Sungai Hanching,
Jln Muara, BC2115
Brunei Darussalam
or
P.O.Box 121
M.P.C, Berakas BB3577
Brunei Darussalam
Tel: 673 2 339609
Fax: 673 2 339612

DENMARK

Consulate of Denmark
Unit 6, Bangunan Hj Tahir,
Spg 103, Jln Gadong
Bandar Seri Begawan
Brunei Darussalam
or
P.O.Box 140
Bandar Seri Begawan, BS8670
Brunei Darussalam
Tel: 673 2 422050, 427525, 447559
Fax: 673 2 427526

FINLAND

Consulate of Finland
Bee Seng Shipping Company
No.7 1st Floor Sufri Complex
KM 2, Jalan Tutong
Bandar Seri Begawan, BA2111
Brunei Darussalam
or
P.O.Box 1777
Bandar Seri Begawan, BS8673
Brunei Darusslaam
Tel: 673 2 243847
Fax: 673 2 224495

FRANCE

Embassy of the Republic of France
(His Excelleny Mr. Jean Pierre Lafosse - Ambassador)
#306-310 Kompleks Jln Sultan,
3rd Floor, 51-55 Jln Sultan
Bandar Seri Begawan BS8811
Brunei Darussalam
or
P.O.Box 3027
Bandar Seri Begawan, BS8675
Brunei Darussalam
Tel: 673 2 220960 / 1
Fax: 673 2 243373

GERMANY

Embassy of the Federal Republic of Germany
(His Excellency Klaus-Peter Brandes - Ambassador)
6th flr, Wisma Raya Building
Lot 49-50, Jln Sultan
Bandar Seri Begawan, BS8811
Brunei Darussalam
or
P.O.Box 3050
Bandar Seri Begawan, BS8675
Brunei Darussalam
Tel: 673 2 225547 / 74
Fax: 673 2 225583

INDIA

High Commission of India
(His Excellency Mr. Dinesh K. Jain - High Commissioner)
Lot 14034, Spg 337,
Kampong Manggis, Jln Muara, BC3515
Brunei Darussalam
Tel: 673 2 339947 / 339751
Fax: 673 2 339783
Email: hicomind@brunet.bn

INDONESIA

Embassy of the Republic of Indonesia
(His Excellency Mr. Rahardjo

Djojonegoro - Ambassador)
Lot 4498, Spg 528
Sungai Hanching Baru, Jln Muara,
BC3013
Brunei Darussalam
or
P.O.Box 3013
Bandar Seri Begawan, BS8675
Brunei Darussalam
Tel: 673 2 330180 / 445
Fax: 673 2 330646

IRAN

Embassy of the Islamic Republic of Iran
No. 2, Lot 14570, Spg 13
Kampong Serusop, Jalan Berakas,
BB2313
Brunei Darussalam
Tel: 673 2 330021 / 29
Fax: 673 2 331744

JAPAN

Embassy of Japan
(His Excellency Mr. Hajime Tsujimoto - Ambassador)
No 1 & 3, Jalan Jawatan Dalam
Kampong Mabohai
Bandar Seri Begawan, BA1111
Brunei Darussalam
or
P.O.Box 3001
Bandar Seri Begawan, BS8675
Brunei Darussalam
Tel: 673 2 229265 / 229592, 237112 - 5
Fax: 673 2 229481

KOREA

Embassy of the Republic of Korea
(His Excellency Kim Ho-tae - Ambassador)
No.9, Lot 21652
Kg Beribi, Jln Gadong, BE1118
Brunei Darussalam
Tel: 673 2 650471 / 300, 652190
Fax: 673 2 650299

LAOS

Embassy of the Lao People's Democratic Republic
(His Excellency Mr. Ammone Singhavong - Ambassador)
Lot. No. 19824, House No. 11
Simpang 480, Jalan Kebangsaan Lama
Off Jalan Muara, BC4115
Brunei Darussalam
or
P.O.Box 2826
Bandar Seri Begawan, BS8675
Brunei Darussalam
Tel: 673 2 345666
Fax: 673 2 345888

MALAYSIA

Malaysian High Commission
(His Excellency Wan Yusof Embong - High Commissioner)
No.27 & 29, Simpang 396-39
Kampong Sungai Akar
Jalan Kebangsaan, BC4115
Brunei Darussalam
or
P.O.Box 2826
Bandar Seri Begawan, BS8675
Brunei Darussalam
Tel: 673 2 345652
Fax: 673 2 345654

MYANMAR

Embassy of the Union of Myanmar
(His Excellency U Than Tun - Ambassador)
No. 14, Lot 2185 / 46292
Simpang 212, Kampong Rimba,
Gadong BE3119
Brunei Darussalam
Tel: 673 2 450506 / 7
Fax: 673 2 451008

NETHERLANDS

Netherlands Consulate
c/o Brunei Shell Petroleum Co. Sdn Bhd
Seria KB3534
Brunei Darussalam
Tel: 673 3 372005, 373045

NEW ZEALAND

New Zealand Consulate
36A Seri Lambak Complex,
Jalan Berakas, BB1714
Brunei Darussalam
or
P.O.Box 2720
Bandar Seri Begawan, BS8675
Brunei Darusslam
Tel: 673 2 331612, 331010
Fax: 673 2 331612

NORWAY

Royal Norwegian Consulate
Unit No. 407A - 410A
4th Floor, Wisma Jaya
Jalan Pemancha
Bandar Seri Begawan, BS8811
Brunei Darussalam
Tel: 673 2 239091 / 2 / 3 / 4
Fax: 673 2 239095/6

OMAN

Embassy of the Sultanate of Oman
(His Excellency Mr. Ahmad Moh,d Masoud Al-Riyami - Ambassador)
No.35 Simpang 100,
Jalan Tungku Link
Kampong Pengkalan, Gadong BE3719
Brunei Darussalam
or
P.O.Box 2875
Bandar Seri Begawan, BS8675
Brunei Darussalam
Tel: 673 2 446953 / 4 / 7 / 8
Fax: 673 2 449646

PAKISTAN

Pakistan High Commission
(His Excellency Major General (Rtd) Irshad Ullah Tarar - High Commission)
No.5 Kampong Sungai Akar
Jalan Kebangsaan, BC4115
Brunei Darussalam
Tel: 673 2 6334989, 339797
Fax: 673 2 334990

PHILIPPINES

Embassy of the Republic of Philippines
His Excellency Mr. Enrique A. Zaldivar - Ambassador)
Rm 1 & 2, 4th & 5th floor
Badiah Building, Mile 1 1/2 Jln Tutong
Brunei Darussalam, BA2111
or
P.O.Box 3025
Bandar Seri Begawan, BS8675
Brunei Darussalam
Tel: 673 2 241465 / 6
Fax: 673 2 237707

SAUDI ARABIA

Royal Embassy of Kingdom of Saudi Arabia
No. 1, Simpang 570
Kampong Salar
Jalan Muara, BU1429
Brunei Darusslam
Tel: 673 2 792821 / 2 / 3
Fax: 673 2 792826 / 7

SINGAPORE

Singapore High Commission
(His Excellency Tee Tua Ba - High Commissioner)
No. 8, Simpang, 74,
Jalan Subok, BD1717
Brunei Darussalam
or
P.O.Box 2159

Bandar Seri Begawan, BS8674
Brunei Darussalam
Tel: 673 2 227583 / 4 / 5
Fax: 673 2 220957

SWEDEN

Consulate of Sweden
Blk A, Unit 1, 2nd Floor
Abdul Razak Plaza,
Jalan Gadong,
Bandar Seri Begawan, BE3919
Brunei Darussalam
Tel: 673 2 448423, 444326
Fax: 673 2 448419

THAILAND

Royal Thai Embassy
(His Excellency Thinakorn Kanasuta - Ambassador
No. 2, Simpang 682,
Kampong Bunut, Jalan Tutong, BF1320
Brunei Darussalam
Tel: 673 2 653108 / 9
Fax: 673 2 262752

UNITED STATE OF AMERICA

Embassy of the United States of America
3rd Flr, Teck Guan Plaza,
Jalan Sultan
Bandar Seri Begawan BS8811
Brunei Darussalam
Tel: 673 2 229670
Fax: (02) 225293

VIETNAM

Embassy of the Socialist Republic of Vietnam
(His Excellency Tran Tien Vinh - Ambassador)
No. 10, Simpang 485
Kampong Sungai Hanching
Jalan Muara,BC2115
Brunei Darussalam
Tel: 673 2 343167 / 8
Fax: 673 2 343169

BRUNEI'S MISSIONS IN ASEAN, CHINA, JAPAN AND KOREA

CAMBODIA
Embassy of Brunei Darussalam
No : 237, Pasteur St. 51
Sangkat Boeung Keng Kang I
Khan Chamkar Mon
Phnom Penh
Kingdom of Cambodia
Tel : (855) 23211 457 & 23211 458
Fax : (855) 23211 456
E-Mail : Brunei@bigpond.com.kh

CHINA
Embassy of Brunei Darussalam
No. 3 Villa, Qijiayuan Diplomatic Compound
Chaoyang District
Beijing 100600
People's Republic of China 1000600
Tel : 86 (10) 6532 4093 - 6
Fax : 86 (10) 6532 4097
E-Mail : bdb@public.bta.net.cn

INDONESIA
Embassy of Brunei Darussalam
Wisma GKBI
(Gabungan Koperasi Batik Indonesia)
Suite 1901, Jl. Jend. Sudirman No. 28
Jakarta 10210
Indonesia
Tel : 62 (21) 574 1437 - 39 / 574 1470 - 72
Fax : 62 (21) 574 1463

JAPAN
Embassy of Brunei Darussalam
5-2 Kitashinagawa 6-Chome
Shinagawa-ku
Tokyo 141
Japan
Tel : 81 (3) 3447 7997 / 9260
Fax : 81 (3) 344 79260

REPUBLIC OF KOREA
Embassy of Brunei Darussalam
7th Floor, Kwanghwamoon Building
211, Sejong-ro, Chongro-Ku
Seoul
Republic of Korea.
Tel : 82 (2) 399 3707 / 3708
Fax : 82 (2) 399 3709
E-Mail : kbrunei@chollian.net

LAOS
Embassy of Brunei Darussalam
No. 333 Unit 25 Ban Phonxay
Xaysettha District
Lanexang Avenue
Vientiane
Laos People's Democratic Republic
Tel : (856) 2141 6114 / 2141 4169
Fax : (856) 2141 6115
E-Mail : kbnbd@laonet.net

MALAYSIA
High Commission of Brunei Darussalam
Tingkat 8 Wisma Sin Heap Lee (SHL)
Jalan Tun Razak
50400 Kuala Lumpur
Malaysia.
Tel : 60 (3) 261 2828
Fax : 60 (3) 263 1302
E-Mail : Sjtnbdkl@tm.net.my

THE UNIION OF MYANMAR
Embassy of Brunei Darussalam
No : 51 Golden Valley
Bahan Township
Yangon
The Union of Myanmar.
Tel: 95 (1) 510 422
Fax: 95 (1) 512 854

PHILIPPINES
Embassy of Brunei Darussalam
11th Floor BPI Building
Ayala Avenue, Corner Paseo De Roxas
Makati City, Metro Manila
Philippines
Tel : 63 (2) 816 2836 - 8
Fax : 63 (2) 816 2876
E-Mail : kbnbdmnl@skynet.net

SINGAPORE
High Commission of Brunei Darussalam
325 Tanglin Road
Singapore 247955
Tel : (65) 733 9055
Fax : (65) 737 5275
E-Mail : comstbs@singnet.com.sg

THAILAND
Embassy of Brunei Darussalam
No. 132 Sukhumvit 23 Road
Watana District
Bangkok 10110
Thailand
Tel : 66 (2) 204 1476 - 9
Fax : 66 (2) 204 1486

VIETNAM
Embassy of Brunei Darussalam
No. 4 Thien Quang Street
Hai Ba Trung District
Hanoi
Vietnam
Tel : (84) 4 826 4816 / 4817 / 4818
Fax : (84) 4 822 2092
E-Mail : bruemviet@hotmail.com

FOOD AND RESTAURANTS

Brunei restaurants, including western style fast food centres, cater to a wide range of tastes and palates.
Visitors can also sample authentic local food offered at the tamu night market in the capital.

The market, along the Kianggeh river, is actually open from early morning. It takes on a special atmosphere at night when crowds throng its alleys to shop and eat at the lowest prices in town.
Tropical fruits like watermelon, papaya, mango and banana are also available.
Locals are fond of the Malay-style satay, bits of beef or chicken in a stick, cooked over low fire and dipped in a tangy peanut sauce.

Brunei's first Chinese halal restaurant is Emperor's Court, owned by Royal Brunei Catering, which caters to Cantonese and Western tastebuds.

A list of restaurants in the capital and Seria-Kuala Belait areas follows:
Bandar Seri Begawan
Aumrin Restaurant, 1 Bangunan Hasbullah, 4 Jalan Gadong
Airport Restaurant, Brunei International Airport
Coffee Tree, Unit 3, top floor ,Mabohai Shopping Complex
Emperor's Court, 1st Floor, Wisma Haji Mohd Taha, Jalan Gadong
Excellent Taste, G5 Gadong Properties Centre, Jalan Gadong
Express Fast Food, 22/23 Jalan Sultan
Ghawar Restaurant, 3 Ground Floor Bang Hasbullah 4
Jade Garden Chinese Restaurant, Riverview Inn, Km 1 Jalan Gadong
Jolibee Family Restaurant, Utama Bowling Centre, Km 11/2 Jalan Tutong
Kentucky Fried Chicken (B) Sdn Bhd, G15-G16 Plaza Athirah
Lucky Restaurant, Umi Kalthum Building, Jalan Tutong
McDonald's Restaurant, 10-12 Block H, Abdul Razak Complex, Simpang 137, Gadong
Phongmun Restaurant, Nos. 56-60, 2nd Floor Teck Guan Plaza
Pizza Hut, Block J, Unit 2 & 3 Abdul Razak Complex
Pondok Sari Wangi, 12 Blk A, Abdul Razak Complex, Jalan Gadong
Popular Restaurant, 5, Ground floor, PAP Hajjah Norain Building
QR Restaurant, Blk C, Abdul Razak Complex, Jalan Gadong
Rainbow Restaurant, 110 Jalan Batu Bersurat, Gadong
Rasa Sayang Restaurant, 607 Bangunan Guru-Guru Melayu
Rose Garden Restaurant, 8 Blk C, Abdul Razak Complex, Jalan Gadong
Season's Restaurant, Gadong Centrepoint
SD Cafe, 6-7 Bangunan Hj Othman, Simpang 105, Jalan Gadong
Seri Kamayan Restaurant, 4 & 5 Bangunan Hj Tahir ,Simpang 103, Jalan Gadong
Seri Maradum Baru, Block C6, Abdul Razak Complex
Sugar Bun Fast Food, Lot 16397 Mabohai Complex, Jalan Kebangsaan
Schezuan's Dynasty Restaurant, Gadong Centrepoint
Swensen's Ice Cream and Fine Food Restaurant, 17-18 Ground Floor Bagunan Halimatul Sa'adiah, Gadong
Tenaga Restaurant, 6 1st Floor Bangunan Hasbollah 4
The Stadium Restaurant, Stadium Negara Hassanal Bolkiah
Tropicana Seafood Restaurant, Block 1 Ground Floor, Pang's Building,Muara
Kuala Belait/Seria
Belait Restaurant, Jalan Bunga Raya
Buccaneer Steak House, Lot 94 Jalan McKerron
Cottage Restaurant, 38 Jalan Pretty
Jolene Restaurant, 83,1st Jalan Bunga Raya
New China Restaurant, 39/40 3rd Floor, Ang's Building, Jalan Sultan Omar Ali, Seria

New Cheng Wah Restaurant, 14 Jalan Sultan Omar Ali, Seria
Orchid Room, B5, 1st Floor, Jalan Bunga Raya
Red Wing Restaurant, 12 Jalan Sultan Omar Ali, Seria
Tasty Cake Shop/Pretty Inn, 26 Jalan Sultan Omar Ali, Seria
Tasconi's Pizza, Simpang 19, Jalan Sungai Pandan

WHERE TO SHOP

For many travellers one of the pleasures of visiting another country is finding something of interest and value for one's self, family or friends. There are many shops in Brunei offering a wide variety of goods at competitive prices. These range from modern department stores to small market stalls where bargaining is still commonly practised.

Modern department stores are found in the major towns of Bandar Seri Begawan, Tutong, Kuala Belait and Seria. In addition to these departmental stores there is a wide variety of old-fashioned shophouses as well as more modern air-conditioned shops.

Most items ranging from the latest electronic goods and imported luxury goods to common household items and groceries can be conveniently found in these shops.

Traditional items that reflect the culture of Brunei like the brass cannon, kris and kain songket, better known as "jong sarat" are excellent souvenirs to bring home from a visit to the country. These can be purchased at the Arts and Handicrafts Centre which is located off Kota Batu, and also at the airport.

Before leaving Brunei make sure you stop by the Duty Free shops at the airport. These offer a wide range of luxury goods, garments, jewellery, writing instruments, perfumes, handicrafts, Brunei souvenirs, books and chocolates at very reasonable prices.

SHOPPING CENTRES

Hua Ho Department Store, Jln Gadong, Bandar Seri Begawan

Kota Mutiara Department Store, Bangunan Darussalam, Bandar Seri Begawan

Lai Lai Department Store, Mile 1 Jln Tutong, Bandar Seri Begawan

Millimewah Department Store (BSB), Bangunan Darussalam, Bandar Seri Begawan

Millimewah Department Store (Tutong),Tutong

Millimewah Department Store (Seria), Seria

Princess Inn Department Store, Mile 1 Jln Tutong , Bandar Seri Begawan

Tiong Hin Superstore,Jln Muara, Bandar Seri Begawan

Megamart,Jln Gadong, Bandar Seri Begawan

Wisma Jaya Complex, Jln Pemancha, Bandar Seri Begawan

First Emporium & Supermarket, Mohammad Yussof Complex, Jln Kubah Makam DiRaja, Bandar Seri Begawan

Seria Plaza, Seria

Seaview Department Store, Jln Maulana, Kuala Belait

TRAVEL AGENTS

BANDAR SERI BEGAWAN

Antara Travel & Tours Sdn Bhd 02-448805/808
Anthony Tours & Travel Sdn Bhd 02-228668
Borneo Leisure Travel Sdn Bhd 02-223420
Brunei Travel Services Sdn Bhd 02-236006
Century Travel Centre Sdn Bhd 02-227296
Churiah Travel Service 02-224422
Darat Dan Laut 02-426321
Freme Travel Services Sdn Bhd 02-234277
Halim Tours & Travel Sdn Bhd 02-226688
Intan Travel & Trading Agencies 02-427340
Jasra Harrisons (B) Sdn Bhd 02-236675
JB Travel & Insurance Agencies 02-239132
JJ Tour Service (B) Sdn Bhd 02-224761
Ken Travel & Trading Sdn Bhd 02-223127
Mahasiswa Travel Service 02-243452
Oriental Travel Services 02-226464
Overseas Travel Services Sdn Bhd 02-445322
Sarawak Travel Service Sdn Bhd 02-223361
Seri Islamic Tours & Travel Sdn Bhd 02-243341
Straits Central Agencies (B) Sdn Bhd 02-229356
Sunshine Borneo Tours & Travel Sdn Bhd 02-441791
SMAS 02-234741
Travel Centre (B) Sdn Bhd 02-229601
Travel Trade Agencies Sdn Bhd 02-229601/228439
Tai Wah Travel Service Sdn Bhd 02-224015
Tenega Travel Agency Sdn Bhd 02-422974
Titian Travel & Tours Sdn Bhd 02-448742
Twelve Roofs / Perusahaan Hj. Asmakhan 02-340395
Wing On Travel & Trading Agencies 02-220536
Zizen Travel Agency Sdn Bhd 02-236991
Zura Travel Service Sdn Bhd 02-234738

KUALA BELAIT

Freme Travel Services Sdn Bhd 03-335025
Jasra Harrisons Sdn Bhd 03-335391
JJ Tour Service Sdn Bhd 03-334069
Limbang Travel Service Sdn Bhd 03-335275
Overseas Travel Service Sdn Bhd 03-222090
Southern Cross Travel Agencies Sdn Bhd 03-334642
Straits Central Agencies Sdn Bhd 03-334589
Usaha Royako Travel Agency 03-334768

SELECTED COMPANIES

- Advance Computer Supplier and Services
- AJYAD Publishing
- Akitek SAA Home Page
- Amalgamated Electronic Sdn. Bhd.
- Anthony Tours & Travel Agency
- Baharuddin & Associates Consulting Engineers
- Beseller Sdn Bhd Homepage
- BIT Computer Services
- BruDirect Business Centre
- Brunei Hotel
- Brupost
- CfBT Homepage
- Compunet Computer & Office Systems
- Dalplus Technologies, Brunei
- DN Private Investigation and Security Consultant
- DP Happy Video House
- Elite Computer Systems Sdn. Bhd.
- Fabrica Interior Furnishing Co
- Glamour Homepage
- HSBC
- HSE Engineering Sdn. Bhd.
- Indah Sejahtera Development & Services
- Insurans Islam Taib
- Interhouse Marketing Sdn. Bhd.
- International School Brunei
- IP and Company
- ISS Thomas Cowan Sdn. Bhd.
- Jerudong Park Medical Centre
- Kristal
- L & M Prestressing Sdn. Bhd.
- Megamas Training Company Sdn. Bhd.
- Mekar General Enterprise Homepage
- Micronet Computer School
- National Insurance Company Berhad
- Paotools Supplies & Services Co.
- Petar Perunding Sdn. Bhd.
- Petrel Jaya Sdn Bhd

- Phongmun Restaurant Homepage
- Poh Lee Trading Company
- Q-Carrier
- Sabli Group of Companies - Brunei Darussalam
- Scanmark Design Sdn Bhd
- SDS System (B) Sdn. Bhd.
- SEAMEO VOCTECH Homepage
- Singapore Airlines
- Sistem Komputer Alif Sdn Bhd
- SPCastro And Associates Sdn Bhd
- Sunshine Borneo Tour & Travel Sdn.Bhd.
- Survey Service Consultants
- Syabas Publishers
- Syarikat Suraya Insan
- Syarikat Intellisense Technology
- Tabung Amanah Islam Brunei
- Tang Sung Lee Sdn. Bhd.
- The Lodge Resort (In Brunei)
- Trinkets Enterprise
- Twelve Roofs / Perusahaan Hj. Asmakhan
- Unicraft Enterprises
- Utama Komunikasi

BASIC TITLES ON BRUNEI

IMPORTANT!

All publications are updated annually!

Please contact IBP, Inc. at ibpusa3@gmail.com for the latest ISBNs and additional information

Global Business and Investment Info Databank: www.ibpus.com

Title
Brunei A "Spy" Guide - Strategic Information and Developments
Brunei A "Spy" Guide - Strategic Information and Developments
Brunei Air Force Handbook
Brunei Air Force Handbook
Brunei Business and Investment Opportunities Yearbook
Brunei Business and Investment Opportunities Yearbook
Brunei Business and Investment Opportunities Yearbook Volume 1 Strategic Information and Opportunities
Brunei Business and Investment Opportunities Yearbook Volume 2 Leading Export-Import, Business, Investment Opportunities and Projects
Brunei Business Intelligence Report - Practical Information, Opportunities, Contacts
Brunei Business Intelligence Report - Practical Information, Opportunities, Contacts
Brunei Business Law Handbook - Strategic Information and Basic Laws
Brunei Business Law Handbook - Strategic Information and Basic Laws
Brunei Business Law Handbook - Strategic Information and Basic Laws
Brunei Business Law Handbook - Strategic Information and Basic Laws
Brunei Company Laws and Regulations Handbook
Brunei Constitution and Citizenship Laws Handbook - Strategic Information and Basic Laws
Brunei Country Study Guide - Strategic Information and Developments

Title
Brunei Country Study Guide - Strategic Information and Developments
Brunei Country Study Guide - Strategic Information and Developments Volume 1 Strategic Information and Developments
Brunei Customs, Trade Regulations and Procedures Handbook
Brunei Customs, Trade Regulations and Procedures Handbook
Brunei Diplomatic Handbook - Strategic Information and Developments
Brunei Diplomatic Handbook - Strategic Information and Developments
Brunei Ecology & Nature Protection Handbook
Brunei Ecology & Nature Protection Handbook
Brunei Ecology & Nature Protection Laws and Regulation Handbook
Brunei Energy Policy, Laws and Regulation Handbook
Brunei Energy Policy, Laws and Regulations Handbook
Brunei Energy Policy, Laws and Regulations Handbook
Brunei Export-Import Trade and Business Directory
Brunei Export-Import Trade and Business Directory
Brunei Foreign Policy and Government Guide
Brunei Foreign Policy and Government Guide
Brunei Immigration Laws and Regulations Handbook - Strategic Information and Basic Laws
Brunei Industrial and Business Directory
Brunei Industrial and Business Directory
Brunei Investment and Business Guide - Strategic and Practical Information
Brunei Investment and Business Guide - Strategic and Practical Information
Brunei Investment and Business Guide - Strategic and Practical Information
Brunei Investment and Business Guide - Strategic and Practical Information
Brunei Investment and Business Guide Volume 2 Business, Investment Opportunities and Incentives
Brunei Investment and Trade Laws and Regulations Handbook
Brunei Labor Laws and Regulations Handbook - Strategic Information and Basic Laws
Brunei Land Ownership and Agriculture Laws Handbook
Brunei Mineral & Mining Sector Investment and Business Guide - Strategic and Practical Information
Brunei Mineral & Mining Sector Investment and Business Guide - Strategic and Practical Information
Brunei Mining Laws and Regulations Handbook
Brunei Oil & Gas Sector Business & Investment Opportunities Yearbook
Brunei Oil & Gas Sector Business & Investment Opportunities Yearbook
Brunei Oil and Gas Exploration Laws and Regulation Handbook
Brunei Recent Economic and Political Developments Yearbook
Brunei Recent Economic and Political Developments Yearbook
Brunei Recent Economic and Political Developments Yearbook
Brunei Starting Business (Incorporating) in....Guide
Brunei Sultan Haji Hassanal Bolkiah Mu'izzaddin Waddaulah Handbook
Brunei Sultan Haji Hassanal Bolkiah Waddaulah Handbook Economic and Foreign Policy Handbook
Brunei Tax Guide Volume 1 Business Taxation
Brunei Tax Guide Volume 2 Personal Taxation
Brunei Taxation Laws and Regulations Handbook
Brunei Telecommunication Industry Business Opportunities Handbook
Brunei Telecommunication Industry Business Opportunities Handbook
Brunei: How to Invest, Start and Run Profitable Business in Brunei Guide - Practical Information, Opportunities, Contacts

BASIC LAWS AND REGULATIONS AFFECTING BUSINESS AND TRADE

COUTRY	LAW TITLE
Brunei	Admiralty Jurisdiction Act
Brunei	Advocates and Solicitors (Practice and Etiquette) Rules
Brunei	Advocates and Solicitors Rules
Brunei	Agricultural Pests and Noxious Plants
Brunei	Air Navigation Act
Brunei	Airport Passenger Service Charge Act
Brunei	Anti Terrorism (Financial and other Measure) Act
Brunei	Antiquities and Treasure Trove Act
Brunei	Application of Laws
Brunei	Arbitration Act
Brunei	Arms and Explosive Act
Brunei	Arms and Explosives Rules
Brunei	Asian Development Bank Act 2009
Brunei	Audit Act
Brunei	Banishment Act
Brunei	Banker's Book Act
Brunei	Banking Act
Brunei	Bankruptcy Act
Brunei	Bill of Sale Act
Brunei	Bills of Exchange Act
Brunei	Biological Weapons Act
Brunei	Bishop of Borneo Act
Brunei	Bretton Woods Agreement Act
Brunei	Broadcasting Act
Brunei	Brunei Board of Examination Act Brunei Economic Development Board Act
Brunei	Brunei Fishery Limits Act
Brunei	Brunei Investment Agency Act
Brunei	Brunei Malay Silversmiths Guild (Incorporation) Act
Brunei	Brunei National Archives Act
Brunei	Brunei Nationality Act
Brunei	Brunei Nationality Act Designation of Areas under Regulation 9
Brunei	Buffaloes Act
Brunei	Burial Grounds Act
Brunei	Business Name Act
Brunei	Censorship of Films and Public Entertainments Act
Brunei	Census Act
Brunei	Chinese Marriage Act
Brunei	Coin (Import and Export) Act
Brunei	Commission of Inquiry Act
Brunei	Commissioner for Oaths Act
Brunei	Common Gaming Houses Act
Brunei	Companies Act
Brunei	Computer Misuse Act

Brunei	Computer Misuse Order
Brunei	Constitution of Brunei
Brunei	Consular Relations Act
Brunei	Contract Act
Brunei	Cooperative Societies Act
Brunei	Criminal Appeal Rules
Brunei	Criminal Law Act
Brunei	Criminal Procedure Code
Brunei	Criminals Registration Act 2009
Brunei	Currency Act
Brunei	Customs Act
Brunei	Debtors Act
Brunei	Defamation Act
Brunei	Description of Land Act
Brunei	Diplomatic Privilege Act
Brunei	Disaffected and Dangerous Persons Act
Brunei	Dissolution of Marriage Act
Brunei	Dogs Act
Brunei	Education (Non-Government Schools) Act
Brunei	Election Offences Act
Brunei	Electricity Act
Brunei	Electronic Transaction Order
Brunei	Electronic Transactions Act
Brunei	Emblems and Names Act
Brunei	Emergency Regulations Act
Brunei	Employment Information Act
Brunei	Evidence Act
Brunei	Exchange Control Act
Brunei	Excise Act
Brunei	Extradition (Malaysia and Singapore) Act
Brunei	Extradition Act
Brunei	Fatal Accident and Personal Injuries Act
Brunei	Finance Companies Act
Brunei	Fire Service Act
Brunei	Fisheries Act
Brunei	Forest Act 2002
Brunei	Geneva and Red Cross Act
Brunei	Guardianship of Infants
Brunei	Immigration Act
Brunei	Income tax Act
Brunei	Intermediate Courts
Brunei	Internal Security Act
Brunei	Internationally Protected Persons Act
Brunei	Interpretation and General Clauses Act
Brunei	Intoxicating Substances Act
Brunei	Inventions Act
Brunei	Investments Incentives Act
Brunei	Islamic Banking Act
Brunei	Kidnapping Act

Brunei	Labor Act
Brunei	Land Acquisition Act
Brunei	Land Code Act
Brunei	Law Reform (Contributory Negligence) Act
Brunei	Law Revision Act
Brunei	Legal Profession (Practicing Certificate) Rules
Brunei	Legal Profession Act
Brunei	Licensed Land Surveyors Act
Brunei	Limitation Act
Brunei	Local Newspaper Act Official Secrets Act
Brunei	Marriage Act
Brunei	Married Women Act
Brunei	Medical Practitioners Dentists Act
Brunei	Merchandise Marks Act
Brunei	Mining Act
Brunei	Minor Offences Act
Brunei	Miscellaneous Licenses Act
Brunei	Misuse of Drugs Act
Brunei	Money-Changing and Remittance Businesses Act
Brunei	Moneylenders Act
Brunei	Monopolies Act
Brunei	Municipal Board Act
Brunei	National Bank of Brunei Act
Brunei	National Registration Regulations
Brunei	Nationality Registration Act
Brunei	Oaths and Affirmations
Brunei	Old Age and Disability Pensions Act
Brunei	Passport Act
Brunei	Pawnbrokers Act
Brunei	Penal Code
Brunei	Pensions Act
Brunei	Petroleum (Pipe-Lines) Act
Brunei	Petroleum Mining Act
Brunei	Petroleum Mining Act
Brunei	Poisons Act
Brunei	Post Office Act
Brunei	Powers of Attorney Act
Brunei	Preservation of Books Act
Brunei	Prevention of Corruption Act
Brunei	Price Control Act
Brunei	Prisons Act
Brunei	Probate and Administration Act
Brunei	Public Entertainment Act
Brunei	Public Health (Food)
Brunei	Public Officers (liability) Act
Brunei	Public Order Act
Brunei	Public Service Commission Act
Brunei	Quarantine and Prevention of Disease Act
Brunei	Reciprocal Enforcement of Foreign Judgments

Brunei	Registration of Adoptions Act
Brunei	Registration of Guests Act
Brunei	Registration of Marriages Act
Brunei	Religious Council and Kadis Court Act
Brunei	Road Traffic Act
Brunei	Royal Brunei Police Force Act
Brunei	Rubber Dealers Act
Brunei	Sale of Goods Act
Brunei	Second-Hand Dealers Act
Brunei	Security Agencies Act
Brunei	Sedition Act
Brunei	Societies Act
Brunei	Specific relief Act
Brunei	Stamp Act
Brunei	Statistics Act
Brunei	Statutory Declarations Act
Brunei	Subordinate Courts Act
Brunei	Subscriptions Control Act
Brunei	Summonses and Warrants (Special Provision) Act
Brunei	Supreme Court (Appeals to Privy Council) Act
Brunei	Supreme Court Act
Brunei	Syariah Courts
Brunei	Telecommunications Act
Brunei	Territorial Waters of Brunei Act
Brunei	Tokyo Convention
Brunei	Trade Disputes Act
Brunei	Trade Marks Act
Brunei	Trade Union Act
Brunei	Transfer of the Functions of the Minister of Law Act
Brunei	Travel Agents Act
Brunei	Trespass on Royal Property Act
Brunei	Undesirable Publications Act
Brunei	Unfair Contact Terms Act
Brunei	University Brunei Darussalam Act
Brunei	Unlawful Carnal Knowledge Act
Brunei	Vicar Apostolic of Kuching Act
Brunei	Water Supply Act
Brunei	Weights and Measure Act
Brunei	Wild Life Protection Act
Brunei	Wills Act
Brunei	Women and Girls Protection Act
Brunei	Workmen's Compensation Act
Brunei	Workmen's Unemployment Indemnity Act

WORLD CONSTITUTION AND CITIZENSHIP LAWS HANDBOOK LIBRARY

Constitution, citizenship, immigration, migration - strategic information, government programs, laws and regulations and more...

Price: $149 each

Afghanistan Constitution and Citizenship Laws Handbook
Albania Constitution and Citizenship Laws Handbook
Algeria Constitution and Citizenship Laws Handbook
Angola Constitution and Citizenship Laws Handbook
Antigua and Barbuda Constitution and Citizenship Laws Handbook
Antilles (Netherlands) Constitution and Citizenship Laws Handbook
Argentina Constitution and Citizenship Laws Handbook
Armenia Constitution and Citizenship Laws Handbook
Aruba Constitution and Citizenship Laws Handbook
Australia Constitution and Citizenship Laws Handbook
Austria Constitution and Citizenship Laws Handbook
Azerbaijan Constitution and Citizenship Laws Handbook
Bahamas Constitution and Citizenship Laws Handbook
Bahrain Constitution and Citizenship Laws Handbook
Bangladesh Constitution and Citizenship Laws Handbook
Barbados Constitution and Citizenship Laws Handbook
Belarus Constitution and Citizenship Laws Handbook
Belgium Constitution and Citizenship Laws Handbook
Belize Constitution and Citizenship Laws Handbook
Benin Constitution and Citizenship Laws Handbook
Bermuda Constitution and Citizenship Laws Handbook
Bhutan Constitution and Citizenship Laws Handbook
Bolivia Constitution and Citizenship Laws Handbook
Bosnia and Herzegovina Constitution and Citizenship Laws Handbook
Botswana Constitution and Citizenship Laws Handbook
Brazil Constitution and Citizenship Laws Handbook
Brunei Constitution and Citizenship Laws Handbook
Bulgaria Constitution and Citizenship Laws Handbook
Burkina Faso Constitution and Citizenship Laws Handbook
Burundi Constitution and Citizenship Laws Handbook
Cambodia Constitution and Citizenship Laws Handbook
Cameroon Constitution and Citizenship Laws Handbook
Canada Constitution and Citizenship Laws Handbook
Cape Verde Constitution and Citizenship Laws Handbook
Cayman Islands Constitution and Citizenship Laws Handbook

Central African Republic Constitution and Citizenship Laws Handbook
Chad Constitution and Citizenship Laws Handbook
Chile Constitution and Citizenship Laws Handbook
China Constitution and Citizenship Laws Handbook
Colombia Constitution and Citizenship Laws Handbook
Comoros Constitution and Citizenship Laws Handbook
Congo Constitution and Citizenship Laws Handbook
Congo, Democratic Republic Constitution and Citizenship Laws Handbook
Cook Islands Constitution and Citizenship Laws Handbook
Costa Rica Constitution and Citizenship Laws Handbook
Cote d'Ivoire Constitution and Citizenship Laws Handbook
Croatia Constitution and Citizenship Laws Handbook
Cuba Constitution and Citizenship Laws Handbook
Cyprus Constitution and Citizenship Laws Handbook
Czech Republic Constitution and Citizenship Laws Handbook
Denmark Constitution and Citizenship Laws Handbook
Djibouti Constitution and Citizenship Laws Handbook
Dominica Constitution and Citizenship Laws Handbook
Dominican Republic Constitution and Citizenship Laws Handbook
Ecuador Constitution and Citizenship Laws Handbook
Egypt Constitution and Citizenship Laws Handbook
El Salvador Constitution and Citizenship Laws Handbook
Equatorial Guinea Constitution and Citizenship Laws Handbook
Eritrea Constitution and Citizenship Laws Handbook
Estonia Constitution and Citizenship Laws Handbook
Ethiopia Constitution and Citizenship Laws Handbook
Falkland Islands Constitution and Citizenship Laws Handbook
Faroes Islands Constitution and Citizenship Laws Handbook
Fiji Constitution and Citizenship Laws Handbook
Finland Constitution and Citizenship Laws Handbook
France Constitution and Citizenship Laws Handbook
Gabon Constitution and Citizenship Laws Handbook
Gambia Constitution and Citizenship Laws Handbook
Georgia Constitution and Citizenship Laws Handbook
Germany Constitution and Citizenship Laws Handbook
Ghana Constitution and Citizenship Laws Handbook
Gibraltar Constitution and Citizenship Laws Handbook
Global Constitution and Citizenship Laws Handbook
Greece Constitution and Citizenship Laws Handbook
Greenland Constitution and Citizenship Laws Handbook
Grenada Constitution and Citizenship Laws Handbook
Guam Constitution and Citizenship Laws Handbook
Guatemala Constitution and Citizenship Laws Handbook
Guinea Constitution and Citizenship Laws Handbook
Guinea-Bissau Constitution and Citizenship Laws Handbook
Guyana Constitution and Citizenship Laws Handbook
Haiti Constitution and Citizenship Laws Handbook
Honduras Constitution and Citizenship Laws Handbook
Hungary Constitution and Citizenship Laws Handbook
Iceland Constitution and Citizenship Laws Handbook
India Constitution and Citizenship Laws Handbook

Indonesia Constitution and Citizenship Laws Handbook
Iran Constitution and Citizenship Laws Handbook
Iraq Constitution and Citizenship Laws Handbook
Ireland Constitution and Citizenship Laws Handbook
Israel Constitution and Citizenship Laws Handbook
Italy Constitution and Citizenship Laws Handbook
Jamaica Constitution and Citizenship Laws Handbook
Japan Constitution and Citizenship Laws Handbook
Jersey Constitution and Citizenship Laws Handbook
Jordan Constitution and Citizenship Laws Handbook
Kazakhstan Constitution and Citizenship Laws Handbook
Kenya Constitution and Citizenship Laws Handbook
Kiribati Constitution and Citizenship Laws Handbook
Korea, North Constitution and Citizenship Laws Handbook
Korea, South Constitution and Citizenship Laws Handbook
Kosovo Constitution and Citizenship Laws Handbook
Kurdistan Constitution and Citizenship Laws Handbook
Kuwait Constitution and Citizenship Laws Handbook
Kyrgyzstan Constitution and Citizenship Laws Handbook
Laos Constitution and Citizenship Laws Handbook
Latvia Constitution and Citizenship Laws Handbook
Lebanon Constitution and Citizenship Laws Handbook
Lesotho Constitution and Citizenship Laws Handbook
Liberia Constitution and Citizenship Laws Handbook
Libya Constitution and Citizenship Laws Handbook
Liechtenstein Constitution and Citizenship Laws Handbook
Lithuania Constitution and Citizenship Laws Handbook
Luxembourg Constitution and Citizenship Laws Handbook
Macao Constitution and Citizenship Laws Handbook
Macedonia,Constitution and Citizenship Laws Handbook
Madagascar Constitution and Citizenship Laws Handbook
Madeira Constitution and Citizenship Laws Handbook
Malawi Constitution and Citizenship Laws Handbook
Malaysia Constitution and Citizenship Laws Handbook
Maldives Constitution and Citizenship Laws Handbook
Mali Constitution and Citizenship Laws Handbook
Malta Constitution and Citizenship Laws Handbook
Man Constitution and Citizenship Laws Handbook
Marshall Islands Constitution and Citizenship Laws Handbook
Mauritania Constitution and Citizenship Laws Handbook
Mauritius Constitution and Citizenship Laws Handbook
Mayotte Constitution and Citizenship Laws Handbook
Mexico Constitution and Citizenship Laws Handbook
Micronesia Constitution and Citizenship Laws Handbook
Moldova Constitution and Citizenship Laws Handbook
Monaco Constitution and Citizenship Laws Handbook
Mongolia Constitution and Citizenship Laws Handbook
Morocco Constitution and Citizenship Laws Handbook
Mozambique Constitution and Citizenship Laws Handbook
Myanmar Constitution and Citizenship Laws Handbook
Namibia Constitution and Citizenship Laws Handbook

Nauru Constitution and Citizenship Laws Handbook
Nepal Constitution and Citizenship Laws Handbook
Netherlands Constitution and Citizenship Laws Handbook
New Zealand Constitution and Citizenship Laws Handbook
Nicaragua Constitution and Citizenship Laws Handbook
Niger Constitution and Citizenship Laws Handbook
Nigeria Constitution and Citizenship Laws Handbook
Northern Mariana Islands Constitution and Citizenship Laws Handbook
Norway Constitution and Citizenship Laws Handbook
Oman Constitution and Citizenship Laws Handbook
Pakistan Constitution and Citizenship Laws Handbook
Palau Constitution and Citizenship Laws Handbook
Palestine (West Bank & Gaza) Constitution and Citizenship Laws Handbook
Panama Constitution and Citizenship Laws Handbook
Papua New Guinea Constitution and Citizenship Laws Handbook
Paraguay Constitution and Citizenship Laws Handbook
Peru Constitution and Citizenship Laws Handbook
Philippines Constitution and Citizenship Laws Handbook
Pitcairn Islands Constitution and Citizenship Laws Handbook
Poland Constitution and Citizenship Laws Handbook
Portugal Constitution and Citizenship Laws Handbook
Qatar Constitution and Citizenship Laws Handbook
Romania Constitution and Citizenship Laws Handbook
Russia Constitution and Citizenship Laws Handbook
Rwanda Constitution and Citizenship Laws Handbook
Saint Kitts and Nevis Constitution and Citizenship Laws Handbook
Saint Lucia Constitution and Citizenship Laws Handbook
Saint Vincent and The Grenadines Constitution and Citizenship Laws Handbook
Samoa (Western) Constitution and Citizenship Laws Handbook
Sao Tome and Principe Constitution and Citizenship Laws Handbook
Saudi Arabia Constitution and Citizenship Laws Handbook
Senegal Constitution and Citizenship Laws Handbook
Serbia Constitution and Citizenship Laws Handbook
Seychelles Constitution and Citizenship Laws Handbook
Sierra Leone Constitution and Citizenship Laws Handbook
Singapore Constitution and Citizenship Laws Handbook
Slovakia Constitution and Citizenship Laws Handbook
Slovenia Constitution and Citizenship Laws Handbook
Solomon Islands Constitution and Citizenship Laws Handbook
Somalia Constitution and Citizenship Laws Handbook
South Africa Constitution and Citizenship Laws Handbook
Spain Constitution and Citizenship Laws Handbook
Sri Lanka Constitution and Citizenship Laws Handbook
St. Helena Constitution and Citizenship Laws Handbook
St. Pierre & Miquelon Constitution and Citizenship Laws Handbook
Sudan Constitution and Citizenship Laws Handbook
Suriname Constitution and Citizenship Laws Handbook
Swaziland Constitution and Citizenship Laws Handbook
Sweden Constitution and Citizenship Laws Handbook
Switzerland Constitution and Citizenship Laws Handbook
Syria Constitution and Citizenship Laws Handbook

Taiwan Constitution and Citizenship Laws Handbook
Tajikistan Constitution and Citizenship Laws Handbook
Tanzania Constitution and Citizenship Laws Handbook
Thailand Constitution and Citizenship Laws Handbook
Togo Constitution and Citizenship Laws Handbook
Tonga Constitution and Citizenship Laws Handbook
Trinidad and Tobago Constitution and Citizenship Laws Handbook
Tunisia Constitution and Citizenship Laws Handbook
Turkey Constitution and Citizenship Laws Handbook
Turkmenistan Constitution and Citizenship Laws Handbook
Turks & Caicos Constitution and Citizenship Laws Handbook
Tuvalu Constitution and Citizenship Laws Handbook
Uganda Constitution and Citizenship Laws Handbook
Ukraine Constitution and Citizenship Laws Handbook
United Arab Emirates Constitution and Citizenship Laws Handbook
United Kingdom Constitution and Citizenship Laws Handbook
United States Constitution and Citizenship Laws Handbook
Uruguay Constitution and Citizenship Laws Handbook
Uzbekistan Constitution and Citizenship Laws Handbook
Vanuatu Constitution and Citizenship Laws Handbook
Vatican City Constitution and Citizenship Laws Handbook
Venezuela Constitution and Citizenship Laws Handbook
Vietnam Constitution and Citizenship Laws Handbook
Virgin Islands, British Constitution and Citizenship Laws Handbook
Wake Atoll Constitution and Citizenship Laws Handbook
Wallis & Futuna Constitution and Citizenship Laws Handbook
Western Sahara Constitution and Citizenship Laws Handbook
Yemen Constitution and Citizenship Laws Handbook
Zambia Constitution and Citizenship Laws Handbook
Zimbabwe Constitution and Citizenship Laws Handbook

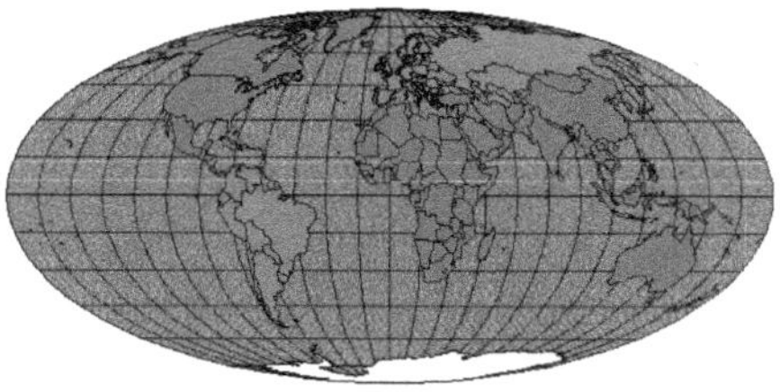

GLOBAL IMMIGRATION AND CITIZENSHIP LAWS AND REGULATIONS HANDBOOK LIBRARY

Price: $149.95 Each

1. Albania Immigration and Citizenship Laws and Regulations Handbook
2. Algeria Immigration and Citizenship Laws and Regulations Handbook
3. Andorra Immigration and Citizenship Laws and Regulations Handbook
4. Angola Immigration and Citizenship Laws and Regulations Handbook
5. Antigua & Barbuda Immigration and Citizenship Laws and Regulations Handbook
6. Antilles (Netherlands) Immigration and Citizenship Laws and Regulations Handbook
7. Argentina Immigration and Citizenship Laws and Regulations Handbook
8. Armenia Immigration and Citizenship Laws and Regulations Handbook
9. Australia Immigration and Citizenship Laws and Regulations Handbook
10. Austria Immigration and Citizenship Laws and Regulations Handbook
11. Azerbaijan Immigration and Citizenship Laws and Regulations Handbook
12. Bahamas Immigration and Citizenship Laws and Regulations Handbook
13. Bangladesh Immigration and Citizenship Laws and Regulations Handbook
14. Barbados Immigration and Citizenship Laws and Regulations Handbook
15. Belarus Immigration and Citizenship Laws and Regulations Handbook
16. Belgium Immigration and Citizenship Laws and Regulations Handbook
17. Belize Immigration and Citizenship Laws and Regulations Handbook
18. Bermuda Immigration and Citizenship Laws and Regulations Handbook
19. Bolivia Immigration and Citizenship Laws and Regulations Handbook
20. Bosnia and Herzegovina Immigration and Citizenship Laws and Regulations Handbook
21. Botswana Immigration and Citizenship Laws and Regulations Handbook
22. Brazil Immigration and Citizenship Laws and Regulations Handbook
23. Brunei Immigration and Citizenship Laws and Regulations Handbook
24. Bulgaria Immigration and Citizenship Laws and Regulations Handbook
25. Cambodia Immigration and Citizenship Laws and Regulations Handbook
26. Cameroon Immigration and Citizenship Laws and Regulations Handbook
27. Canada Immigration and Citizenship Laws and Regulations Handbook
28. Cayman Islands Immigration and Citizenship Laws and Regulations Handbook
29. Chile Immigration and Citizenship Laws and Regulations Handbook
30. China Immigration and Citizenship Laws and Regulations Handbook
31. Colombia Immigration and Citizenship Laws and Regulations Handbook
32. Comoros Immigration and Citizenship Laws and Regulations Handbook
33. Cook Islands Immigration and Citizenship Laws and Regulations Handbook
34. Costa Rica Immigration and Citizenship Laws and Regulations Handbook
35. Croatia Immigration and Citizenship Laws and Regulations Handbook

---

For additional analytical, business and investment opportunities information, Please contact Global Investment & Business Center, USA at (202) 546-2103. Fax: (202) 546-3275. E-mail: rusric@erols.com

36. Cuba Immigration and Citizenship Laws and Regulations Handbook
37. Cyprus Immigration and Citizenship Laws and Regulations Handbook
38. Czech Republic Immigration and Citizenship Laws and Regulations Handbook
39. Denmark Immigration and Citizenship Laws and Regulations Handbook
40. Dominica Immigration and Citizenship Laws and Regulations Handbook
41. Dominican Republic Immigration and Citizenship Laws and Regulations Handbook
42. Dubai Immigration and Citizenship Laws and Regulations Handbook
43. Ecuador Immigration and Citizenship Laws and Regulations Handbook
44. Egypt Immigration and Citizenship Laws and Regulations Handbook
45. El Salvador Immigration and Citizenship Laws and Regulations Handbook
46. Equatorial Guinea Immigration and Citizenship Laws and Regulations Handbook
47. Estonia Immigration and Citizenship Laws and Regulations Handbook
48. Falkland Islands Immigration and Citizenship Laws and Regulations Handbook
49. Fiji Immigration and Citizenship Laws and Regulations Handbook
50. Finland Immigration and Citizenship Laws and Regulations Handbook
51. France Immigration and Citizenship Laws and Regulations Handbook
52. Georgia Immigration and Citizenship Laws and Regulations Handbook
53. Germany Immigration and Citizenship Laws and Regulations Handbook
54. Gibraltar Immigration and Citizenship Laws and Regulations Handbook
55. Greece Immigration and Citizenship Laws and Regulations Handbook
56. Grenada Immigration and Citizenship Laws and Regulations Handbook
57. Guam Investment & Business Guide
58. Guatemala Immigration and Citizenship Laws and Regulations Handbook
59. Guernsey Immigration and Citizenship Laws and Regulations Handbook
60. Guyana Immigration and Citizenship Laws and Regulations Handbook
61. Haiti Immigration and Citizenship Laws and Regulations Handbook
62. Honduras Immigration and Citizenship Laws and Regulations Handbook
63. Hungary Immigration and Citizenship Laws and Regulations Handbook
64. Iceland Immigration and Citizenship Laws and Regulations Handbook
65. India Immigration and Citizenship Laws and Regulations Handbook
66. Indonesia Immigration and Citizenship Laws and Regulations Handbook
67. Iran Immigration and Citizenship Laws and Regulations Handbook
68. Iraq Immigration and Citizenship Laws and Regulations Handbook
69. Ireland Immigration and Citizenship Laws and Regulations Handbook
70. Israel Immigration and Citizenship Laws and Regulations Handbook
71. Italy Immigration and Citizenship Laws and Regulations Handbook
72. Jamaica Immigration and Citizenship Laws and Regulations Handbook
73. Japan Immigration and Citizenship Laws and Regulations Handbook
74. Jersey Immigration and Citizenship Laws and Regulations Handbook
75. Jordan Immigration and Citizenship Laws and Regulations Handbook
76. Kazakhstan Immigration and Citizenship Laws and Regulations Handbook
77. Kenya Immigration and Citizenship Laws and Regulations Handbook
78. Kiribati Immigration and Citizenship Laws and Regulations Handbook

79. Korea, North Immigration and Citizenship Laws and Regulations Handbook
80. Korea, South Immigration and Citizenship Laws and Regulations Handbook
81. Kuwait Immigration and Citizenship Laws and Regulations Handbook
82. Kyrgyzstan Immigration and Citizenship Laws and Regulations Handbook
83. Laos Immigration and Citizenship Laws and Regulations Handbook
84. Latvia Immigration and Citizenship Laws and Regulations Handbook
85. Lebanon Immigration and Citizenship Laws and Regulations Handbook
86. Libya Immigration and Citizenship Laws and Regulations Handbook
87. Liechtenstein Immigration and Citizenship Laws and Regulations Handbook
88. Lithuania Immigration and Citizenship Laws and Regulations Handbook
89. Luxemburg Immigration and Citizenship Laws and Regulations Handbook
90. Macao Immigration and Citizenship Laws and Regulations Handbook
91. Macedonia, Republic Immigration and Citizenship Laws and Regulations Handbook
92. Madagascar Immigration and Citizenship Laws and Regulations Handbook
93. Malaysia Immigration and Citizenship Laws and Regulations Handbook
94. Malta Immigration and Citizenship Laws and Regulations Handbook
95. Man Immigration and Citizenship Laws and Regulations Handbook
96. Mauritius Immigration and Citizenship Laws and Regulations Handbook
97. Mauritius Immigration and Citizenship Laws and Regulations Handbook
98. Mexico Immigration and Citizenship Laws and Regulations Handbook
99. Micronesia Immigration and Citizenship Laws and Regulations Handbook
100. Moldova Immigration and Citizenship Laws and Regulations Handbook
101. Monaco Immigration and Citizenship Laws and Regulations Handbook
102. Mongolia Immigration and Citizenship Laws and Regulations Handbook
103. Morocco Immigration and Citizenship Laws and Regulations Handbook
104. Myanmar Immigration and Citizenship Laws and Regulations Handbook
105. Namibia Immigration and Citizenship Laws and Regulations Handbook
106. Netherlands Immigration and Citizenship Laws and Regulations Handbook
107. New Caledonia Immigration and Citizenship Laws and Regulations Handbook
108. New Zealand Immigration and Citizenship Laws and Regulations Handbook
109. Nicaragua Immigration and Citizenship Laws and Regulations Handbook
110. Nigeria Immigration and Citizenship Laws and Regulations Handbook
111. Northern Mariana Islands Immigration and Citizenship Laws and Regulations Handbook
112. Norway Immigration and Citizenship Laws and Regulations Handbook
113. Pakistan Immigration and Citizenship Laws and Regulations Handbook
114. Panama Immigration and Citizenship Laws and Regulations Handbook
115. Peru Immigration and Citizenship Laws and Regulations Handbook
116. Philippines Immigration and Citizenship Laws and Regulations Handbook
117. Poland Immigration and Citizenship Laws and Regulations Handbook
118. Portugal Immigration and Citizenship Laws and Regulations Handbook
119. Romania Immigration and Citizenship Laws and Regulations Handbook
120. Russia Immigration and Citizenship Laws and Regulations Handbook
121. Samoa (American) Investment & Business Guide

122. Samoa (Western) Immigration and Citizenship Laws and Regulations Handbook
123. Saudi Arabia Immigration and Citizenship Laws and Regulations Handbook
124. Scotland Immigration and Citizenship Laws and Regulations Handbook
125. Singapore Immigration and Citizenship Laws and Regulations Handbook
126. Slovakia Immigration and Citizenship Laws and Regulations Handbook
127. Slovenia Immigration and Citizenship Laws and Regulations Handbook
128. South Africa Immigration and Citizenship Laws and Regulations Handbook
129. Spain Immigration and Citizenship Laws and Regulations Handbook
130. Sri Lanka Immigration and Citizenship Laws and Regulations Handbook
131. St. Helena Immigration and Citizenship Laws and Regulations Handbook
132. Sudan Immigration and Citizenship Laws and Regulations Handbook
133. Suriname Immigration and Citizenship Laws and Regulations Handbook
134. Sweden Immigration and Citizenship Laws and Regulations Handbook
135. Switzerland Immigration and Citizenship Laws and Regulations Handbook
136. Syria Export Import & Business Directory
137. Taiwan Immigration and Citizenship Laws and Regulations Handbook
138. Tajikistan Immigration and Citizenship Laws and Regulations Handbook
139. Thailand Immigration and Citizenship Laws and Regulations Handbook
140. Tunisia Immigration and Citizenship Laws and Regulations Handbook
141. Turkey Immigration and Citizenship Laws and Regulations Handbook
142. Turkmenistan Immigration and Citizenship Laws and Regulations Handbook
143. Uganda Immigration and Citizenship Laws and Regulations Handbook
144. Ukraine Immigration and Citizenship Laws and Regulations Handbook
145. United Arab Emirates Immigration and Citizenship Laws and Regulations Handbook
146. United Kingdom Immigration and Citizenship Laws and Regulations Handbook
147. United States Immigration and Citizenship Laws and Regulations Handbook
148. Uruguay Immigration and Citizenship Laws and Regulations Handbook
149. US Immigration and Citizenship Laws and Regulations Handbook
150. Uzbekistan Immigration and Citizenship Laws and Regulations Handbook
151. Venezuela Immigration and Citizenship Laws and Regulations Handbook
152. Vietnam Immigration and Citizenship Laws and Regulations Handbook
153. Serbia Immigration and Citizenship Laws and Regulations Handbook

www.ingramcontent.com/pod-product-compliance
Lightning Source LLC
LaVergne TN
LVHW080038210926
848481LV00011B/3225
* 9 7 8 1 5 1 4 5 1 6 4 8 5 *